BEYOND GRIEF

A Guide for Recovering from the Death of a Loved One

by
Carol Staudacher

Publisher's Note

This publication is designed to provide accurate and authoritative information in regard to this subject matter covered. It is sold with the understanding that the publisher is not engaged in rendering psychological, financial, legal, or other professional services. If expert assistance or counseling is needed, the services of a competent professional should be sought.

ISBN 0-934986-43-6 (paperback)
ISBN 0-934986-44-4 (hardcover)

First Printing February, 1987, 6,000 copies
Second Printing July, 1987, 11,500 copies
Third Printing January, 1990, 3,000 copies
Fourth Printing November, 1990, 5,000 copies
Fifth Printing May, 1992, 5,000 copies
Sixth Printing August, 1993, 5,000 copies

In memory of my parents, Rachel Alviso Pascoe and Sherman Blair Pascoe, whose premature deaths provoked in me the initial impulse to examine the abyss, to get *beyond,* and to create an alternative.

Acknowledgments

I would like to thank and extend my admiration to all of those who allowed me to inquire into their lives with the trust and hope that their experiences could be used to help others. My gratitude to George Fuller, Joan Knego, Steve Knego, Wendy Chapler, and Robert Chapler for their extensive and valuable contributions. I am also deeply appreciative for the exceptional contributions of Joseph Silverman, Ph.D., M.D.; Jill Ginghoffer, Leah Ferraro, Melanie Coon, Margaret Coombs, Marcie Pais, Beverly Mc Gowan, Jil Platner, Dana Clark, Lisa Jones, Patricia Harder, Caroline Davis, Amber Coverdale-Sumrall, Lucy Diggs, Jan Carlton, Teresa Franklin, Mary Decker, and to those who also shared but wish to remain entirely anonymous.

My deepest gratitude goes to those whose professional contributions were germinal to this project. These people shared their knowledge, experiences, insights, and opinions regarding the needs of survivors: Sister Jane Marie Lamb, S.H.A.R.E. Founder and Program Facilitator, St. John's Hospital, Springfield, Illinois; Jo Ann Siemsen, Executive Director, Santa Cruz County Hospice Caring Project; Robin Wolfe, R.N., Director of Hospice, Alta Bates Hospital, Berkeley, Calif.; Rev. Gerald Hill, Ph.D., Director of Pastoral Care and Bereavement Program Coordinator, Mt. Diablo Medical Center, Concord, Calif.; Father Barry Brunsman, St. Francis Xavier Catholic Church, Seaside, Calif.; Teresa Koetters, R.N., M.S., Oncology Clinical Nurse Specialist, Kenneth Koenig, Ph.D., M.D., psychiatrist in private practice, Aptos, Calif.; Judith Dunlop, Former Program Director, Home Care Hospice, Children's Hospital, Oakland, Calif.; Lee Morrison, Director of Pastoral Care, Dominican Hospital, Soquel, Calif.; Tom Pinkson, Ph.D., Center for Attitudinal Healing, Tiburon, and private practice, Mill Valley, Calif.; Judy Dellar, M.F.C.C., and Suzanne Nicholas, counselor, Loma Prieta School.

Many of the professionals and survivors who are mentioned above also shared or directed me to pertinent resources.

Others who supplied useful resources were Steve Turner, Sandra Lampe, Jeanne Lohman, Greg Keith, Debbie Shayne, George Fuller, Dorothy DeLacy, Lucy Diggs and Jo Walz. Also Charlotte Hullinger, Former Executive Director, Parents of Murdered Children (P.O.M.C.), and Robert Hullinger, Editor, *Survivors* newsletter, P.O.M.C.; Sally Gedney, L.C.S.W., Director of Social Services, Peninsula Hospital and Medical Center, Burlingame, Calif.; Gretchen Kucserka, Helping After Neonatal Death (H.A.N.D.); and those at the National Institute of Mental Health, National Committee on Youth Suicide Prevention and International Association for Suicide Prevention.

To Jan Sturtevant, who kindly made the initial contact for several of the survivor interviews, I am appreciative.

To those in the field of human services who gave generously of their time to read and evaluate the final manuscript, I am extraordinarily grateful: Jo Ann Siemsen, Executive Director, Santa Cruz County Hospice Caring Project; Rev. Gerald K. Hill, Ph.D., Director of Pastoral Care and Bereavement Program Coordinator, Mt. Diablo Medical Center; Robert Keet, M.D., Ethics Task Force Chairman, Dominican Hospital, private practice, Aptos, Calif.; Sister Jane Marie Lamb, S.H.A.R.E., Founder and Program Facilitator; Margaret Coombs, Regional Director, Parents of Murdered Children, Illinois; Rev. John D. Golenski, Ph.D., Medical Ethicist, Kaiser Foundation, Oakland, Calif.; Julia Sullivan, Executive Director, Candlelighters Childhood Cancer Foundation, Washington, D.C.; Shirley Karnovsky, Executive Director, The Samaritans, Boston; Therese Goodrich, Executive Director, Compassionate Friends, Oak Brook, Illinois; Jill Ginghoffer, Administrative Officer, Women's Crisis Support, Santa Cruz, Calif.; Alice Mestemacher, M.S., L.M.F.C.C., Hospice Caring Project, Santa Cruz County; and Edith Mc Shane, National Director of Chapter Development, National SIDS Foundation, Landover, Maryland.

I extend my appreciation to H.A. Slatoff, Professor Emeritus, California State University, Hayward, for reading the manuscript in its various forms, offering helpful editorial suggestions, and providing encouragement.

A warm thank you is due my daughter Susan, whose supportive presence I always feel, regardless of where she is, and who never fails to maintain enthusiasm for my work, despite the burdensome circumstances it often imposes.

Finally, I am fortunate to have as an editor, Dr. Matthew McKay, whose interest in this book arises from a genuine and deep concern, both professional and personal, for the well-being of the survivor. And finally, thank you to both Dr. McKay and Patrick Fanning whose faith in me made *Beyond Grief* possible.

Table of Contents

III. GETTING AND GIVING HELP

Preface

What does the grieving person need to *know, have,* and *be able to do* in order to successfully work through the pain that accompanies the death of a loved one? Exactly *which* perspectives, insights, strategies, resources, and courses of action will ease the survivor's burden? As I formulated answers to these two challenging and enduring questions, *Beyond Grief* was born.

This book reaches out, as much as possible within the limits of the printed page, to serve as a guide and extensive aid, and as a small although inanimate support system. It is intended to be equally useful to the survivor as well as the many dedicated lay persons and professionals who work with great perserverance, skill, and compassion within the area of human service.

Beyond Grief is the product of three major pursuits: First, in-depth research into the valuable and scholarly written resources within the field. Second, direct interviews with numerous lay people and professionals — Hospice administrators and volunteers, counselors, psychologists, clergy, psychiatrists, and nurses — who work with the grieving, and know, intimately and profoundly, the survivor's concerns and needs. Third, a series of powerful and illuminating personal interviews with people dealing with the death of a loved one.

Many of my observations and conclusions were drawn after compilations and comparisons of hundreds of hours of conversations with survivors. These people of varying ages, backgrounds, education, circumstances, and religious beliefs, generously shared the firsthand experiences of their loss. The spectrum of their loss includes the death of a spouse, child, sibling, parent, loving companion, or friend; loss during childhood; and loss as the result of an accident, terminal illness, suicide, or murder.

The information from this spectrum is organized to be easily accessible to every reader, regardless of his or her type of loss. Specifically, Section I, *The Conditions of Grief: Understanding and Coping,* examines the origins and nature of grief-related responses, interprets the information, and provides positive, dependable coping strategies for dealing with grief's many conditions. This section provides information and resources for *any survivor* regardless of the type of death he or she is surviving.

Section II, *Surviving Specific Types of Loss,* examines specific characteristics of each type of loss. It provides additional information and strategies related to surviving that *particular* loss, such as an accidental death, the loss of a parent during adult life, or the loss of a loved one.

Section III, *Getting and Giving Help,* is designed to meet the needs of all survivors and caregivers regardless of their specific circumstances. It addresses the issue of getting help outside one's self. It also offers guidance for relatives, friends, and counselors whose aim is to assist the survivor.

In summary, any survivor will find in *Beyond Grief* information to meet his or her *general* as well as *specific* needs.

For example, parents who have lost a child in an automobile accident will find relevant information in all of Section I. It provides the foundation for understanding and dealing with the total grief experience, regardless of the type of loss. It is equally relevant to each survivor. In Section II, two chapters discuss the specific needs and situations of parents who have lost a child in an accidental death: *Surviving the Loss of a Child* and *Surviving an Accidental Death.* Further, if the parents have a surviving child, *Surviving Loss During Childhood* will help them by delineating the child's needs. It also provides step-by-step guidance for the child's caregiver. In Section III, the parents will find guidelines for starting their own support group, or for locating appropriate professional help. Here the parents may also evaluate their grieving processes by using those guidelines which indicate a positive, successful outcome to grief.

On a more personal note, grief is by no means a topic nor a condition I have approached from a lone, clinical perspective. I have been *there,* in grief, deeply and resolutely. I have experienced grief's constriction as well as its impetus for personal change and growth. I mention this in order to affirm for you, the reader, that this book is not merely the product of analytical research; rather, it has evolved as well from the mind and heart of one who has traveled the same general course as the reader, though not precisely in the same way. Without my own personal experience, it is certain I could not have worked with such intensity on, nor dedication to, this project.

To those whose grief is with them at this very moment, I want to say: "Let's begin now. Let's explore this, understand it, and find some ways to ease those painful aspects of grief from which there seems to be no relief and which may seem to have no end."

Santa Cruz, California
July 1986

I.

The Conditions of Grief:
Understanding and Coping

1

Grief as the Stranger

At some point there is a moment at which you realize the person is not coming back and your original self is never going to be complete or the same. You will spend the rest of your life living with a major loss and it is going to be okay. You can do that. It's not going to be so aching and so terrible that you can't function, that you can't re-create your own life.

MOTHER OF A TEENAGED ACCIDENT VICTIM

In the midst of your grief it may be impossible for you to imagine that one day you too will experience a "turning point." You may find it difficult to believe that the majority of people who experience loss are eventually able to say, "Even though I will never be the same, it is going to be okay."

When your grief begins, the aching and the terror are insistent. At times you think you will never function normally again. You want desperately to be rid of grief and all of its accompanying symptoms — mental and emotional pain, physical weakness, confusion, possibly even contempt for your own life, your own *alive*ness.

There is, however, only one way for you to *live* without any *grief* in your lifetime; that is to *exist* without *love*. Your grief represents your humanness, just as your love does. It is that humanness which now causes you to wonder how long you will have to endure all the agony that mourning brings. The days go on and on, endlessly, relentlessly. And each day, in its own way, is unpredictable. You don't know what it will bring, or what it will require of your inner resources.

> Every day, after someone dies, you have a different feeling about it. I don't know how long this continues but it changes from morning to evening and from day to day. *(Father of six year old leukemia victim)*

A mother of a seventeen-year-old son who was killed in a sailing accident reflected on her grief one year after the death.

> Grief is much more profound than I ever thought, and much more complicated. It is still the major thing in my life and I don't know how much longer it will be that way.

There is no schedule for recovery. While you can generally be expected to experience some emotional healing between the end of the sixth month and the beginning of the second year, you will have your own timetable. You will do it in your own way, depending upon your individual personality, character and situation.

Each *person* is unique and each *situation* is unique. Even the *relationship* between the survivor and the deceased is unique, but the *needs of a bereaved person are universal.* A sixty-five-year-old widow in Billings, Montana, makes the same observations about her feelings and expresses the same desires, guilts and despair as a thirty-five year old woman survivor in Atlanta. A Portland man who has been devastated by the sudden death of a teenaged son in an automobile accident expresses the same wishes, frustration and anger as his counterpart in New York.

The Unfamiliarity of Grief

For most bereaved people, their grief has no predecessor. They are not familiar with the grieving process when they are first thrust into it. Grief is like a stranger who has come to stay in both the heart and mind.

Even if you had anticipated the death of your husband, or friend, or child, you could not have anticipated all the feelings the loss brought.

How do you cope with them? How do you know what to expect, what to do? A nurse, widowed at the age of thirty-two, told of her experience immediately after the unexpected death of her husband.

> I went back to work a week later and the doctors asked me what I was doing there. That upset me because I didn't know what else to do. I said, "I don't know what I am supposed to do. I've never lost anyone in my life."

What to expect and what to do are not the only dilemmas. The tormenting questions go on and on. Why am I so angry? How do I convey my pain to others so they'll understand me? Where do these bizarre, disturbing feelings come from? Why do I see or hear the person who is dead? Am I losing my mind? Will I ever be able to function normally?

This book answers these and the other questions that are most commonly raised by those who are mourning the loss of a loved one.

To begin with, it is necessary to recognize that *your grief is not a stable thing; it is a process.* The conditions which make up that process are common to everyone, regardless of the individual's personality, character, or situation. The grief process includes — but is not limited to — anguish, fear, denial, despair, sadness, anger, anxiety, changing identity and longing. You may experience only a few of these conditions. You may proceed from one condition to another; but more likely, you will move back and forth between two or more conditions, or will experience several of them simultaneously.

Some grief theorists have delineated stages of grief. The major benefit of this structuring has been to make survivors and professionals more aware of grief's components. To assume, however, that these components fit into any definite order or into any predictable series is an error. Generally, survivors experience three major phases: shock, disorganization and reorganization; but not even these hold true for everyone. Some survivors, for example, do not experience shock and numbness after the loss of a loved one.

As you experience grief, one day you may withdraw into your closed room, feeling hopeless and despairing. The next day you spend six hours shopping and doing errands at a frantic pace. One day you resent your own life. The next day you have a desire to plan for the future. You may remain extraordinarily angry or guilty for a very long time. You may have to deal with a lot of doubt, anxiety and fear before you can begin to function in any normal way. Most important, you and your situation are unique and because of this there will be no definite pattern to your grieving process and your healing cycle.

There is, however, one solid fact which remains true for everyone: *You must not walk around the perimeter of loss.* Instead, you must go through the center, grief's very core, in order to continue your own life in a meaningful way.

As you make your way through grief, you need understanding, information and assistance. These needs are addressed throughout Section I, which has two objectives: 1) *to explore the conditions of grief*, and 2) *to offer some coping strategies* for dealing with the various conditions of grief. Ultimately, you will find that you can go through grief, right through the center of it, and come out on the other side ready to resume your life as a changed person who is able to say, "Even though I am not the same, it is going to be okay."

An attorney who had been orphaned as a child reflected on her strongest personal need during the grieving process. Her words echo those of countless survivors, regardless of their age or the nature of their loss.

> I wanted so much to talk. Other people assume that if they don't talk about your loss, you will not *think* about it. Which is exactly the reverse of what is true. The more you talk about it and get it out, the sooner you will not need to talk about it. You will be able to transfer your thoughts to something else, and finally rediscover and reinvent your own life.

So let's talk about it, and as we do, let's examine some of the ways in which you can successfully deal with it.

2

The Grief Experience

The days were a blur. Everything was hazy and unreal. Sometimes people who spoke to me were almost faceless, without an identity. I remember waking up in the morning, sitting up on the side of the bed and looking down at my feet. Then I would think, "Okay. Now. My feet are on the floor. I can see them there. Okay, now walk." And then I would get up and walk. All day there would be something else that is hard to describe: It was a sameness *to everything—comfort and discomfort, heat and cold, noise and silence, because nothing really mattered anyway. I guess I was numb both inside and outside.*
WOMAN WHOSE HUSBAND AND SON WERE
KILLED IN A PLANE CRASH

Immediately upon being notified of your loved one's death you may have reacted with, "Oh no, this is a mistake. You have the wrong person." Even if you were expecting the death, you may have tried to delay its reality with questions. "How do you know? Are you certain? I just left his room at the hospital. I just spoke to him a few moments ago." You were really saying, "This horrible thing is not possible and it will not happen." You chose not to believe because disbelief made your life bearable. Within a few hours or days, you knew, intellectually and rationally, that your loved one was dead; however, you may have continued to resist accepting the fact. You may have found yourself feeling numb, moving as if in a dream.

Experiencing Disbelief and Numbness

Sometimes the disbelief and numbness you experience upon the death and at the funeral itself are so strong that you cannot accurately remember what happened. One grieving couple accused two of their boy's teenaged friends of missing their son's funeral. The teenagers had, in fact, attended. A week after her husband's memorial service, a middle-aged widow completely forgot that two of her cousins had stayed overnight in her home for two days and had taken care of responsibilities after the funeral.

If you can identify with this, if you have "shut off" for periods of time, what you have said is, "If I don't see, hear, taste, or touch, then nothing is really happening." It is as if you had chosen to become unaware or to disassociate yourself from events, to deaden your physical and mental self in order to avoid emotional death. Further, this kind of numbing allows you to suppress such uncomfortable emotions as rage or guilt which might otherwise be very prominent.

Besides avoiding the emotions which result from loss, there is another major motivation which may cause you to deny your loved one's death. This is the reluctance to admit your own mortality. Acknowledging and accepting the death of someone close to you means that you accept, also, your own inevitable death. You must say to yourself, "We are not permanent; we are temporary." Depending upon the beliefs you hold in regard to life after death or rebirth, this temporary condition on the earth will foster in you varying degrees of denial.

In the early stages of survival, belief and disbelief frequently operate simultaneously. Looking for a lost loved one is part of a common antithetical situation in which the bereaved often find themselves. This situation was described by a young woman whose fiance was killed in an automobile accident which also resulted in the amputation of one of her legs.

When I got out of the hospital and saw a van that looked like Phil's van, I would turn around and follow it. It was like the phantom pain of my limb loss. The limb was still there even though it wasn't. It was the same with Phil. He was with me even though I knew, intellectually, that he wasn't.

While you may actively search for, or imagine seeing, the dead person, part of you knows that he or she is not alive. The disbelief you experience is produced by the part of your mind that helps you to endure the unendurable. You are protecting yourself.

Sensing the invisible presence. You may find yourself hearing the noises your son would make if he were coming up the back steps and into the kitchen. You may feel the touch of your husband's hand on your shoulder. Months after her death, you may catch the scent of your wife's perfume in the bathroom. These kinds of experiences are as normal as dreams. In dreams your subconscious allows things to happen which you fervently wish would actually occur. You are now experiencing this same phenomenon during your waking state.

Because your longing is deep and unfulfilled, you may create an illusion to fill the void, to stave off sadness and the psychic pain you cannot yet bear.

> I had a feeling that he was with me and the feeling stayed with me for about a year. It was like having a comfortable shawl around me. Even though I was anxious, I felt he was with me. *(Thirty-two year old widow)*

> I would awaken and see him standing in the doorway. He would say, "I love you and want to be with you, but I can't." *(Young woman survivor)*

Some bereaved people set up a method for communicating with their loved ones. A retired teacher created signals that indicated to her that her dead husband was in the room. A child talked to her pillow for years, pretending it was her father. A widower sat in the living room every night and told his deceased wife about his day, what he was feeling and doing.

The Duration of disbelief. The period of time you remain in this mode, and the degree to which it occupies you, may vary greatly from those of other family members. Some bereaved people find that occasional bouts of disbelief continue to surface in their lives for a couple of years.

> The second year was more difficult than the first. You think that he'll walk through the door. Maybe God will change his mind. *(Mother of a teenager killed in an accident)*

If, in the first few months or even throughout the first year or two, you find yourself hanging onto the idea that the dead person is still alive, or if you keep personal possessions of the deceased in the hope that he or she will use them, don't be alarmed. What you are doing is providing yourself with a sort of temporary comfort. However, disbelief or denial which is totally encompassing, that continues for an extended period of time, is not normal. It will, in fact, stop your necessary grieving process and impede your ability to function.

An example of an extreme case of disbelief is the widow who kept her husband's coat hanging in the same spot for twenty years. One day she was horrified to notice that the coat was moth-eaten and had fallen apart. When the woman realized the extent of her subconscious denial, she cried, "Look how I've tried to keep my husband alive with an old moth-eaten coat. Why don't I just get rid of it? I don't need it any longer!"

One of the predecessors to successful grief is the final ritual, the funeral, the memorial service, some form of thorough good-bye.

Modern Western society is severely deficient in its treatment of death. In contrast, many other cultures have definite rituals which promote the exhibition of emotion and provide adequate time for mourning. In these cultures it is uncommon for the bereaved to exhibit pathological symptoms such as chronic depression or grief-precipitated physical illness.

The Need for Ritual

In order to fully realize a death, it is imperative for you to see some evidence of it. For example, a mother who is notified by telephone of her son's death in a drowning accident in which the body was not recovered, will be less likely to accept death as readily as a mother who is summoned to the hospital to identify the body of her son who was killed in an automobile accident. However traumatic it may be, viewing the body of the deceased allows you to take the first step from disbelief to belief, particularly if the death has been unexpected or sudden.

You have heard bereaved people say such things as, "I want to remember my daughter *as she was* when she went out the door to the prom." "I want to remember my husband *the way he was* before his last business trip." "I want to remember grandma *as she used to be,* joking around with dad." It is desirable to have these kinds of loving memories because they provide emotional warmth, but they need to be viewed in the proper perspective. "As she was," and "the way he was," and "as she used to be," all have one factor in common: Those ways were as a *living* person and the person is *not living*. That distinction is assimilated more easily when you see that the person is not alive or when you attend some form of final service. You will be less likely to deny something you have seen or participated in.

The terms used in the mortuary industry often contribute to your wish to deny death. The dead person is placed in the "slumber room" where people file by, pretending they are viewing the person taking a "long rest." This delicacy can be appreciated at one level, but at another it makes absurd the finality of the person's bodily presence.

The funeral should begin the separation of those who are alive from the dead person. Its function is not to separate the sleeping from the waking.

Of course, the funeral does much more than validate your loved one's death. It serves also as an acceptable outlet for a physical show of emotion, and perhaps even more important, it provides a forum for sharing the person with others, sharing what the person loved, enjoyed, and gave. The funeral not only says, "good-bye," it also says, "I'm hurting," "I'm missing," "Thank you for having lived," and "Your life has left this effect upon your relatives and friends, your part of the world."

As the funeral publicly acknowledges the end of the person's life in the way that the family and friends knew it, it reunites those people whose lives touched because of the loved one. This final service or memorial puts together an immediate, though temporary, support group.

After the funeral is over and the members of your temporary support group have returned to "life as normal," you will experience a number of emotions. Just as there are no definite stages of the grieving process, there are seldom, if ever, any absolutely pure emotions. It would be rare to find a person who is feeling sadness and *only* sadness, or fear and *only* fear. Feelings arise from a provocative event or condition in your life. During the grieving process, you may feel a jumble of emotions. Some of them will be ones with which you are familiar because they are a part of your emotional history. You have felt them many times before under stressful conditions. Other feelings may come as a surprise to you and to those around you, and these unfamiliar feelings may be even more dominant than those which are familiar. Among these strong emotions is anger.

Experiencing Anger

> Mark was at a party when he was told of his older brother's fatal accident. He became angry and started hitting people. By the time he was convinced to get into the car, he was paralyzed, unable to move, so he was taken to the hospital and treated. *(Mother of a teenaged accident victim)*

Your loved one is supposed to live, to enjoy life, to have more time. Then what is supposed to happen doesn't happen. Your spouse, sister, child, or friend dies. When this death occurs, it seems to be an error of the greatest magnitude. You had your ideas and suppositions about your loved one's life. You were involved in it and now that person isn't even here. Your perception of the way things are has been changed to the way things really are. You have been proven wrong. Because your belief system has been damaged, it makes you angry.

As you confront this new reality with hostility, you are behaving quite normally as a bereaved person. Anger is not only a logical and natural part of *your* grieving, it is a part of the whole history of grieving.

Expressions of anger, aggression, and hostility have long been linked to death. In *On Death and Dying,* Elizabeth Kubler-Ross points out that ". . . the early American Indians talked about the evil spirits and shot arrows into the air to drive the spirits away. Many other cultures have rituals and take care of the 'bad' dead person, and they all originate in this feeling of anger which still exists in all of us, though we dislike admitting it . . . though we call the firing of guns at military funerals a last salute, it is the same symbolic ritual as the Indian used when he shot his spears and arrows into the skies."

So today, we too shoot our spears and arrows. But they are personal and allegorical. They may take the form of fists or words, letters or lawsuits.

The direction in which your anger is focused will vary depending on your situation, your personality and even your gender. You may ba angry at God and religion, the unfairness of "the world," other people, yourself, or even the deceased. It helps to see how your anger works in each case.

Anger at God

"How could God do this?" is frequently asked by those suffering the affects of a loved one's death. If this is a question you have wrestled with, your thinking may follow these lines: "After all, God is supposed to do things right and suddenly the Almighty has been ruthless." To make matters worse, well-meaning friends and relatives try to placate you with, "It was God's will" . . . "The Lord needed him" . . . "She was such an angel, she was just too good to live" . . . "It is all in God's Plan."

If you are among those who do not find comfort in these words, "God's Plan" may seem to be synonymous with punishment and then you wonder what you did wrong; otherwise, why would you be punished? A woman who lost her fiance shortly before they were to be married asked, "How could God do this to me? Wasn't I a decent person? Why was this happening to me?"

Hearing that a death, particularly a premature death, is "God's Plan" only compounds your anger at God and religion. If God is supposed to be loving, how could this unloving act be committed?

A mother whose son was killed in an automobile accident on the way to a high school dance told about listening to her surviving son, who was in a fit of rage over his brother's death.

He was so angry. He was in the bedroom and was pounding on his bed. He was calling God every name in the book. At that point the priest stopped by our house. When he entered I said, "Oh, Father

Michael, just *listen* to him!" He put his hand on my shoulder and said, "Don't worry. God is big enough to take care of himself."

In recounting this anecdote the mother smiled and said, "It was such a relief to know that taking care of God was one thing I didn't need to worry about."

Of necessity, her son was channeling and finding a release for his sorrow. This expulsion took the form of anger at God in particular, and religion in general. By venting his rage he reduced the possibility of living with a trauma which could have resulted in any one of a number of pathological conditions, such as chronic depression, accident proneness, or alcoholism. This does not mean that grief is so simple that hitting your bed and calling God names will guarantee good mental health, but it is definitely true that venting your anger accelerates emotional healing.

Anger at the Unfairness of the World

Closely related to the anger directed toward God and religion is anger at some unknown force in the world, the force that is supposed to keep things *fair*.

This line of reasoning causes you to ask, "If a power exists that is *just,* how could this great injustice be levied against me?" "Where is all the morality of life I have been taught to believe exists?"

Death of a loved one feels extremely unfair; it is not something either you or the other person deserved.

Why did my daughter die? Why did she have to give up her life when she was leading it so successfully and was such a loving person? She was a good student, helped around the house, had lots of friends and a good sense of humor. If somebody on that bus had to die, why couldn't it have been that girl across the street? She cuts school, takes drugs, and drives her poor parents crazy with worry. Why not her instead of Lisa? *(Mother of a teenager killed in a bus crash)*

At the same time this mother expressed such a blatantly frustrated and anguished cry, she also recognized that it was illogical and morally wrong to suggest that another person's death could have been substituted for that of her daughter. She was voicing her discontent regarding the unfairness of life and, simultaneously, directing her anger toward another.

As you try in vain to answer the unanswerable questions regarding the timing or conditions of your loved one's death, anguish, bitterness, disillusionment and occasional irrationality become part of your emotional and mental state.

Anger Toward Others

The others who suffer chastisement, verbal abuse, and perhaps even physical violence, may be anyone who is *not dead*. That is, linked with your anger at the unfairness of death is a contempt for other people around you whose lives go on as usual. Because they have not been devastated as you have (or you *think* they haven't), you want to extract from them some kind of dues for your loss. You want to punish them for being alive, perhaps even for causing the death of your loved one. Often the routine involvement of ambulance drivers, paramedics, nurses, or doctors is viewed as *participation* in your loved one's death.

You may feel that your loved one's illness was misdiagnosed, that he or she had not been adequately tested. You conclude that if only the symptoms could have been recognized at an earlier stage, the death would not have occurred.

In case after case, the hospital staff seems to have taken the wrong action. They took away the clothes of your deceased before you had a chance to get them. They were unresponsive to your daughter's pain before she died. They forgot to give your brother his prescribed medication. They didn't tell the truth about your child's illness and they didn't answer your questions.

A woman who lost her fiance in a crash which also resulted in her own hospitalization recounted the following:

> Brian had been asking for me in his conscious moments. He had called my name. I always felt if the hospital staff had let me go to him and let me hold his hand it might have changed things.

Anger is also incited by the passiveness or avoidance exhibited by others when you most need support. Often, as soon as the funeral is over, or shortly thereafter, friends, relatives, or community members act as if nothing has happened. This is particularly true if the death was that of an infant or if the death occurred as a result of a suicide. Regardless of the cause or type of death, it is important to have your loss acknowledged.

One husband and wife whose teenager was the victim of a fatal accident developed their own method for handling friends' avoidant behavior.

> We had friends in the grocery store just turn the other way and walk off when they saw us. It was very irritating. By not saying anything they were denying that anything ever happened. That made us even madder. If in five minutes Craig's name was not brought up, we would bring it up.

Recognition of a traumatic event is extremely important to you. You want the other person to recognize your sorrow, not to pretend that everything is as it always has been; because for you, the survivor, things will never be the same again.

One bereaved mother expressed her anger toward people who told her how well she was coping. As she saw it, she was just getting through the day the only way she knew how.

> They'd look at me and say, "Oh Betty, you're so strong!" I thought if one more person tells me I'm strong, I'm going to smash him right in the mouth.

It adds to your bitterness if you sense that the other person is searching for a way out of an uncomfortable situation by complimenting you on your strength. As an older widow put it, "Strong? What's strong? You either keep on living or you don't. It's that simple."

Anger Toward Yourself

Studies have shown that males more often direct their anger outward, while women direct it toward themselves. Women are less prone to telling someone off, initiating a lawsuit, or displaying violent anger. Instead of chopping down a tree or smashing up the car, they will find reasons to punish themselves.

Sometimes the anger is so severe and illogical that the bereaved person may feel mentally ill, particularly if the individual does not ordinarily feel anger, let alone express it. If your anger is of this type, you may worry that it will never dissipate. It is true that if your anger is self-directed and does not seek an outlet, it may ultimately produce another undesirable condition such as physical illness, severe depression, or self-destructive behavior. But if your anger has an outlet, it will eventually weaken.

Anger Toward the Deceased

Anger doesn't respect any boundaries as far as its "target" is concerned. You can even be angry with your loved one who has died. Widows and widowers frequently feel they have been *deserted*. It is this feeling of being victimized by the deceased that causes the survivor additional anguish.

Typically, widows say, "He left me with this mess." Almost immediately they have to deal with insurance policies, social security, monthly payments with which they are not familiar, and death benefits. They have to begin sleuthing for their basic economic survival by identifying and making decisions regarding any available financial resources. Sometimes this means discovering that the resources are nonexistent and they have to create them.

The young widow may have to manage her preschoolers, find a babysitter and full-time employment. The forty- or fifty-year-old widow may have to return to school in mid-life to acquire new marketable skills.

A Hospice administrator made this observation about women who have lost their spouses:

Lots of wives are angry at their husbands for having left. Older women in particular. They have been married for thirty or forty years. The death is equivalent to desertion. That may not be true in future generations as women become more involved in all tasks and are increasingly independent. But now I often hear, "Why didn't I learn to drive?" "Why didn't I pay more attention to our securities, our banking?" "Why didn't I return to finish college when the children were in school?"

Widows certainly do not have a monopoly on anger. Anger can be directed toward the deceased from any of their loved ones. It can come from husbands, boyfriends, sisters or any survivor who feels that the traumatic situation he or she is now in is the responsibility of the one who died.

Children and Anger

Children who lose siblings or parents not only feel anger, they often express it more easily than adults. In Jill Krementz' *How It Feels When A Parent Dies,* a fifteen-year-old boy talked about his feelings toward his mother who was killed in an auto accident.

I was really mad at Mom. I never blamed the taxi drivers. I don't know why, but I didn't. I just took it for granted that accidents happen and it wasn't their faults, but Mom should have known better. She should have jumped back more quickly like Timmy did. Timmy was mad, too—mad that he hadn't been able to pull her back. He felt hopeless that he couldn't help her, and that was rough. I even asked Dad, "Do you think Mom knows she's ruined our lives?"

If a child's anger is not expressed at the time he or she first begins to feel it, this hostility may continue in one form or another for years.

From Rage to Recuperation

Regardless of where your anger is directed—at the medical community, at yourself, your best friend, your mother, the neighbor, or the person who survived the accident in which your loved one was killed, you can experience relief. You do not have to feel stuck in this energy-depleting condition for months. There are numerous concrete ways in which you can vent, dilute, or otherwise weaken the anger that will ultimately weaken *you* if you don't get rid of it.

A mother whose young son was killed in an accident found that talking about her anger, expressing her rage, provided great relief.

If something hurts me, I'm going to let it be known *now*. I'm not going to put it back inside. The death of Allan has taught me to bring out anger whether or not it seems appropriate. Whether or not it is even right.

Another woman vented her anger in a less direct way, but one which was equally effective. Her son had been drowned while on a rafting trip in Washington. Shortly after his death, she realized she had no recent picture of him. When his possessions were returned from the camp, she was surprised and relieved to find eight rolls of film which she took to be developed. When she went to pick them up, she was told that the film was damaged, "nothing came out." Weeks later when she was cleaning her son's room, she discovered a movie film he had taken shortly before he left to go on the trip. With renewed hope she took the film to be processed at a different photo store. When she went back to pick it up she was told, "We're sorry. The film was defective. We'll give you a replacement role."

Later still, she found a snapshot of her son. In response to requests from others who also wanted a recent picture, she prepared to have it copied. This time she called a professional for advice about the best place to do the job. On her way to the photo lab her purse was stolen and, along with it, the snapshot. Her last hope for an image of her son was destroyed.

Months later, this series of events became a focal point for anger and despair. She expressed her feelings by writing them out in a poem which, in turn, served as her sounding board and allowed her to share her feelings with members of a writing group to which she belonged.

Often, very deep feelings like these can be expiated by writing them out. (Various kinds of writing and their benefits are discussed further in Section II.)

An activity that requires physical endurance, such as running, swimming, biking, or tennis, will also help. But your activity doesn't *have* to be sports oriented or even "socially acceptable." It is okay to hit inanimate objects as long as you don't cause harm to yourself or anyone else.

It is permissible to show anger in public, as long as you don't stop an airplane in midflight or hurl heads of lettuce all over the local supermarket. If you are provoked, avoided, or not listened to, you'll feel better if you express how you feel. In other words, you can be *human* when you're out in public.

It is also okay to go off alone and scream. An English woman who had been raised to be "proper" told of her experience in expressing her anger. As a child growing up, she had been admonished by her father whenever she began to display any emotion. "Remember dear," he would say, "after all, you ARE *English*." When, in her mid-fifties, she was notified of her father's death, she found herself in an extremely emotional state. Her story is one of insight and humor.

> When daddy died I went down through the trees and walked along the riverbank yelling and screaming. I had never done that before. I ranted and raved for a very long time. Then, suddenly, I looked up at the clouds and I could hear daddy's voice admonishing me, "Quiet down, dear. After all, you ARE *English*!"

Regardless of how you have been trained, if your anger can be diffused you will be able to look more deeply into yourself at what lies below the layers of accusation and rage. For example, you may, in time, be able to admit that your anger is caused by more than "those people out there" who failed to keep your loved one alive, who misdiagnosed, or drove too fast, or encouraged him to go somewhere he shouldn't have gone.

Feeling Powerless and Abandoned

In general, anger results from feeling abandoned and powerless. Ask yourself where your emotional pain is coming from. What information do you get? Talk about that information with a supportive friend, relative, or counselor. For example, a widowed teacher found that his anger stemmed from viewing his wife as a punisher. She had given him a bad time when she was alive and, by dying, had ruined the rest of his life. However, *at the same time,* he had been dependent on his wife. The two of them had shared a consistent closeness for seventeen years. In discussing his feelings with a close friend he uncovered his own ambivalence. He was able to accept that his wife was neither a saint nor a devil. He viewed her as a whole person with attributes as well as deficiencies. With his new perspective, his anger lessened and he began to progress through the grieving process.

Feeling powerless means you perceive yourself as a victim. The way to change your "victimization" is to give yourself some sense of power. This is not as difficult as it may sound. You gain power by exerting control, and there are numerous ways in which this can be done. An example of this on a national scale is the mother who founded MADD, Mothers Against Drunk Driving. Her devastating experience produced an organization which lobbies for stricter laws and enforcement in regard to driving under the influence of alcohol. Of course, you don't have to start a national organization to vindicate your anger. You can first look at your experience in dealing with your particular loss. Next, you can examine that experience and identify what could have possibly prevented it or made it less confusing or painful. It may be that you convince a local group, agency, or institution to make modifications or to develop new procedures. "All of this is fine," you may say, "but what can I do? I'm too angry, too upset." Actually, the list of things you can do is endless. Consider, for example, these ways in which others have put their anger into action and eliminated their own powerlessness:

- The sister of an accident victim *convinced* the hospital counselor to establish improved procedures for dealing with survivors of a sudden, unexpected death.
- A father *proposed* that warning signs be posted at the scene of his son's drowning to reduce the possibility of another similar accident occurring.
- A grandmother *requested* that educational material be offered to the parents of young cancer victims.
- A middle-aged son who lost his seventy-three-year-old father *organized* bimonthly entertainment for a local convalescent home.
- A young hospital clerk *formed* a support group for women who were survivors of neonatal death.
- A college student who lost her three-year-old daughter *solicited* toy contributions from friends, neighbors and merchants for a local pediatric ward.

Notice the key words here: *convinced, proposed, requested, organized, formed* and *solicited*. They all denote action. If you can force yourself into action, regardless of how small and insignificant your effort may at first seem to be, you will experience both relief and a sense of control. You will, in time, find your anger supplanted by positive feelings that enrich your life.

Anger and Responsibility

You have been encouraged here to find ways to dissipate your anger, to vent your rage. For when anger is grounded, when it is focused and released, it will begin to slow, to lose energy, and you can begin to heal. However, it would be injudicious to suggest you can do anything and everything that serves to release your anger. Even though the majority of survivors are likely to err on the side of restraint, rather than on the side of overindulgence, it is necessary to mention some limitations.

The boundaries for safe and legitimate anger are simple. First, your anger should not be directed at someone who will predictably retaliate with *greater* anger and aggression. You will only escalate your own frustration and anger when you try to defend yourself. This does not mean pick on people who can't defend themselves. It means don't inflate the *cause* for your anger by antagonizing someone who you can change and who may use verbal or physical tactics which will intensify your rage and anguish.

Second, your accusations or revelations should not be directed toward someone who could suffer unjustly from them. That is, it would not be appropriate to be accusatory toward your mate who was driving the car in which your child was killed. It would, however, be appropriate to focus and channel your anger toward a judicial system which allowed your daughter's assailant to be released from prison.

In summary, nothing is gained by exerting anger which has at its base cruelty, or by publicly venting anger which could provoke cruelty toward yourself.

If you question the normalcy or the therapeutic value of your own anger, you can assess your situation by posing these two questions: Is my anger giving me temporary energy or is it depleting what small amount of energy I have? Am I using my anger or is it using me? If your answers indicate that you have an anger that drains, consumes, or "manipulates," you would benefit by sharing your feelings with a professional counselor. By getting a new perspective on your anger and by learning some personal strategies which fit your unique situation, you will then be able to help yourself more adequately.

In addition to anger, guilt can also overwhelm you during your grieving period. Guilt may hit without warning, or it may gradually insinuate itself into your thoughts until you are thinking of little else.

Feeling Guilty

> I feel so guilty because I made funeral plans ahead of time. It is almost as if I wished him dead. *(Sixty-three-year-old widow whose husband had been diagnosed as terminally ill six months prior to his death)*

This woman is reflecting a guilt reaction common among widows who, after learning that the death of their spouse is imminent, give some preparatory thought to their husband's funeral.

Guilt, however, is not limited to widows. In fact, of the many conditions which occur during the grieving period, guilt seems to affect the broadest segment of the bereaved population and arises from the widest variety of sources. People can generate many reasons to make themselves feel guilty. A new reason for guilt can be adopted every day of the grieving period, and each new guilt will seem as valid as the one which preceded it.

Those who have no guilt about the death of a loved one are in the minority. Unless you belong to that minority, you are no doubt experiencing some debilitating feelings. Regardless of the actual cause of death, the age of the deceased, and the extent of your actual control over your loved one's life, *chances are you have decided you have done something wrong for which you should feel guilty.* These self-accusations arise from a variety of circumstances and a limited perspective.

- Why did we insist on him having surgery?
- I knew the kids might have been drinking beer. Why didn't I stop them from driving?
- If only I had paid more attention to his complaints and had not shrugged them off.
- Everyone knows how dangerous surfing can be. Why did I let him talk me into buying a surfboard?
- If only I had not let his brother drive my car to the game. Why didn't I just tell him no?
- Why did I give her the option? Why didn't I demand that she have chemotherapy?
- If I had not insisted on her being on time for dinner, she would not have been running across the street.

Regardless of the blame with which you now burden yourself, what you are saying is this: You should be in charge of what happens in the world. Blaming yourself takes away the responsibility of others. It also says that the one who is dead had no control over his or her life situation. Usually, this is not the case.

Besides feeling that in some way you were responsible for the death, you may also feel that you should account to other survivors.

I had trouble seeing his brothers. I felt like I took him away from them when he died. I felt like his death was my fault even though it wasn't. *(Young widow whose husband died of a sudden heart attack)*

Your Changed Lifestyle

After the death you may have received something material — money, a house, or some jewelry. This produces another guilt.

I have the money to buy a new car now, but I feel guilty doing it. *(Middle-aged widower who inherited his wife's life insurance)*

Now I have both the money and time to take the trip to Russia with our study group, but I don't feel as if I should go without him. I couldn't really enjoy myself, thinking that I could go and he couldn't. *(Widow of a retired political science professor)*

Death may change your daily circumstances significantly, either by making your life materially easier or by allowing you more time for your own personal use. It may be the first time you have been able to leave the house for longer than an hour at a time. It may allow you to see old friends you have not been able to visit with during the long illness of your child, husband, or mother. You may take up a hobby or recreation, but you cannot enjoy one minute of it because you perceive the activity as being the outcome of your loved one's death. Each time you pick up a paintbrush or a golfclub, go to a movie or have coffee with a friend, you may feel a pang of guilt. If the pangs become too intense, you stop doing whatever it is that you would otherwise enjoy.

Parental Guilt

The loss of a child almost always produces excessive guilt in the surviving parents or parent. The reasons for this guilt are endless. If your child died of an illness that is, or could be considered to be congenital, you may feel guilty about allowing the child to have been conceived. If your child died as the result of an accident, regardless of the *type* of accident, you may feel guilty about not preventing the tragedy. You can torment yourself for months, even years, with, "How could that have been avoided? What could I personally have done to eliminate any possibility of that accident occurring?"

If you somehow see yourself as an active participant in the tragedy which resulted in your loved one's death, your guilt will be even more profound. If you were driving the car, flying the plane, encouraging the sport permitting the sailing, financing the mountain climbing trip, swimming in the same river, you may feel you could have prevented the loss of your child. When the results are tragic and you assume guilt for the death, you often experience guilt in relation to other family members as well.

> I felt as if I owed Dan for killing his son. After all, I was driving the car. *(Mother of a teenaged son killed in a sporting accident)*

> I feel guilty about not spending enough time with her at the end, but the full time job I had was probably my saving grace. *(Mother of a teenaged cancer victim)*

After someone dies, there is no such thing as *enough* time. No amount of time would have been sufficient. Nothing less than the rest of your life would seem as if it were truly *enough*.

Children's Guilt

Children can be just as critical of themselves as adults. When a parent dies a child may condemn himself for having caused the parent to worry over trivial things, for not being affectionate, for refusing to mind, or for failing to help around the house. In *When a Parent Dies,* by Jill Krementz, a sixteen-year-old girl expressed her feelings about her mother's death.

> Sometimes I feel guilty too. I hate Saturday mornings because before my mother died, I used to watch television and my mother used to ask me to make her coffee and I used to say, "Yes, later,

later..." She used to practically beg me to make her coffee and so after she died I felt bad.

You would have a difficult time convincing the girl that neglecting to make her mother's coffee had nothing to do with her mother's death, or that it was not an act of cruelty. In circumstances such as these, the good and generous acts are rarely remembered.

Children can also feel a tremendous and lasting guilt about the death of a sibling. Remorse covers a lot of territory in the children's world. Their self-punishing thoughts go something like this:

- Last week he wanted to borrow my baseball mitt and I didn't loan it to him.
- My sister interrupted my phone call and I screamed at her.
- The baby cried and I was busy talking to my friends in the driveway so I didn't tell my mother. She was just next door.
- He got a D in Math and I laughed at him and made fun of him because all my grades were high. I called him, "Stupid."
- After my sister was born, I was really jealous. I wanted things to be the way they were before her birth.

For the most part, the surviving children will, at one time or another, ferret out reasons to see themselves as selfish, mean, or careless in regard to their dead brother or sister.

If the surviving sibling has longed to be the *only child* prior to the brother's or sister's death, the survivor will feel especially and profoundly guilty. The child thinks, "I wished her away. She died because I wanted it to happen or *thought* I wanted it to happen." In some cases, the child reflects, "I wished him away and now my life is better. But I don't deserve for my life to be better because I am a bad person."

It is not uncommon for a child to perceive of his or her life as having improved after the death of a brother or sister. This is especially true if the survivor gets more attention from the parents, gains a long-sought freedom or a new privilege, or is given more money, toys, clothes, trips, or other material things.

The child who sees his or her changed life situation as more pleasant and gratifying, may actually exhibit positive personality changes after the sibling's death. The surviving child may be happier, demonstrate increased confidence, be more talkative or more spontaneous without the presence of a brother or sister.

Survivor Guilt

War, accidents, and disasters such as train and airplane crashes, earthquakes, and floods produce a special form of remorse in those who were involved in the tragic event but did not die. This remorse is called survivor guilt.

The statements which follow illustrate both the circumstances as well as the thought processes which produce this type of guilt.

> When we got on the plane, my husband offered me that seat next to the window, but I said for him to sit there. I wanted to be on the aisle.

> *Translation:* By not sitting in the seat, I condemned my husband to death.

> We had been together for a year in the same platoon. We were both making our way uphill under enemy fire. Before I knew it, there was a loud blast and Brad's body went flying through the air. He had been my best friend. One minute there we were, the two of us, the next minute he was gone.

> *Translation:* We were both equal but I was chosen to survive. I was given priority over him.

> People were dying all around us every day and every day we wondered which of us would go, too. We talked about what we would do if we escaped death. We talked about what we would eat, who we would try to locate, what we would do and say if we found them. I got out of Auschwitz and did some of those things. She went to the ovens.

> *Translation:* There was a competition to survive. Some did and some didn't. I competed with her and won.

Survivor guilt emanates from the same belief, regardless of the specific details of the situation; the belief is that one death has somehow been exchanged for another, that one person was allowed to live *at the cost of* another's life.

Those who suffer the pain of survivor guilt may remain preoccupied with the deceased, and may go so far as to assume the characteristics of the one who has died.

The survivor may also exhibit any number of a wide variety of symptoms including, most commonly, depression, low self-esteem, poor physical health or alcoholism.

Regardless of the type of guilt or its origins, it must be explored and understood before one can successfully be rid of it.

Understanding and Dispelling Your Guilt

The Death Exchange

While you may genuinely wish your own life could have been substituted for that of your child, spouse, parent or friend, it is important to recognize that death is not the result of an exchange or competition. You may readily agree, saying to yourself, "Of course, everyone knows that." Yet at a certain level of consciousness many survivors do *not* seem to know that. Along with other prominent feelings, these survivors undergo remorse based on the idea that the death was going to occur, but the wrong person was taken.

Commonly, survivors seem to indicate that a certain amount of suffering and death has been allotted to a particular family, town, group, or even a nation, and that *someone else* within that unit could have been taken to spare the life of a loved one. If you find yourself identifying with this reaction, it may help to remind yourself that *death has no scoreboard.* Proof of this is all around us. Consider, for example, several tragedies involving the deaths of U.S. citizens within less than a seven week period, from December 12, 1985, to January 28, 1986: Six family members were killed in Mount Clemens, Michigan, when a suicide of one member went awry and carbon monoxide fumes leaked into the house, killing the remaining five family members. Two hundred forty-eight U.S. soldiers, on their way home from a peacekeeping mission in the Sinai, were killed when the DC-8 in which they were flying crashed. All seven crew members of the Challenger Space Shuttle were killed when the vehicle exploded in space.

Incidents such as these certainly confirm that the inevitability of any one person's death is not determined by how many people within that person's family, or group of associates, have *not* died. Tragically, there is no limit to how many family members, residents of a town, or people in a nation can die at one time. You could not, therefore, substitute yourself for the life of another person because *there is no quota to be filled.*

Another common lament among survivors is, "But I am so much older, why couldn't I have gone?" Or, "I am not in good health, anyway." Or even, "I've been a bad actor in my day and she was always such a good person. Why couldn't..." People are not "selected" for death because of their age, physical condition, or morality. To assert that it would have been more sensible for you (or the neighbor, or the miserable juvenile delinquent in your child's school) to have died may indeed seem logical, especially if you compare the quality or quantity of your life (due to illness, age, or other limitations) to the quality or quantity of your loved one's life. When you feel guilty to be alive, remind yourself that not only does death have no quota; *death has no selection process.* Further, if you are trying to impose some logic on what has occurred, you have created for yourself a limitless challenge — for you are striving to make sense of the oldest and most unfathomable mystery of humankind.

Cause and Effect Syndrome

As mentioned earlier, you may suffer from the belief that perhaps you could have prevented the death. *If only* you had performed some specific act or had some specific conversation, your loved one would still be alive.

A first-year college student whose single mother collapsed at home and died instantly of a heart attack felt he should have known how to save her.

> I didn't know CPR. I tried to revive her but I didn't know how. Then I panicked and dialed the wrong emergency number. I *should* have known CPR. I should have been able to have better control when I was trying to call for help. Even though part of me knew I hadn't killed my mother, another very big part of me felt as if I *had*. For the first couple of months after her death, whenever I saw a sheriff's patrol car in our neighborhood, I thought they had found me out and were coming to pick me up for questioning.

This nineteen-year-old had constructed for himself a whole scenario of cause and effect. I did not do *this* and *this;* therefore my mother died. While this idea made his life tortuous, it also made it *neat*. He could assume all the blame and deny reality—the reality that *no one* was responsible for his mother's death.

This type of thinking is not surprising, given the human need for harmony; that is, most people have an inherent need to believe that a kind of order exists in our universe. That order says that someone is responsible for things that happen. This belief produces this kind of thinking: "If someone had done something differently, then that would not have happened. If *I* had done *this,* then *that* would not have occurred. If you, as a survivor, are feeling guilty for what you think you did or did not do, you are burdening yourself with debilitating guilt, rather than admitting there is no cause and effect order at work in our universe and that *no one* is responsible.

When you feel guilty for *not being dead,* or *not stopping* or *causing* the death of a loved one, you are choosing to inflict pain upon yourself. Subconsciously, you are constructing this plan of action: "I will take responsibility for this terrible loss. Then there will be a reason it happened, and I can cope with reasons. I cannot, however, cope with the hard fact that reason does not exist in this case and that my world is not orderly and secure, as I had previously thought."

Consider the guilt you are experiencing. Remember your guilt is a choice. Ask yourself if it helps you to generate and then magnify your own anguish. Think about the consequences you may have to endure as a result: physical illness, depression, unabating rage, extreme sadness or disillusionment.

Not Being Good Enough

You may view yourself, after your loved one's death, as being inattentive, selfish, or cold, even cruel. Your husband was in a coma and you didn't go to the hospital every time you had an opportunity to do so. Your child wanted a new bicycle and you told her the old one was good enough. Your sister begged you to go on a trip with her and you opted to spend the weekend with your boyfriend instead. Your mother always wanted you to finish college and you dropped out to join the army. You could have helped your brother paint his house, but you stayed home to watch the Super Bowl game.

Guilty feelings are just as likely to arise from an absurdly miniscule incident. "My husband wanted spinach and I cooked broccoli instead." Then the widow, whose husband died the day after the spinachless dinner, expands on her theme of selfishness: "I never did what he wanted. I always did things my own way. Why didn't I do what he wanted once in a while? What difference did it make if we had spinach or broccoli? I was just being mean."

This line of thinking does its best to build a case for the prosecution, but if you examine the opposite side of your behavior, this self-blame will not survive. For example, consider trying this writing exercise: Get a blank notebook. Take some time to mentally review your relationship with your loved one. Try to recall every bad action, deed, or conversation you initiated. Screen out those on the borderline and include only those about which you have no doubt.

If you're a widower, you may start (as many do) with, "I didn't tell her I loved her enough." Or, "I got angry at her over every little thing." A widow may begin with, "I complained about him being too lethargic . . . or too overweight . . . or too serious . . . or too sexual." When your list is complete, read it over to yourself.

Now take another sheet of paper and follow the same procedure for every positive or kind action, for every enjoyable, supportive conversation you can vividly remember. Take your time. Your list might look something like this: "I nearly always shopped for her favorite food." "I supported his career change." Or, "I often complimented her on her sales skills . . . or cooking . . . or mechanical ability." "I encouraged her to return to school," or, "I bragged about him at the office." Instead of denying any good element of your behavior, go to the source. Pin down what you did. Be thorough.

You now have two lists. Before you is the evidence that nothing is all one way or the other. You were not completely terrible nor completely wonderful because unless you felt no closeness to the individual, your relationship was a blend of good and bad.

One counselor capsulized it this way, "The good wouldn't be much *good* if you didn't have anything to compare it to." And then she quoted from a poem by Robert Frost: "It was by having been contrasted/that good and bad so long had lasted." Again, accept yourself as human. Remind yourself that there is much in your history to contradict the actions and feelings which produced your guilt.

Feeling High

More than a few mourners confide that they experience guilt for having felt a kind of euphoria, a high, upon the death of their loved one. "How could I have been happy when my husband was dying before my eyes?" "How could I have floated out of the hospital with a smile on my face when my child just died?" these people ask. "It was as if I was on some kind of drug," they will tell you — and indeed they were. The "drug" was adrenaline. Though actually a hormone, adrenaline closely resembles an amphetamine in its effect. When under stress the body releases adrenaline (as well as other hormones) which may energize the person, produce a rush, and give a feeling of extreme well-being.

This euphoria can be produced by at least two other factors. First, a survivor may feel as if he or she witnessed a very spiritual and peaceful death. Indeed, the death may have appeared to the observer to have been an extremely beautiful transition to something incomprehensibly superior to life. If you were fortunate enough to be present during an experience such as this, it is no surprise that you were pleased and felt uplifted.

Another possibility is that even though you didn't identify with any spiritual aspect of the death, you felt tremendously thankful that the pain, fear, or confusion of your loved one was over.

If you recognize that your euphoria was caused by either this *enchantment* or *relief,* you will probably not feel guilty. It is when you are euphoric but don't quite understand what produced it that you will berate yourself so severely.

Inherited Guilt

If you were the recipient of material goods from your loved one, you may feel that receiving the car, money, house, or other possessions, is the equivalent of *collaborating with death.* You may even feel that you are an unworthy recipient. These, then, are facts for you to consider:

You cannot cause or sanction a death by taking what has been willed to you. Further, you have no right to judge who would be a "worthy recipient." Your loved one's will is a validation of that person's personal priorities and affirmations in regard to all the individuals he or she knew. You should honor the validation.

Often, those who spend an inheritance in great haste are regarding their money as tainted, something to be gotten rid of as quickly as possible. If kept and used as normal income, the money would be a constant reminder of the dead loved one and, consequently, of the survivor's loneliness or sadness.

Janet, a thirty-two-year-old married legal secretary who had a close, loving relationship with her parents, was deeply affected by their deaths, which occurred within a two year period. Upon the second death, that of her father, she inherited a great sum of money.

Janet had been a model mother, wife and friend. She had also excelled at her job, exhibited a charming wit, and had been sensitive to the needs of others. Economically, she had led a middle-class life. The inheritance from her parents provided her with a chance to give herself and her family a few personal luxuries, to make long-term investments, and to ensure exceptional educational opportunities for her three children, who were all gifted students. Instead, she began drinking excessively and lost her job. Within two years, her marriage ended, and she lost custody of her children.

Her need to get rid of the money outside her family became obsessive. During the course of her pathological grieving, Janet went into a supermarket, filled three grocery carts with steaks and roasts, returned to her apartment building and distributed her purchases door to door. Of course, her neighbors, who were not needy, were confused and she got little satisfaction from her action, if any.

Janet's lifestyle prior to the deaths had not included "bar-hopping." However, with plenty of money in hand, she bought drinks for the house in bar after bar, night after night. As you might expect, soon her inheritance was completely depleted.

"It was blood money," Janet's psychiatrist reflected. "She had to get rid of it. She was, in her own way, 'getting rid' of the deaths at the same time."

Unfortunately, she was also getting rid of herself because in addition to having forfeited her children, marriage, and money, she had sunk deeper and deeper into a destructive lifestyle. My last word of Janet was that she had confessed to a murder which she had not committed.

Changing Your Perspective

All of the guilts which have been considered here are those which arise from a limited and self-punishing perspective; that is, these guilts grew from thoughts that were either distorted or illogical. In direct contrast, you have been presented with a new perspective based on facts. In summary, these facts are as follows:

- Death is not the result of an exchange or competition.
- Death has no scoreboard and no quota.
- Death has no "selection" process.
- You are not collaborating with death by enjoying an inheritance.
- All human relationships have both good and bad components. The bad components in your relationship will not kill your loved one.
- Enchantment with the process of your loved one's death, or even euphoria at or after the death, are not abnormal nor necessarily undesirable reactions.

Guilt That Won't Go Away

If your guilt is terribly deep and immobilizing, or if it continues for a prolonged period during which you see practically no change, chances are you have some ambivalence, either recognized or unrecognized, in regard to your loved one. This is not to suggest that you did not genuinely love him or her, nor that you do not experience a deep sense of loss. It is to suggest, instead, that you may have some negative feelings in regard to your relationship with your loved one. These feelings are bringing you to an emotional halt.

It is not uncommon for a survivor to confide that he or she had, in a burst of frustration or outrage, wished the loved one dead. Having had this thought, even having *voiced* this wish to the loved one, did not cause the death. The message to a survivor grappling with this memory is this: You are not powerful enough to cause someone to die in this way. Your wish for the death, regardless of how intense it was at the time, and the actual deed of killing the person are two separate actions entirely. Your *wish* is not the *deed*.

Don't continue to try to coexist with the emotional pain your guilt causes. Consider discussing your feelings with a counselor. Counselors are accustomed to helping survivors deal with ambivalence or extreme remorse. Both can be resolved.

Experiencing Fear and Anxiety

Fear and anxiety are the source of much emotional pain and concern among survivors. Many experts make a distinction between fear and anxiety, and an even more finite distinction among the various types of anxiety. However, for purposes of discussion which will meet your needs as a survivor, only one general distinction is made here. Fear, within this context, refers to a feeling of extreme fright or alarm which is related to a definite object (act, event, person or thing). You fear crying in public. You fear the dark. You fear failing at something — getting lost on your way to an appointment, talking to your children about your feelings, performing tasks your wife used to do. In contrast, anxiety refers to that state of extreme apprehension which cannot be directly related to any one thing, person, or event. This anxiety is described by the wife of an accident victim:

> I would go to bed at night and huddle to myself and shake. The thought of having to cope with anything, anything at all, was overwhelming. My heart beat fast. I ached, my body felt tense. I couldn't really explain why I felt the way I did or what was bothering me, but the feeling was horrible and immobilizing.

This woman's experience could be referred to as a "panic attack," or extreme anxiety. She seemed to sense that something horrible was going to happen, but she didn't know what it was. Many survivors confide that they have these same feelings and sensations.

> For a long time, maybe for three to four months, I was on guard. I had the feeling that things were not right, that I wasn't walking on firm ground. *(Man whose young daughter died suddenly)*

> Wherever I would go, whatever I would do, I would feel an anxiousness. I would feel it in my stomach. It would lay in my stomach, and eventually cause stomach cramps. *(Young widow whose husband died suddenly of a heart attack)*

These feelings of trepidation and anxiousness are common and they can produce disturbing physical symptoms which include the following:

- heart palpitations
- loss of appetite
- ringing in the ears
- digestive problems
- nausea
- dizziness
- nightmares
- constriction in the throat
- muscular pain
- impeded concentration
- poor memory
- damp hands
- dry mouth
- insomnia

It is evident that any part of your body can be affected by the stress of anxiety. As you grieve, you may find yourself caught unaware by sensations you never would have expected to experience. In C.S. Lewis's *A Grief Observed,* he states:

> No one ever told me that grief felt so like fear. I am not afraid, but the sensation is like being afraid. The same fluttering in the stomach, the same restlessness, the yawning. I keep on swallowing.

You may be experiencing one or more of the above symptoms— either on a regular basis, or occasionally. You may feel as if you are constantly traumatized and apprehensive. If so, you may, as a middle-aged attorney put it, be "annoyed at the idea that you are going through these feelings of panic and you don't know *why.*" There is, however, a way to sort this out. Your anxiety, in fact, is a normal outcome of your experience. You have real reasons for feeling the way you do. You have recently been the victim of a circumstance beyond your control. This situation has caused you to be less sure of yourself and your environment than you once were. The uncertainty and fright are even more pronounced if you have lost someone unexpectedly, such as by Sudden Infant Death Syndrome, an automobile accident, an airplane crash, or by suicide or homicide.

Feeling victimized. You now feel as if you have little or no power over what happens or does not happen. The brother of a man who died suddenly of undetermined causes, put it this way: "You are everything's victim. Anything can get you. You don't even have to know what it is." This feeling of powerlessness, of victimization, coupled with a subconscious belief that there is some mysterious zone in which anything can happen, will indeed produce an anxiety which seems to have no focal point.

Feeling disassociated. Your anxiety can be produced, too, simply by the separation of yourself from the other person. The two of you were close, then suddenly the other one is gone and only you remain. A sixty-seven-year-old widow described this state from her personal perspective:

> You are told when you marry that you are *two* people who combine to make *one* unit; one family with shared love and goals. For forty years the *two* of you are *one*. What happens when all of that is subtracted? What are you supposed to do when *one* becomes *one half*? Nobody tells you that.

It is as if your base has been knocked out from under you and you're supposed to build an instant foundation to support yourself. The separation you experience is twofold: You have been permanently separated from the *person* you love and, in addition, you are cut off from *what you were together*. It is frightening and you feel inadequate. At about this same time you may feel intense longing for the other person, a longing so strong that it is almost tangible.

Identifiable Fears

In contrast to experiencing anxiety whose origins may be impossible for you to identify, you may experience some very concrete fears. For example, a parent may be afraid of losing another child in an accident. A widow may be terrified of someone breaking into her house. A widower may be anxious and fearful about his domestic survival. A survivor of a loss due to illness may fear that he or she will also become fatally ill. Many survivors of *all* ages fear they will die soon after the death of a loved one.

All of these fears can be categorized as "fears of impending doom." For the most part, the anticipated situations are not likely to occur. It is unlikely that a parent would lose two children in separate accidents. A widow's house is not more likely to be robbed because there is one resident rather than two. It is unlikely that a widower would not be able to learn how to cook well enough to keep himself alive, or how to operate the washing machine. And unless an illness has been already transmitted or is genetic, it is not realistic for the surviving friend or relative to anticipate becoming ill. Further, this fear can be quickly put to rest by a physical examination.

There are a limitless number of things for a person to be afraid of. In fact, there are as many objects of fear as there are actions, people and things in the world. When it comes to fear, people can be extraordinarily imaginative. One widow worried that she would be poisoned by canned food if she didn't mark the dates of purchase on the cans. A young boy was afraid he would just disappear like a snowman in the hot sun because his older brother had told him his father "disappeared."

A woman who lost her parents tells this story:

> I felt so vulnerable to disaster for a long time. A couple of months after the deaths, I went to Washington D.C. on business. The room that had been reserved for me was on the fourth floor of a popular and picturesque hotel which had no elevator. There was a fire escape outside my window, but that did nothing to alleviate my fear. I was terrified and panicky.

Frightened, the woman called a friend who listened and kindly assured her, "I know that hotel. It hasn't burned down in a hundred years. That is more than thirty-six thousand days. What would be the odds of it burning down the two days you are there?" Afterwards, the woman was able to be more rational and disregard her fear. Her perspective had changed.

All people, however, cannot change their perspective that quickly or easily. The material which follows details specific strategies for coping with foreboding states and situations.

Reducing Fear and Anxiety

Fighting Anxiety of Unknown Origin

To begin with, let us consider anxiety. It is intense but does not seem to be associated with any one person, place, thing, or situation; further, it does not seem predictable. It is as if one is dealing with the ghost of fear. Just as it seems possible to catch it in sight, it vanishes.

If you are having feelings and experiences such as these, there are several important facts for you to remember:

- Everything you feel cannot be explained.

- Your feelings of fright are not permanent.

- You will not "go crazy."

You can experience success in reducing an anxiety of unknown origin. There are three simple procedures which will help you to achieve that goal: 1) allowing yourself an emotional purging, 2) meeting miniature challenges, and 3) being discriminating about your diet.

Allowing yourself an emotional purging. The young widow who complained of "an anxious feeling in my stomach," and of stomach cramps, told how she coped with those conditions and sensations.

> I had to learn to cry. When I did, the anxiousness went away and the sadness took its place. I know people think you are crazy, but I had to learn to cry and sigh. That was part of it. I was literally holding my breath.

It is crucial to recognize that your feeling of anxiety is not operating independently without the support of other feelings. Sadness is most often "standing in the wings," ready to come on and replace anxiety.

Once you begin to exhibit a few of those ignored emotions, such as sadness, you will experience relief, and the relief will continue to grow as each buried emotion is vented in some way. For example, you may have wanted to pine and long for your loved one but you have not done it. You feel such behavior is irrational, too self-indulgent, or disturbing to others. There are those who would agree that it is indeed all of those things, *but* it is also an instinctive need. Many other cultures set aside time for pining and longing because they acknowledge these behaviors as an acceptable part of mourning. Accept them as a part of your mourning, also; recognize them as important instincts which will aid your healing process. Identify a place in which you can vent your feelings without disturbing others. Give yourself a certain amount of regular uninterrupted time for several days, weeks, or even months if you need to. Say what you have been holding in. Say it aloud. It is all right to long for your loved one. Give yourself permission to do it.

> For weeks I would cry and wail all night, "Gary, Gary, come back, come back." All night I would go on without stopping. Living alone made it easier for me to do that. I don't know what I would have done if another person had lived in the house. I only know I had to do that and I did it. I used to wonder if I was going crazy, but I know it made me feel better. It definitely helped me function during the day. *(Wife of an accident victim)*

Eventually your need for expressing longing and sadness will begin to lessen. It does not mean you love the person less, or miss him or her less, it only means your energy is supporting other feelings which will help with your recuperation. *Remember, you have a whole gamut of emotions and if you are to grieve in a healthful way, none will be ignored.*

Meeting Miniature Challenges

It seemed as if I couldn't do anything. For no reason at all, I would ust panic about driving to the store, or meeting a friend who had invited me to lunch, or seeing a neighbor who might stop and say hello. I just felt immobilized by strange feelings. I wanted to get in bed and pull the sheet over my head. *(Teacher who lost both of her elderly parents within a year)*

This statement is rephrased in similar ways by many survivors. It should be stressed here that it is *not just women* who want to withdraw from it all. Men too, want to "pull the sheet" over their heads (and some do). It is easy, when death occurs, to forget that men feel victimized, powerless and vulnerable. They too, can become so anxiety-ridden that they are immobilized. As one male survivor put it, "I don't feel as if I can make anything work out. I feel as if I don't have command over anything—at home, at work, *any*where."

One of the strategies you can use to reestablish your feelings of personal power, and thus reduce your anxiety, is to contract with yourself to meet small challenges. This is the way it works:

First, select some action or conversation that is *necessary,* but *currently very difficult* for you to perform. The smaller it is, the better. For example, it may be taking your suit to the cleaners, going to the post office, photocopying some financial documents, requesting a prescription, writing a thank-you note, getting your hair cut, returning a telephone call, throwing out wilted flower arrangements, changing your sheets, or getting the car filled with gas. The key requirements are that the action *needs to be done* and *it is hard for you to do.*

Now set up a contract with yourself for the next five days. First decide on five necessary actions. On a sheet of paper write the names of the next five days and next to each day write one action you will perform. The list should look embarrassingly easy to anyone else. At another time and under other conditions it would be easy for you; but for now, you need to start where you are, in terms of rebuilding your capability and power. This contract of miniature challenges allows you to do that.

Nobody else needs to know about your list. It is a contract with yourself. At the beginning of each day, read the item you have listed for that day. Next, give yourself a time limit within that day for performing the task. Record that time limit. For example, you might write, "By two o'clock I will have called the insurance company." You might allow yourself as much as five or six hours in which to take action, but make sure you do it. Then cross off the item on your contract. Follow the same procedure for each day. At the end of the fifth day look back at what you have been able to do without help, without encountering disaster, and without breaking down.

You may be wondering, "But what if I *do* lose control when I try to order a perscription or call the insurance company?" The answer is, as long as you complete the action, you cross it off. Your insurance agent will not be harmed if you cry; neither will you. Some things will naturally be less stressful and go more smoothly than others. The objective of this exercise is to regain your power by exerting control over events in your life. Even if you accomplished your goal *only* by extreme effort, you have exhibited capability and some degree of power.

When the first contract is completed, set up another contract for the next five days. This time select two miniature challenges per day. Take precautions not to include actions that are likely to overwhelm you. For example, don't schedule yourself to go look at the coroner's report or pick up your child's personal possessions from school. Keep your requirements reasonable and varied. Soon you will find yourself feeling as if you have more and more command over your life. Your helpless feelings will subside.

When your contract grows to five or six actions a day, you will be back to a fairly normal operational level. By then, you may like to maintain this schedule-making for a while. When you are going through grief, your memory is often undependable. This contract, therefore, has secondary benefits. It serves as an aid to counteract your easily distracted or forgetful nature which, though temporary, is annoying.

Being Discriminating About Your Diet. Feelings of anxiety can also be intensified by certain foods. Don't allow your diet to magnify your psychic tension and uneasiness. More than a minimal amount of stimulants (coffee, tea, or soft drinks with caffeine) should be eliminated.

If your appetite is so poor that you do not eat unless someone insists upon it, you are in danger of suffering from low blood sugar, which can cause tiredness, depression, and anxiety.

Desserts, jams, jellies, and syrups should be eaten in moderation since too much sugar can cause a high energy level followed by a lower-than-normal low.

Alcohol should, of course, be used with caution. It may be more apt to intensify your anxiety than temporarily relieve it. If drink is only a disguise, recognize it as such and keep track of the feeling it is disguising; *that* is what you need to examine.

Coping with Specific Fear

In direct contrast to feeling a general anxiety, you may fear *specific* actions, procedures, and events. A certain degree of fear during the grieving process is to be expected and may subside as quickly as it arose;

however, pervasive and insistent fear that haunts you during the day or keeps you awake at night must be explored. If it isn't, it will impair your ability to experience other feelings that are necessary to your recuperation.

First, pinpoint the exact object of your fear. Here are some fears of other survivors:

- I am afraid to go into my son's room. *(Mother of a teenaged accident victim)*

- I am afraid of interacting with other people. *(Widowed bank teller)*

- I am afraid of going back to work. *(Middle-aged father of teenaged accident victim)*

- I am afraid my house will be broken into when I'm sleeping. *(Fifty-seven-year-old widowed store owner)*

- I am afraid to have another baby. *(Twenty-six-year-old mother whose baby died at four weeks of age)*

Write a statement identifying your fear, starting with, "I am afraid..." Next, write what you *think* or *visualize* that makes you afraid. Following are three examples.

Fear	*What I Think or Visualize that Makes me Afraid*
• I am afraid to go into my son's room.	• I might break down and fall apart.
• I am afraid my house will be broken into when I'm sleeping.	• A person could break into my house, beat me, and rob me — maybe even kill me. I wouldn't have any way to protect myself.
• I am afraid to have another baby.	• The baby might die.

Notice that all of the things the survivors think and visualize reflect catastrophe. Realistically, most people don't experience multiple catastrophies. Most of the actions which occur in your life on a day-to-day basis take place along a continuum of experience. Think of it this way: At one end of the continuum is the event taking place normally and smoothly; at the other end of the continuum is the catastrophe. *In between,* are numerous other ways in which the event could progress. The normalcy or smoothness of the event could be impaired, but that is a long way from a *total* catastrophe. Here is the way this continuum might look for the man who said, "I am afraid to go back to work."

NORMAL PROCEDURE	I return to work, greet my co-workers, and have a normal day at the office.
	I go to work and get butterflies in my stomach when I have to face everybody. I greet everyone and go into my office. I feel self-conscious and nervous.
	I go to work. A co-worker says he's sorry and I get tears in my eyes. We talk for a few minutes and I get a little choked up. Then I say good-bye and go into my own office.
CATASTROPHE	I go to work. A co-worker says he's sorry. I break down and lose all control. I can't work and people think I'm unstable. I'm in danger of losing my job.

There are some differences in each event. Notice that only one of the events is completely positive and only one is totally negative. The event most likely to occur will be a mix of both positive and negative. This is the way it is with the object of your fear, also. Think about it as being along a continuum. Visualize the ways in which it could occur, including the catastrophe. Now write down your new event. Be realistic about what will be likely to happen. Consider this fear, for example, "A person will break into the house, beat me, and rob me—maybe even kill me." *Realistically,* it will be, "With new locks on my doors and windows it is unlikely that anyone could break in easily; if they did break in they would have to make a lot of noise. I would have time to call the police, or leave the house and go to the neighbors."

Now when you experience your old fear creeping up on you during the day, or landing with a resounding thud on your nervous system in the middle of the night, visualize the continuum of experiences. See all the various events with their mixtures of positive and negative. Think only about the event which is most likely to occur. Selecting catastrophe is not realistic. While you visualize this realistic event, concentrate on completely relaxing your body and your breathing. (See the section on *Affirming Your Physical Well-Being* below.)

Fears That Become Phobias

If, after several months, your fear has not subsided you may need to gauge the degree to which your fear is affecting your life. If your fear is dominating your time, affecting your relationships, seriously affecting your physical condition, limiting your mobility, or forcing you to do things the hard way (such as avoid going over bridges, or taking elevators, or passing your dead child's room), then it would be wise to seek counseling.

A pathological disturbance which sometimes arises if symptoms of anxiety and fear continue to magnify, is agoraphobia. The world, to an agoraphobic, is terrifying. It is seen with dread, a place where anything can happen. For example, a girl who has lost her mother may feel that as long as she stays with her father, his life will not be in danger; neither will he die. "No one can die," thinks the girl, "if I'm at home watching."

Whenever any severe and prolonged symptoms are manifested, counseling is recommended. Fears may perpetuate withdrawal, or prevent you from releasing other emotions which are necessary to successful grieving.

Affirming Your Physical Well-Being

You will recall the variety of physical symptoms cited earlier. Some of them may be ones you experience either consistently or intermittently. Think about them. You may be tense. Your hands may shake. You may be nauseated, or find it difficult to swallow. Determine which part of your body is feeling the brunt of your anxiety and fear. Think about exactly how that part of your body feels. "My heart feels like a butterfly, fluttering in my chest." "My throat feels as if it is closing up." "I feel as if I'm losing my balance when I walk." "My mouth is constantly dry." Write a sentence that describes each disturbing physical sensation you experience.

Next, you are going to contradict those statements. Beside each one, write a statement that reflects a *normal* physical sensation for that part of your body. For example, next to, "My heart feels like a butterfly..." you may write, "My heart is beating with regularity and strength." Next to the statement, "My throat feels as if it is closing," you will write, "My throat feels relaxed and open, and I find it easy to breathe and swallow."

Visualization. For at least twenty minutes every day, and at a specific time, follow this procedure. (1) Get in a completely comfortable position. (2) Concentrate on relaxing your body, starting from the top of your head and progressing to your toes. Say to yourself, "I feel loose and relaxed. My face feels relaxed; my jaw is loose and open. I am relaxing the muscles in my neck and shoulders..." Continue thinking about total relaxation as you loosen your body, gradually feelng your muscles relax all the way down to the end of your toes. As you progress, do a mental inventory of how your body feels and concentrate for a longer period of time on relaxing any part which still feels tense or resisting. (3) When you are completely relaxed, close your eyes and say your affirmation to yourself. ("My throat is relaxed and open..." etc.) *At the same time,* visualize the specific part of your body which corresponds to your affirmation. Visualize it as healthy, without any irregularity. (4) Do not let yourself think about anything other than your affirmation. Continue this exercise until your physical symptom subsides.

You cannot, of course, follow this exercise and expect it to work if you do not utilize the other strategies discussed in the preceding material; that is, it is unrealistic to think you can get rid of any symptom without getting rid of its cause. Employing the other strategies which are relevant to your anxiety or fear—purging emotions, meeting miniature challenges, being discriminating about your diet, and coping with specific fear—makes it possible for you to eradicate your state of fright and replace it with one which is neither disquieting nor taxing.

Experiencing Sadness

> I didn't know it was possible to feel such sadness. I have been unhappy before, but never like this. Sometimes the sadness is almost like physical pain. In fact, I wish it were. I think it might be easier to get rid of. Sometimes I think maybe I'm not going to feel that way any more. Then it comes back. *(Father of a nine-year-old son who died as the result of a burst blood vessel in his brain)*

You may have successfully pushed away thoughts of your loss for a few hours. You may even be able to go several consecutive days without "breaking down." Then, just when you think you are beginning to function without showing how you feel inside, something triggers all the emotion that has been waiting for an outlet. Perhaps you see a child who reminds you of your deceased son or daughter. You may hear your boyfriend's favorite song on the radio, see your wife's best friend driving down the street, or find a forgotten birthday card from your sister. Suddenly all that feeling that you had so successfully suppressed rushes to the surface. It is then that you are reminded of the deep sadness which you carry with you as a constant, but not always evident companion.

Unanticipated tears. Your feelings may spill forth at times when there seems to be no outside source to provoke such a reaction. For no obvious reason, you may begin to cry in the supermarket, while driving home from work, or while dining in a restuarant. During ordinary activities such as these you find yourself in tears so suddenly you are astonished. When this happens, you are at a loss to explain exactly what it is you are crying about.

> After my son died, many times when we went out to dinner at another couple's house, or to a party, I would go into the bathroom at the other people's houses and cry. *(Mother of an accident victim)*

> I would go to the bank, or to see the accountant, and I would start to cry. I would just stand there and cry and I knew people felt awkward, but I couldn't control it. *(Young widowed nurse)*

Bereaved people usually think they owe others an explanation for crying without giving "prior notice." However, there isn't any way a grieving person can convey the deep source from which personal sadness erupts. Each individual's emotions will be triggered by incidents that he or she least suspects would recall the loss.

A young mother whose eight-year-old son was killed in an automobile accident relates an incident that occurred several months after the death when she went to the races with her husband.

> We were in the stands when a young boy fell in the crowd. He started to cry for his mother, and when he did, I began to cry. That boy was my son crying for me.

A middle-aged woman whose father died when she was six tells of bursting into tears one evening when she was attending a retirement dinner at which a band was playing.

> I stood there in the dining room with people all around me and I began to cry. My father had been a musician. I had few memories of him, but one of the few I had was of him playing onstage in a band. There was something about the way one of the men was smiling and tapping his foot. For that moment, he could have been my father. Even though my father had been dead for forty years, it made me feel my loss and I began to cry.

There may be similar occasional incidences of spontaneous crying throughout your life. Generally, however, your bursts of unexpected tears should be less frequent after about the first eighteen months of your loss.

Releasing Your Sadness

If, during your grieving period, you are working hard at repressing your sadness, you are only delaying the necessary expiation which must precede healing. The more you allow yourself to cry, the more possible it will be for you to progress through the mourning period. Remember the statement of the young widowed nurse who was experiencing anxiety.

> I had to learn to cry. When I did, the anxiousness went away and the sadness took its place.... I even had to learn to sigh because I

had been letting the anxious feeling lay in my stomach and it was causing stomach cramps.

For the first six months every time I looked at something that had belonged to my wife, I began to cry. But the crying was good. I had to do it. It doesn't help to hold in how you feel. *(Retired air force captain who lost his wife of forty years)*

Because grief has to show up somewhere, it will manifest itself in someway, even if you are determined (or someone else is determined) to keep it from being evident. Suppressed emotion can result in sleeplessness, heart palpitations, a choking sensation, irregular breathing, and weight loss as well as a number of other physical symptoms.

I couldn't get the grief out in the hospital because when I started to cry and get it out they gave me medication. I had to wait until I got home, which was four months later. Then I went back to the house where we had been living and indulged myself thoroughly. I cried and ranted and raved. *(Young woman accident victim whose fiance was killed)*

If you don't cry, chances are you are trying to protect those around you from any discomfort, you are taking medication, or you are making a concerted effort to be a "strong person."

The word "strong" is much distorted when discussing the actions of the bereaved. "He shows such strength through all of this," or "She is such a strong person," implies that if the survivor showed feelings, *honestly* showed them, he or she would be the opposite of strong, which is *weak*.

When a friend or relative whom you know well and trust, asks you how you are, you don't have to reply with, "Fine," if you're not fine. If you feel sad, talk about your feeling. Share your thoughts. Mention the experiences that are making you feel sad.

There are also benefits to be gained by joining a support group. In the company of others who have had a similar experience, you can say you feel sad and you don't need to tone down your sadness or apologize for it. (See *Getting and Giving Help* in Section III.) The participants of the group will be aware of your needs and will not cause you to feel uncomfortable. They won't insist that you "get over that now," or that you "quit feeling sorry for yourself." They know you have every right in the world to feel sorry for yourself. You have been hurt. Your life has been altered. You miss the person who is gone.

If it is difficult to express your feelings aloud and you feel more at ease writing about them, then do that. Get a notebook and "talk it out" on paper. It should be pointed out that keeping a journal or writing a poem is not exclusively a female activity. Many men write poems which deal with the loss of a loved one. For some men, it seems safer to write about loss, than talk about it. Unfortunately and historically, men have had — the pressure is lessening — to be overly concerned with appearing strong at all costs. Sometimes the cost is their health, job or marriage.

Being "strong" (and silent) after death has been an unrealistic expectation of our particular culture. However, as professionals and human service agencies become more attuned to the psychological effects of death, this expectation diminishes. This attitudinal change, though gradual, reflects a more realistic view of mourning, one which is long overdue in our Western culture.

Experiencing Despair

> There are still times when I think, God, I'm never going to feel good. It is so much effort to go on. *(Mother speaking on the one-year anniversary of her teenaged son's death)*

One day in the midst of research for this book, I had just completed seven hours of interviews with bereaved people. The last person with whom I had talked, a middle-aged man who had lost two children — one to cancer, the other in an automobile accident — had been questioning the purpose of life. He asked, "Is all this agony really worth it?"

I was thinking about this as I drove toward home. Then, almost as if it had been prearranged, a battered pickup truck pulled in front of me and rattled down the highway, bearing a bumper sticker which read: LIFE IS HARD. THEN YOU DIE.

In the following weeks as I continued to interview people experiencing deep dispair, the message of that bumper sticker kept reoccurring. Often, after a death, people feel that the human experience is an equation with zeroes on both sides. Life is perceived as being "as empty as death" and death as final as a void, a zero. During the first year or so of bereavement, people having this kind of reaction may feel as if they are drowning. They consider the smallest everyday task such as getting dressed, washing their hair, or answering the telephone to be nearly impossible. Merely getting out of bed can be a long and arduous process that requires not minutes, but hours.

Awareness of mortality. Along with the despair you feel, you also experience the psychic shock that accompanies the full realization of your own mortality. This realization is the inevitable outcome of losing someone close to you.

As you reflect upon this inevitability, you assess and evaluate many of your actions, desires and goals. You ruminate about what you will do now, and what your limitations are in the future. It may seem as if you have to chop your way through an impenetrable forest in order to reach a clearing. And worse, you don't know what to expect when you get there. You think, "What is it all for?" You find yourself tired, dismayed, and feeling hopeless.

During this period, you may also reflect temporarily on the unknown aspects of death. You may ask, "Just what *is* death, anyway?" "What happens when you die?"

Trying To Make Sense of Death

Death often seems grossly "unfair." It certainly does not follow any accessible logic. Depending upon the content and degree of your religious or metaphysical beliefs, death may be viewed as anything from a completely mysterious state about which *nothing* is known, to a state which is only slightly perplexing because *most aspects* of it are *assumed*. For most people, however, death represents a realm which has few, if any, definitive characteristics. Bereaved people commonly feel they have no answers to any of the major death-related questions: "What does death mean to the individual?" "What happens in terms of the separation of the spirit and body, or of the soul and body?" "What is the possibility of 'life' after death?" "What is the possibility of rebirth, punishment, or reward?" Trying to make sense of what happens would be easier if it were possible to answer the seven-year-old boy who, when told of his mother's sudden death, asked, "Where *is* death?"

If it were possible to give absolute answers to *what* death means and *where* it is, two of the biggest mysteries of all time would be solved. For those whose religious beliefs provide answers to these questions, any exploration may be seen as entirely unnecessary. However, research has shown that most bereaved people welcome any attempt at an investigation into the invisible realm of death.

People's beliefs about the meaning of death can be seen as quite distinct, one from another. In trying to make some sense of death, most people have adopted one of the following orientations:

- Death is being with God in heaven.

- Death is an invisible force that takes you when it is your time to go. Death is the grim reaper.

- Death is a time of judgment during which your life is evaluated and you are consigned to either a heaven or hell.

- Death is only non-living. It is the ultimate existential experience.

- Death is an elevation to another life, a continued existence in a realm without the consequences of human frailty—hostility, materialistic values, etc.

- Death is a rebirth. It is beginning again in a new and different life. (Voltaire wrote, "After all it is no more surprising to be born twice than it is to be born once.")

- Death is the state between two other states, as sleep is the state between two waking states.

You will be inclined to believe one of these more than the rest because the core content of one orientation diminishes or precludes belief in the content of another. In addition to holding a particular belief, there are several predispositional factors which may lessen your interest in boldly examining death. These factors stem from several lines of thinking: 1) If I do not fear death, then I do not completely respect its power. I must respect death because before it, I am helpless. 2) I am presumptuous to think I can fathom the unfathomable. We can never really *know* anything about death; we can only guess or fantasize. 3) If I can explain and define death, then I am reducing the magnitude of my loved one's death and am minimizing my own personal loss.

So if we think of death as the greatest of all dilemmas, to be feared, contended with, or used as a measurement for suffering, we can't observe or examine it.

Of course, we all "capitulate" to death as physical bodies. But this does not mean that we must also ignore death, mentally and emotionally. Beginning in the 1970's, studies were undertaken to examine the *what* and *where* of death. These scientific inquiries were conducted among subjects who had what are termed "near-death experiences."

The near-death experience. These subjects had been considered "clinically dead"; they lacked any respiration or pulse, or they were as close to death as you can get without being clinically dead. These men and women had come near to death, or had experienced apparent death as a result of a serious illness, an accident, or an attempted suicide. They were of various ages, incomes and educational backgrounds. Some of the people were religious, others were not. When interviewed privately these people described what they saw, felt, heard, and understood while they were in the near-death state.

The research disclosed a remarkable phenomenon. Individuals who had never met, and who had no access to one another's interviews, told of experiences which were so nearly identical that they could not be dismissed as coincidental, or having been suggested or imagined. This does not mean that this research is a definitive ultimate or that it will offer every one of us a glimpse of what death is and where it is. But we cannot completely ignore the common and similar experiences of people who are otherwise different in background, behavior, and belief.

The survivor's independent descriptions of the near-death experience provided researchers with sufficient material to advance many hypothesis regarding the pattern of dying as well as the quality of death. Following are several characteristics of near-death experience which may be of particular interest to those considering the *what* and *where* of death:

- The experience is positive, sometimes even euphoric, with a stabilizing calmness, sureness, and deep peace.

- There is no loneliness.

- There is no pain.

- The dying person often views, as if from a distance, the "end" of life; that is, the individual may witness others frantically trying to save his or her body.

The person who is entering the realm of death is so at peace there is no desire to return to physical life on earth. Many of the near-death subjects returned because they felt it was imperative for them to continue their lives. They were needed to take care of someone, to finish some work which they had begun, or to fulfill some other purpose. They had decided to *come* back, or they were *sent* back by an unspoken directive that issued from within the realm of death. Some people felt they had been *called back* to life by someone.

> I felt as if I was moving toward a light. I wasn't aware that I was dead. I felt very determined to reach the light and the closer I got to it the more ecstatic I felt. There was an overwhelming sense of joy. There is a feeling of love about the light—there is no way of putting it into language. I don't remember anything other than that my determination was to reach the light. Then, I heard my daughter, who was one and a half years old at the time, calling my name. At first, I was annoyed because I was distracted from the light. As she called, "Mommy, mommy," the light seemed to be withdrawing. When I returned I was in my hospital room and felt as if I had been tricked into staying there because my daughter wasn't there. Then I realized that she needed me, whether or not she was there in the room. *(Young mother who experienced a near-death experience when hospitalized with Guillain-Barré syndrome)*

None of the people who had a near-death experience expressed any fear or uncertainty regarding death. The *what* and *where* were no longer beyond their imaginings. They fathomed death and found it an experience completely devoid of negative feelings and unpleasant sensations.

You are free, of course, to accept or reject these selected findings. They are presented here in the belief that they constitute a valid offering, one which permits a survivor to reflect with less sadness and despair on what he or she may previously have seen as the existential void or terror-filled "fate" of a loved one.

Experiencing Confusion and Disorientation

> We tried at first to be just as we always were. For me it got increasingly difficult to go out and pretend I never had the son I had. Now, it's easier than it was. *(Mother of a six-year-old leukemia victim)*

Sometime after the death you will realize that you cannot be as you were before. You may find yourself confused about your changed identity since your loved one's death. It takes more than a few months to gradually develop a different perspective on your life and, specifically, on *who you are now.*

A Changed Identity

Before you experienced this recent death, your life proceeded in a certain way; now that way has been altered. Your schedule, environment, and circumstances have changed. Because of this, you too are not exactly as you were. You have lost a person who was a part of your identity. You were Michael's mother, or John's uncle, or Ann's sister. Now that part of you no longer actively exists. Even though you continue to be John's uncle or Ann's sister in your heart and memory, the reality is that you are no longer interacting with John or Ann. *The loss of the person has subtracted from you part of your self-definition.*

To compound this confusion, a new and possibly even undesirable identity is thrust upon you as a result of death.

I was this woman who had just lost this child. That is who I was. *(Mother of a young cancer victim)*

I was the girl whose father had just died. People said it to each other and I overheard them. I heard people talking in the neighborhood, at school, everywhere I went. Only my mother seemed to treat me as a regular person. *(Teacher reflecting on her father's death when she was five years of age)*

In our small community I was the young widow. I was aware of other people watching me to see if I behaved as a young widow should but I didn't know what that behavior was. All I knew was that my life had drastically changed forever. *(Accountant widowed at twenty-eight years of age)*

In addition to your life circumstances being altered, and your activities changing as a result of your loved one's death, you have definite *feelings* about the role you played as the deceased's wife, husband, sibling or friend. You had a place for this role in your emotional make-up. For example, you may have been *proud* to be the mother of a boy who played the violin in the youth symphony, or was awarded a college scholarship, or scored a touchdown. You got *satisfaction* from being your little brother's idol. You felt *important* when your niece preferred your company to that of the other relatives. You *enjoyed* the *respect* you received as the husband of an accomplished, popular wife. But these elements of gratification have been cancelled out by your loved one's death.

A psychologist working with the bereaved commented on this state, during which redefinition becomes necessary.

So much of us is defined by what we do in the world and who we are in the world; losing a child or a partner changes that. Often, a lot of self-esteem is tied in with the other person.

Sometimes your identity can be so affected that it seems as if you no longer really have any identity at all. In May Sarton's *Shadow of a Man,* the main character, Frances Chaubrier, has just experienced the death of his mother.

He was here on the steps of his mother's house, Francis Adams Chaubrier, and yet he asked himself, "Do I exist?" For the last few hours it had seemed as if his very existence were suspended. There was no simple answer to this philosophical question, and even as he asked it, he proved his existence at least as a physical being, by walking quickly down the hill, listening to his own footsteps as if they were somehow reassuring.

He must, of course, assure himself that he is still alive; that he does indeed exist, though not in the same way as before. Death has also revised your identity and it is necessary for you to reestablish *for yourself* who you are, what you want, and what your methods for achieving your goals are.

A Changed Perspective

Almost without exception, the bereaved person changes his or her priorities in regard to social participation and personal goals. You may now find yourself taking a look at exactly how you have spent the precious years of your life. As you compare the past to the present, your perspective changes. What once seemed important, such as a party, your club, shopping, a golf game, possibly even your occupation, may no longer have the same importance. In fact, you may place no value on it whatsoever.

What really matters is people, their relationships, love and caring. Nothing else really matters—money, power, and all that. It means nothing. *(Mother of an accident victim)*

I recognize when I get lost in my cerebral activities and then I consciously make myself pay more attention to the other part of me. *(Woman survivor of an accident in which the driver was killed)*

I'm not as social as I was. I don't want to do as much. I don't like big parties. I don't like small talk. I've always been a little bit that way but now I am more so. *(Mother of a teenaged accident victim)*

I had seen how everything could be wiped out in a minute and I wasn't going to do anything I didn't really believe in anymore. It makes living more immediate for me. *(Woman who survived an accident which took the life of another passenger)*

Working Toward Clarification and Redefinition

After a period of assessing your life to date, you will likely adopt a revised set of values, or even a *new* set of values. This may mean that your life structure will be greatly altered. You may, for example, have no desire at all to relate to particular individuals with whom you once spent much of your time. You may not want to devote as many hours to domestic chores, church duties, or business dinners. You may think it a waste to expend as much energy participating in sports. You may not even want to continue the same career.

> I changed my job because I felt it wasn't relevant to my life any more. That is why I went back to school. I wanted to be trained so I could do something in the helping, feeling field. *(Parent who left sales to get a degree in social work)*

Commonly, a survivor has less interest in social functions or materially oriented activities, and an increased interest in those areas of life concerned with human values, such as love, compassion, assistance to others, or political or social activism. Many people in the field of bereavement are those who have redirected their careers after being affected by the death of a loved one. Businessmen who have been through loss often spend less time with their associates and more time with their families. Homemakers return to school to undertake study in the field of psychology and sociology. Bereaved siblings become social activists or volunteers in human services organizations.

All priority changes are not major ones such as these. They come in various degrees. Your own changes may be extremely ambitious or quite modest. They may also be so instinctive that you don't notice them. For example, you may no longer accept invitations to large gatherings or spend as many weekends working on your boat, or watching television. Instead, you may devote more time to something that seems more valuable to you, such as helping your child with homework, pursuing your own education, or having "quality visits" with older family members. You may treat yourself and a companion to a picnic in the woods, a walk on the beach, or a lovely dinner. You may take time off for a leisurely trip.

What you do for yourself will change continually as your personal needs change. You will find your grief producing growth—a growth that is almost indiscernible at first, but as the days progress, redefinition and restructuring will become increasingly evident.

II.

Surviving Specific Types of Loss

3

Surviving the Loss
of a Spouse

*It was very, very hard to go to work and
come home to my house whtn the sun was
going down. That was the hardest thing to
handle...coming back to that empty house
up on a hill in the country, unlocking the
door, and walking in...*

WIDOW

*The house isn't even a house without her. I
can't look forward to her coming
home...walking in. I'm just getting through
the days one at a time the best I can. We
were married for thirty eight years. It's like
part of me is missing. Part of me is* missing.

WIDOWER

When surviving spouses share their feelings following the death of a
husband or wife, they usually speak of the extremely debilitating effects
of feeling entirely *alone* and *incomplete*.

If you have experienced these feelings, you know that the sense of
having lost an essential part of yourself is painful and disorienting. The

immediate world often seems odd and distanced. You are not sure how to cope with life in general. Sometimes you may not be sure you want to *try*.

During the period immediately following your spouse's death, you will be most likely to experience a depressed mood, prolonged and excessive crying, and insomnia. As sadness, despair and exhaustion pervade your daily life, you may also feel a futility which affects you physically and emotionally. A sixty-five-year-old widow said, "There is no use trying because you can't get anywhere anyway. I'm so tired all the time. Everything is too much effort."

A widower tells of being a gourmet cook before his wife died. For several months following her death, he was unable to get his own breakfast, or even brew a cup of coffee. His inability had nothing to do with lack of skill; it was caused by lack of motivation and the helplessness that comes with depression. He reports that he "no longer felt complete." His breakfast partner wasn't there. He was alone and resented it.

There are inumerable ways in which a spouse reacts to loss. Your own feelings and concerns in this regard are influenced by your personality, your unique characteristics, the nature of your marital relationship, the duration of your marriage, the cause of your spouse's death, previous losses you have endured, and your age and gender, as well as other factors.

The section which follows explores the most common responses of widows and widowers.

Feelings and Concerns Following the Death of a Spouse

In addition to reporting that they felt incomplete and alone, surviving spouses summed up their major feelings and concerns in the following statements:

- I feel as if I have lost my best friend.
- I am angry.
- I feel guilty about something (or many things) I did.
- Now I think about my own death more frequently.
- I feel very old.
- I feel sick all the time.
- I am afraid.
- I worry about money.
- I'm going through an identity crisis.
- I feel relieved after the death.

You will identify with some of these statements and not with others. You may also find yourself silently adding statements which reflect some of your own unique feelings and concerns.

To more fully understand the effects of losing a spouse, it helps to examine the dynamics behind each of the above reactions. In this way, you can gain an awareness of how your own responses are being shaped. Is is easier to cope when you know exactly what you are coping *with*. Let's explore the statements to learn what forces are operating to produce these strong feelings and concerns.

I feel as if I have lost my best friend. When your spouse has also been your best friend, you experience a loss which has many components. First, you have lost the companion with whom you shared activities. Even if your spouse did not participate in an activity with you, he or she acknowledged it and accepted your need to do it. The majority of your activities, therefore, were supported by your husband or wife—either by his or her direct involvement or through compliance.

Secondly, you had a language that was familiar and shared by both of you. You used the same references, anticipated one another's topics of conversational interest, and perhaps enjoyed the same sense of humor.

Thirdly, you received daily (nonsexual) physical contact to which you may have become so accustomed, you didn't miss it until it was gone: the pat on your shoulder when you worked in the kitchen, the hand on your elbow when you went down the steps, the smoothing of your hair, the straightening of your tie. As one widower noted, "Nobody ever touches me any more. Not sexually, but just as another human being."

Fourth, you were the recipient of the kind of loyalty that is provided by a best friend. This is the loyalty of the trusted supporter and "co-conspirator" who backed you up, explained you to others and served, if necessary, as your active defender.

All of these components add up to an interaction that was, above all, enormously familiar and highly valued.

I am angry. Anger arises from a wide variety of feelings, beliefs and situations.

When you have been left by someone you trust, interact with and depend on, it is natural for you to feel abandoned. Some husbands and wives are successful in convincing themselves that their spouses died on purpose, deliberately and mercilessly leaving them in a state of loneliness, disarray and confusion. Whether this is a conscious or a subconscious conviction, it can produce a great degree of anger. Further, spouses may feel that the desertion of their partner has robbed them of their future as they wanted or *expected* it to be.

Anger can just as easily be directed toward the self. You may, for example, be angry at yourself for not loving enough, not getting a different doctor (treatment, hospital, clinic, etc.) for your spouse, for not working harder and assuming a larger share of the economic burden, or for not having children. You may even be angry because you let yourself "get so attached" to another person, and be so "completely vulnerable."

Regardless of the source of your anger or the direction it takes (self or others), it is important to find *healthy* ways of expressing your angry feelings. (See *Experiencing Anger,* in Section I.)

I feel guilty about something (or many things) I did. It has been emphasized repeatedly that anger and guilt often operate side by side. For example, the man who feels angry at himself for not loving his wife enough may also feel *guilty* because his love was insufficient and inadequately expressed.

You may feel guilty about being too quick to criticize, about being disloyal, about not earning more, or about being a poor listener. A spouse can feel guilt about anything. One woman criticized herself for not granting her husband's request to stop at his favorite coffee shop "hang out" when they were returning from a trip to a nearby medical clinic. "That was the last time he expressed any desire at all to be out in public. He probably was trying to prove to himself he could go on with life as usual, but I said we had to get home because I needed to call a real estate client. I could have done that later — or not at all. It wouldn't have made any real difference."

When the survivor is suddenly the recipient of death benefits the new financial gain can cause tremendous guilt.

> It was difficult for me to have money all at once. My husband and I didn't have any savings and we were selling our house to have a savings. It was as if all at once I exchanged him for money. It was a horrible guilt. I was being practical with the use of the money, but I still felt as if I shouldn't have the money. Because I'm not working full time and doing what society says I should do I still feel guilty using the money to live on. *(Widow)*

In a survey conducted among widowers it was found that most of them felt uncomfortable with any financial assets due to them resulting from their wife's death. If they inherited money they did not need to raise their children or to pay off medical bills, they gave the inheritance away to children or their wife's relatives.

When a spouse dies of illness, the survivor feels that if only his or her care would have been better, the death would not have occurred. A wife thinks she took her husband to the wrong specialist. A husband believes his wife would have lived if he had insisted on an earlier diagnosis.

Regardless of the *reason* for the guilt, every guilt arises from one of two premises: 1) that you would have made your spouse's life *happier* if you had done a certain thing, or, 2) that if you had not done one thing, another thing would not have occurred; that is, if you had done or not done something your spouse *would not have died.*

Many assumptions are based on the belief that your actions would have made all the difference. This belief leads to the issue of personal control. By feeling guilty you are making yourself believe that you had control over the death. Having the conviction that you are guilty is preferable to accepting the fact that death is beyond your control. (See *Understanding and Dispelling Your Guilt* in Section I.)

Now I think about my own death more frequently. Because your spouse's life ended against your will, you realize that your own life can do the same. Your mortality is underscored, and your death may seem to be approaching rapidly. Even though your death is not any more imminent than it ever was, you may find yourself thinking about it more than ever.

You may, in fact, have less fear of dying or even wish to die so you can join your partner. (These wishes usually dissipate within the first few months, but if they are obsessive, counseling should be sought.)

I feel very old. Usually, the feeling of being very old accompanies the preoccupation with death. Worse yet, if you are experiencing this feeling, your "oldness" is reinforced on a daily basis. For the most part, the lithe-bodied, younger generation is featured in billboard, magazine, and newspaper advertising as well as TV commercials. Further, eighty percent of the actors on television are between the ages of twenty-five and forty. As you look out at the world in general, it can seem as if you have no valued place in society. In advertising, for example, the senior citizen's only concerns seem to be denture cleaner, antacids, medical insurance, life insurance, and telephone calls which come to them from across the miles as they rest their weary bones in rocking chairs.

No wonder you feel ancient or ill. it is as if that is what you are expected to be. (See *Transforming the Mourning Process into the Nurturing Process* in this chapter.)

I feel sick all the time. Insomnia, extreme tiredness, anorexia, headaches, indigestion, chest pains, and heart palpitations are symptoms frequently reported by survivors.

In a noteworthy study conducted with people who were experiencing conjugal bereavement, it was found that the subjects had depressed T-cell function. This means that their immune response was impaired and the subjects were more likely to be susceptible to infections.

In the six month period following the death of a spouse, your loss can physiologically manifest itself in many ways. When your general health changes, there naturally occurs a reduced capacity to care for yourself, to carry on with domestic chores or a job. In this sense, your perception of self-worth becomes suddenly and drastically changed. So the problem of poor health ultimately affects all aspects of life — psychological, emotional, social, and mental.

I am afraid. Any person who is experiencing a major change or loss will feel afraid. Fear may be a strong reaction during the first few months after the death of your spouse. You may fear taking care of yourself or fear being emotionally alone for the rest of your life. You may fear shopping alone, driving by yourself, or sleeping in your house alone. A widow who lost her husband after forty-two years confided, "I'm afraid at night because I've never gone to bed in an empty house. I lived at home with my parents until I was nineteen. Then I married and lived with Don. I've never been by myself."

This type of situation can be very frightening to someone who is already experiencing the stress produced by loss. (See *Experiencing Fear and Anxiety* in Section I.)

I worry about money. Numerous financial situations occur following the death of a spouse. First, more often than not, financial matters are not in order when a husband dies. Approximately fifty percent of the property owners in this country die without leaving a will. Second, when the spouse who dies has been the financial planner and money manager, the surviving spouse may not be aware of the location, amount and distribution of the resources. Third, even if financial matters have been attended to and all resources clearly delineated, they may be shockingly insufficient. Fourth, from the spouse's point of view, property may be inequitably or irrationally distributed among the survivors.

Financial complications or insufficient resources can produce a variety of reactions in the spouse survivor, including anxiety, fear, shame, and anger. For some, emotional energy can be completely consumed by the economics of survival.

I am going through an identity crisis. There are many ways in which people establish their identity. A man gains his identity largely through his occupation (lawyer, teacher, truck driver, artist, etc.). Next, his identity is partly established through his recreation or avocation (golfer, pilot, bowling champ, volunteer fireman, etc.), his memberships (Rotarian, Mason, Elk, Jaycee, church officer, local union representative, etc.) and his role as husband and father. The order in which these facets of the man's identity are established depends, of course, on the individual, but most males will gain their major identity through their employment.

In contrast, a woman's identity more often starts with wife and mother, and *then* includes identity through occupation, or association with community groups, recreation, or women's networks. Though this identity structure for women is changing, the change is very gradual, especially in some areas of the country where *who* a woman is married to is far more important to society than *what* a woman does for a living. The result, therefore, is that a married woman's identity is usually much more closely linked to her husband, than the husband's is to his spouse. It does not mean the husband loves his wife less or misses her less, but it does mean that more of his self-definition, his identity in the world, remains intact after the death of his spouse. The more sources of positive identity, the more sources there are of self-esteem and gratification.

In this regard, the woman who has established a role outside of the home will not have lost her sole source of identity; but the woman who has been Dr. William's *wife, Mrs. Richard* Burke, or the *Shirley half* of

Jack and Shirley, may have quite a struggle with identity following the death of her spouse. A widow is no longer a "couple." She is a single individual who now reminds others that their own "couple-ness" may be in jeopardy. A widow is a visual reminder that one half of a couple (who were former friends) is now missing. As a result, a widow may experience a new kind of loneliness, that which comes from being excluded from dinner parties, bridge nights, tennis games, group camping trips or senior citizen couples' functions. Weekends or nights that were once spent with other couples are now spent alone.

In addition, the widow often feels different without her spouse and because of this she removes herself from her former friends.

> I still find it hard when I'm with people who knew us together. I expect Ted to walk in. I know that although they're nice to me there is a part of the puzzle that is missing. He was a great conversationalist and had a good sense of humor and I know they miss that. I know I can't fill that gap. I just don't want to be around them. *(Thirty-two-year-old widow)*

Surviving spouses often find it emotionally easier to interact with new people or those friends who didn't know the deceased spouse. Six months after the death of her husband, one widow described her feelings in this regard:

> It's hard for me to be around people who both of us cared for. I see the person and I start to cry. I can't even go back to our family doctor. It's easier to go to someone who never knew Jim.

I feel relieved after the death. There are many spouses who experience relief upon the death of a husband or wife. This relief may have come from any number of causes: 1) the spouse was terminally ill and was experiencing great distress, discomfort, or pain; 2) the spouse was an accident victim whose injuries had reduced life to nothing more than existence, 3) the deceased spouse was abusive, or, 4) the spouse was suffering from a chronic addiction which made it impossible to have a quality relationship.

> My husband drank excessively and abused the children. He promised to change and attempted to change, but didn't. When he died, I felt relief. It was as if the children and I were free. We had lived in fear of him for so long. Yet, part of me knows I'm supposed to be sad. All I feel is pity for him, and I feel strange because I was married ten years and I think I'm kind of disloyal not to miss him. Sometimes I wonder if I'll be punished for it. *(thirty-year-old widow and mother of three children, ages 8, 6, and 4)*

. A feeling of relief is not easily admitted, and, quite obviously, is difficult to bear because it brings with it the burden of guilt and often the confusion generated by the spouse's own unacceptable reactions.

Expressing Your Feelings

As noted at the beginning of the chapter, during the first few months following the death you will no doubt feel depressed, are likely to do a lot of crying, and may experience sleep disturbance. These are the reactions most commonly reported by surviving spouses. At this same time, you are dealing with many other feelings, reactions, and concerns which occur as a result of your loss. Now, the task is coping with those responses in a way which will ultimately facilitate your healing.

Talking About Your Feelings

First, it is imperative to recognize that healing cannot take place if you do not express what you are feeling and thinking as a result of your loss. Both positive and negative responses need to be shared. You will benefit by talking of your loneliness, your missing, and you will review the final days of your loved one's life. Allow yourself to talk about the type of person your husband or wife was, about things your spouse did and said, and about the activities, interests, qualities and opinions the two of you shared.

You may feel ambivalence about some aspect of your life together. You may want to vent your anger.

> I thought I knew how to handle it. I knew I was going to go through anger. I knew I was going to go through periods of being vulnerable. Even though I intellectualized it, I still had to go through it and experience it. *I made myself sick physically because I wasn't letting my feelings out. (Widow whose forty-two-year-old husband died suddenly of a heart attack)*

Expression is equally important to widows and widowers. Our societal expectations, however, make it more difficult for the widower to discuss or convey his feelings and concerns. For example, men generally do not have the same kind of peer support that women have. Talking is viewed by men as an activity which is necessary to accomplish a specific task. Talking should serve an acceptable, legitimate function. It should take care of business, convey useful information, or set forth plans, but a man should not just talk because he wants to; for the most part, this is viewed as aimless activity.

Certainly, a man is allowed to "get it off his chest" once in a while, but that is the exception rather than the rule. If he unburdens himself frequently, he may be seen as weak, vulnerable, or "womanly."

A male survivor explained his feelings on the subject.

> I can talk to my sister about the macho thing and a woman can be very understanding, very sympathetic, but it doesn't mean a hell of a lot unless it comes from another man.

Women are more accustomed to establishing relationships through the benefit of verbal expression. Talk is perceived as a way to form a stronger bond with a friend, to intensify a needed relationship. Women are used to bonding that builds from a conversational exchange. Any bonding that men do usually results from an activity. Perhaps the strongest examples of this are seen among men who are in the armed services, serving in the same companies, squadrons, or platoons. It is also prominent in the case of police officers who serve together on the same force. Interestingly, it is often action or the threat of potential violence that binds the men together.

Unfortunately, very real consequences emerge from *not* expressing feelings. Studies have shown the mortality rate is higher among those who do not exhibit grief.

This discrepancy in grief-related behavior between the genders will diminish as a younger generation of men become influenced by a more psychologically aware society, and as they are exposed to the increasingly acceptable concept of counseling and therapy to facilitate emotional and psychological growth.

The inhibited expression of the young widow and widower. When a man or woman loses a spouse in a premature death, there emerges a major challenge. The spouse survivor must often provide emotional support to the children at the time of his or her own grieving. A man may be expected to comfort his wife's mother and sister as well as his children. The young widow must keep herself from exhibiting any severe grief or sadness because she fears it will hurt her children. To the contrary, when the children see her grieve, they will not be afraid to voice their own feelings, to do their own necessary crying. A withdrawn parent who denies his or her own feelings makes it more difficult for the surviving children. (See chapter six, *Surviving Loss During Childhood.*)

Consoling others and getting relief for yourself can result in a precarious balance, but when honesty provides the basis for expression, the task of how to grieve and the choice of what is permissible will prove less difficult.

Some survivors ask, "How long will I want to talk about this? What is normal?" The answer is that you may want to talk about your loss for a very long time. Talk about it as long as you like and as much as you like. Stop only when you don't want to talk anymore. For some people, this will be six months. For others, it will be two years or longer.

Identifying the appropriate listener. The listener who will ultimately be the most helpful to you will be someone who is

- Nonjudgmental
- Accepting
- Able to hear the bad as well as the good.
- Not afraid of anger.

The listener who is not helpful

- Says that talking doesn't do any good.
- Counsels not to be weak (i.e., express to much pain or sadness).
- Urges the spouse to think of others who are worse off.
- Sees the female's expression of anger as "unladylike," not maternal, frightening, or sexually unattractive.
- Sees the male's expression of sadness, longing, or despair as being unmanly, a waste of time, an indication of impending collapse.
- Urges the spouse to focus on tomorrow and forget the past.

If there is no friend, relative, or neighbor to fill the role of listener, do not withdraw and try to "get through it alone." Seek out a minister, priest, rabbi, or counselor.

If you don't feel comfortable in a one-to-one situation, try attending a widows and widowers support group. There you do not have to worry about pleasing or embarrassing your listener, or refraining from tears. You don't have to be concerned about someone else's expectations for your behavior, or worried that you are keeping your listener from important responsibilities. The group participants will be familiar with your feelings and needs, and will be working to facilitate the grieving process—yours, as well as their own. They will invite you to share but will respect your silence when you wish to listen and merely share the same space with them for a while.

Some hospitals have support groups for people who are suffering loss due to one specific cause, such as cancer. A member of one such group told the group's sponsor of her personal gain.

> With the help you gave me at the meetings and the support of others who were there, I think I have gained enough confidence now to go on without my husband by my side.

Many Hospices, churches, and senior citizen's centers offer support groups for widows and widowers. In a group of over one hundred survivors who were questioned about their participation in a support group, only one expressed any negative feelings.

Writing About Your Feelings

In addition to expressing yourself verbally, you may seek to express yourself in writing. Your writing does not need to be organized, or in any way self-conscious. It needs only to accurately reflect your feelings, the thoughts that occupy you during the days and nights of your grieving, and the concerns which trouble you. You may find yourself writing without really intending to. One woman survivor gave this advice, "Follow your instinct. Mine was to sit in my room and cry and write things. It made me feel better."

If you would like to try expressing yourself on paper, you may consider using one of the following exercises to help you get started. Once you have begun, you will follow your own lead, based on your individual needs and grief reactions.

- Ask yourself what your major feeling is in regard to your loss. Is it loneliness, incompleteness, anger or guilt? Write about this feeling, saying everything you think about it. Follow the feeling to its source. Don't be afraid to say the bad things as well as the good. Explore the feeling; don't deny it.

- Write a farewell piece to your spouse as a way of saying an in-depth, completely thorough good-bye. Tell what you are feeling, what you will miss most, what you will always remember with fondness. Write about what the relationship gave you and about how your life will be influenced by having known and loved that person.

- Write a description of your spouse, creating it as if it were for someone who had never met your husband or wife. Include descriptions of all aspects of your loved one's personality, character, abilities, speech, gestures, habits, preferences, appearance, intelligence, humor, etc. Include everything that made your spouse unique.

There are some husbands and wives who, finding themselves faced with the inevitable loss of a spouse due to terminal illness, begin to chronicle the end of their spouse's life through a private journal or poetry. This type of writing releases emotional pain they can't allow the spouse to witness.

The following excerpt, for example, is from a poem written by a woman who was forced to endure her own strong dichotomous feelings as her husband's health continued to fail.

Oh when will you dream it through and go on
past the bullies who wait on nightmare corner,
to the other side of the brilliant colored capsules,
the knives and injections, the humming machinery
of research, past anyone's efforts to help?

It is time, I tell you, to risk it, Go over,
my love, and check out the country....

...When you go, I will never be ready.
Not now, for these words.

Or then, for the music
I will go down on my knees and beg for.

"Regardless," *Granite Under Water,* Jeanne Lohmann

In addition to helping you express how you feel, your writing can serve as a small private memorial to your love, your relationship, and your two lives that were shared. Whether or not the writing is read by anyone else is not important. What is valuable is that it gives you a safe place to express what you are feeling and that it offers you an alternative outlet to verbal expression.

Meeting the Unique Challenges

Widows and widowers report several situations which require an inordinate amount of personal courage: 1) coping with recurring unpleasant memories, 2) being compelled to avoid certain rooms in the house, 3) experiencing hallucinations in which the dead husband or wife is seen or heard, and 4) trying to gather the emotional and physical resources necessary to deal with the spouse's personal effects. (Whenever these situations follow the loss of any loved one, they seem to present a pronounced challenge to spouse survivors.)

Unpleasant memories. Spouses usually have a wide variety of unpleasant death-related memories. There may be the painful images that come from having watched a spouse drift into a steady decline. Several widowers reported the frustration of not knowing if their words of encouragement and love could be heard in the final stages of their wife's illness. A widow recalled the fright she experienced when her husband asked her not to let him die alone and urged her to "go with him."

When a spouse is terminally ill, a certain dynamic usually occurs between the husband and wife; during the illness, their relationship will peak in one direction or another. Simply put, a good relationship will tend to get even better and a bad relationship will tend to get worse. This *intensity* of the relationship prior to the death magnifies the loss.

Many couples, for example, talk about how the illness greatly improved their relationship. Their goals, needs or desires became clarified. Their determination to make life better vastly increased. The couple, for example, may have decided to take their dream vacation, remodel the house, or spend more time with their grandchildren. One of them may have decided to leave a job. When the death occurs, the situation is even more tragic because the spouse dies just when the relationship seems to be better than ever. The mutual gains, benefits, and pleasures which seemed to be accessible are suddenly out of the question, an impossibility. When their new future is not realized, the resulting sense of deprivation is severe.

Any kind of memory can cause residual pain after your spouse's death. As stressed earlier, it will help you to talk about it, write about it, and if it continues to dominate your thoughts for an extended period of time, or if it affects your capacity to function, discuss the memory with a professional. You will then be able to explore, with someone who is objective, your reasons for not being able to let go of the obsessive thought or image.

Avoiding rooms. If you are avoiding sleeping in your bed, walking through a certain area in your house, or using a specific piece of furniture, you do not need to force yourself to do something you dread. You are merely protecting yourself against additional stress. You fear that the emotional response to sleeping in the bed without your wife, or passing your husband's favorite chair will be felt too intense.

A widower told of his feelings which continued for six months following his wife's death:

> I knew I couldn't stand to go into our room at night knowing that she was not already in bed, in her dressing room, or coming down the hall. It was the same as if you asked me to cut my heart out with a knife. I couldn't do it.

A widow explained,

> For months I didn't sleep in the bed because the room felt different and empty. He was in the bathroom, in the bedroom. He was everywhere.

If you are concerned about your own behavior and are wondering how you can never face a certain room, or area, or chair again, don't try to set a time limit on yourself; that is, don't push yourself or become more miserable with expectations you can't meet. When your pain has sufficiently diminished, you will, once again, be able to enter the room, sleep on her side of the bed, or drive his car.

Only in a very small minority of cases does this behavior take on pathological implications. You can challenge yourself periodically to see if you feel differently about what you are avoiding. Test yourself from time to time to see if you notice yourself growing stronger in your resolve to return to a more practical, natural routine. Of course, if your life is seriously inhibited by your behavior you might like to talk with a professional to investigate alternative behavioral patterns which are suited to your individual situation.

Experiencing hallucinations. If you sense an invisible presence, see your loved one, or talk with him during the first year or so following the death, you are not losing your mind. Survivors do occasionally experience these visitations for which there are a wide variety of "explanations." Some researchers think the presence is the product of sensory recall; others consider the vision or voice to be the actual visit of the person's spirit. The explanations of *why* these experiences occur are less important than the fact that they are very real to the people who experience them.

Such an illusion eases your pain, gives you reassurance, and provides brief relief from your loneliness. (See *Sensing the Invisible Presence,* in Section I.) Some survivors, in fact, report having occasional visits from their loved ones throughout their lives.

A well-known author tells of her life being threatened following her prominent public involvement in a political demonstration which met with much disapproval. She was standing at the window of her empty apartment, looking out, when suddenly she felt two hands, one on each shoulder. The hands pushed her down just in time to avoid the bullet that came blasting through the window, shattering glass and imbedding itself in the room's interior. The hands, she believed, were those of her deceased father.

A widow tells of seeing her husband in the doorway, dressed in his favorite robe, looking pleasant and composed. She was with her mother at the time and even though the vision was extraordinarily vivid, the widow did not mention it to her mother. Later, however, her mother confided that she had seen her daughter's husband and described what he had been wearing and how he looked on that same day.

Stories such as these often go unreported (or *unconfided*) because the survivor fears being ridiculed, or classified as "crazy." Again, the fact is that incidents like these do happen and the reason they happen is less important than the fact that they are not harmful, nor are they an indication of abnormality.

Dealing with a spouse's personal effects. Some survivors are able to deal with the disposition of their spouse's personal effects several weeks after the death; others find the task difficult to accomplish. If you are procrastinating about going through your spouse's clothes and personal belongings, do not force yourself to do it. Take your time. If it takes a year to clean out a clothes closet, it is okay.

You may not have the physical energy nor the emotional stamina to handle the clothes and personal effects of your spouse. You may not know what to do with them or who to give them to. You may like to consider some of these options when you get ready for the task: Ask a close friend or relative to assist you, or to sit in the room and talk to you while you go through things. Collect several empty boxes ahead of time and designate them for the disposition of various possessions. You may have one for things to keep, articles to be given to a certain person (a child, brother, or sister), one for donations to the Salvation Army, Goodwill, the church clothes box, or a private charity organization.

You may not want your spouse's possessions to be used by anyone else; in this case, you will discard or store them.

Remember that it does not hurt anybody or anything to leave your spouse's belongings where they are. Most likely, when you have the energy to deal with them, you will. If, however, you never seem to be able to face the task, you may find that the best solution is to ask your grown child, your spouse's sibling, or a close friend to accomplish it for you.

The Individual Memorial

Having a meaningful memorial service helps to acknowledge your loss as final and to integrate the death into your present life. It makes prolonged denial less likely to occur. (See *Expressing Disbelief and Numbness,* in Section I.)

You can also, for your own emotional comfort and pleasure, commemorate your spouse's life. If he or she liked to garden, then plant a tree or flower that reminds you of your loved one. If your spouse admired a certain type of art, acquire a work as a memorial piece and hang it in your home. In other words, examine your spouse's likes and choose something to incorporate into your own life as an appropriate personal memorial.

You may like to tape record your memories, or to ask other people to record their anecdotes and stories of your loved one. This gesture of love and respect for your spouse will serve as a tangible memorial for you to keep and enjoy.

Anticipating Milestones

Some days will be much more difficult to endure than others. These are the birthdays of your spouse, your wedding anniversary, major holidays, Father's Day or Mother's Day, or private milestones. These occasions may reawaken painful emotions. They may seem interminable and tortuous, bringing on great sadness, spells of crying, and intense despair.

You can help yourself through these milestones by taking control of the day *in advance.* Don't be the day's victim. Make a plan of action, being specific about where you will go and what you will do. You may plan to visit someone. You may even make sure you are invited somewhere on that dreaded day. Don't be passive about how you will spend it. If you can be around other people, so much the better; but if you don't think you can be in a social situation, plan to talk on the telephone with someone you trust and love. Support group members are extremely cognizant of survivors' needs on special days. If you belong to a group, you can arrange for your favorite group member to contact you. Many tell of the comfort they felt when another survivor called to express empathy and to visit on a day that was a difficult milestone.

Problem-Solving Alone

One of the most arduous challenges after the loss of a spouse is making decisions alone, without the benefit of your loved one's advice, opinion, and knowledge. If you make a decision that has an unfavorable outcome, you will bear the consequences alone—or the anguish, fear, guilt, or confusion.

It is necessary to realize that in the first year following the death of your spouse, your ability to be objective and rational is impaired. For that reason, no major decisions should be made. You should not sell your house, quit your job, enroll your children in different schools, or take a new person or people into your home to live permanently. If you *must* move because of changed financial status, or other serious and unavoidable circumstances, seek the advice of objective and knowledgable relatives or friends who will be able to help you make the smoothest transition possible.

While you will probably be able to postpone major decisions, you will not, realistically, be able to avoid solving normal daily problems.

> The hardest emotional issue during the first year was the reality that I was on my own, that I didn't have somebody with me any more, that I had to make major decisions by myself. *(Widow)*

Principles of problem solving. When the problem you have can be approached *in degrees* it will not seem as overwhelming. It is only when you view the problem as *one insurmountable entity* that it becomes unsolvable. There is one major procedure which can be followed when solving any major problem. Consider the steps below as a guide to problem-solving alone. A series of questions makes progress possible.

- *What is the problem?*
  Identify the problem exactly. Don't carry an unidentified burden. ("A whole lot of things are piling up that I can't deal with.") Pinpoint what needs to be solved. For example: The car needs major engine repair, but the car is three years old and I don't know whether to have it repaired or buy a used car.

- *What is the goal?*
  Identify what you need to achieve to eliminate the problem.
  Example: I need to have a dependable car with the least possible expenditure.

- *What are the possible solutions to your problem?*
  Identify the various means by which you can achieve your goal.
  Example: Get the car repaired. Buy an economical used car.

- *What are the advantages and disadvantages to each solution?*
  Obtain specific information about each solution and make a direct comparison of the advantages.
  Example: A rebuilt engine for my car will cost $1,150. Any dependable used car which would be equivalent to the car I now have will cost about $6,500. (Cost advantage to the rebuilt engine.) The rebuilt engine is guaranteed for 12 months. It is possible to get a warranty on the used car for 24 months. (Advantage to used car.)

- *What important factors might I have overlooked?*
  Review your information. Ask if there is anything you have failed to take into account to accomplish your goal.
  Example: I don't know how much it will cost to install the rebuilt engine.

- *Follow up on overlooked details.*
  Look into any major factor which will influence your choice.
  Example: The cost of the rebuilt engine along with the cost of installation is higher than the down-payment necessary for the used car.

- *What is my informed and final choice?*
  I will purchase the used car since the initial cash outlay is lower, the warranty is double that of the rebuilt engine, and the used car is newer than my present car.

- *Implement your goal.*
  Start visiting car dealerships or reading classified ads for used cars.

Each step of this problem-solving procedure, though clear-cut and easy to follow, may require extreme effort at a time when your physical and mental energy is already low. However, if you look at any problem *in segments,* rather than as one overpowering, debilitating force to be reckoned with, you will find it easier to work your way through it.

This car problem is a practical one actually solved by a fifty-seven-year-old widow who not only had never had the responsibility of managing an automobile, but had never learned to drive. After she had bought her used car, she took driving lessons. As a result she could rely more on her own resources and less on friends and neighbors. By meeting a challenge independently she gained important personal benefits. "Every time I get in that car and drive downtown, I'm so proud of myself I can hardly stand it," she said. "If Don's watching, I know he's smiling."

Each time you surmount a crisis, make a major decision, and implement a goal — regardless of what your goal is — you will gain satisfaction and self-assurance through your own competence.

Coping with Financial Dilemmas

The multilayered financial responsibilities after the death of a spouse are both complex and time-consuming, especially for unemployed widows. Surviving spouses report feeling "over-burdened," "drained," "angry," and often believe their efforts to clear up financial matters are futile. At a time when the emotional and mental states are already feeling the effects of stress, the surviving spouse may need to 1) immediately locate all existing sources of income, 2) pay staggering medical expenses, and 3) identify and investigate *potential* financial resources.

Locating All Existing Sources of Income

Immediate emergency needs. Some surviving spouses find themselves with no existing sources of income. This happens in extreme cases when, for example, the husband's salary was the only source of income and it was terminated by his death. In such a situation social service agencies should be contacted immediately. The necessary paper work can then be expedited and benefits such as Aid To Families With Dependent Children, Social Security, and other forms of social assistance may be obtained. When necessary, charity organizations and religious organizations can be contacted for immediate temporary food donations.

If a deceased spouse did not receive a last check prior to death, the employer should be contacted immediately and a request should be made for the spouse's final check to be issued as soon as possible. A request should also be made for any unpaid commissions or bonuses that are due to the spouse and appropriate compensation should be issued for accrued vacation time or sick time.

In some cases, the survivor is a beneficiary of a life insurance policy which will be paid, once the claim is processed, but the survivor needs the money immediately for the mortgage payment, utility bills, gasoline, or food. The survivor is often allowed to receive a check for up to ten percent of the policy amount. If, for example, the husband had $75,000 worth of life insurance, the wife could receive a maximum payment of $7,500 prior to the claim being processed. Although *all life insurance companies do not offer this service,* many do, and it can remove a considerable burden at a particularly stressful time.

Regular financial needs. A typical survivor will be entitled to benefits from a variety of sources.

Following is a list to help you review any possible sources of income which may be available to you.

- life insurance policy
- employer compensation, unpaid bonuses, commissions, unpaid sick time, death benefits
- Social Security benefits
- Medicare
- Veteran's benefits
- Individual Retirement Account
- Keogh Plan
- Stocks and bonds
- Private unpaid loans

You will probably find yourself entitled to one or more of the above benefits, as well as others. It is essential for you to realize that you must *apply* for the benefits. Only in exceptional circumstances will you receive benefits for which you have not applied. Most sources of income are not automatically dispersed.

Tracking down all the necessary documents you must have in order to apply for benefits is a long and arduous task. For instance, if you are a widow filing a Social Security claim, you will need your husband's Social Security card, death certificate, your marriage certificate, your husband's birth certificate, the birth certificates of any children your husband fathered in a previous marriage, and your W-2 form for the last year.

To make an insurance claim you will need your husband's death certificate, his Social Security card, his life insurance policy, and your own birth certificate.

To make a veteran's claim you will need your husband's birth certificate, your marriage certificate, your husband's death certificate, and the birth certificates of your children and any children of your spouse by a previous marriage. Your husband's military discharge papers, and his VA claim number are also needed.

You will make it easier on yourself if you gather the documents and make a set of photocopies. (You can obtain copies of the death certificates from the registrar of vital statistics of the city, county or state where your spouse's death occurred.) Put the original documents together in a large envelope. This will be your resource for seeking claims. Keep the photocopies of the documents in a safe place separate from the originals. You can use them for reference if any of the originals become lost or damaged and need to be replaced.

It is important to recognize that some benefits will be reduced after a certain period of time has elapsed. For that reason, gather your material together as soon as you possibly can. If you have a knowledgable friend who can offer practical assistance, accept help. If you can't get all documents together for several months, start the claim's procedure by notifying the appropriate agents. Take the initial steps toward gaining benefits. For the most part, receiving benefits and tapping your resources will not be a quick process; for example, your first social security benefit may take more than 60 days.

Paying Medical Expenses

Once you have identified your sources of income, you may have to attend to medical expenses which accrued during your spouse's long-term illness.

Considering the length of time it takes most companies to process claims, you should file for health insurance benefits as soon as you can.

If you need financial assistance with medical payments, contact the local social service office in the hospital in which the expenses accrued. The hospital's representative will be able to explain any payment options you have; also, sometimes assistance is available from a discretionary fund which has been provided by the hospital by private donations.

If you have medical expenses which seem insurmountable and you are unable to obtain help from agencies or charitable organizations, contact the billing department of the hospital, clinic, or laboratory. Briefly, but clearly explain your financial situation. Emphasize your intent to pay and assure the department representative that you are earnest in your desire to work out a mutually agreeable plan for payment of the debt. You may, for example, begin the discussion by volunteering that it would be possible for you to pay off the debt in a specified number of months, with equal payments of a certain amount. When you have reached an agreement, ask the name of the person to whom you are speaking. Follow up your telephone call with a note to that person summarizing the verbal agreement and thanking the person for his or her help. Include a payment to be applied to your account. Your note will go into your file to show proof of your intent to pay.

If you have health insurance or Medicare and find yourself unable to file claims, monitor the progress of reimbursements, and keep accurate records, there are, in some geographical areas, companies which provide (for a fee) professional claim service. In California, for example, Medi-Bill, Inc., is a professional claim service which reviews and summarizes health coverage, prepares and submits medical claims, and follows up on claims and reimbursements. Medi-Bill also maintains records of submitted claims, insurance payments and related correspondence, as well as accounting to be used for tax purposes. To find out if such a service is available in your area, contact the social services office in your local hospital.

Investigating Potential Financial Resources

You will probably have neither the desire nor the energy to think about future resources and investments for quite some time. Also, as noted previously, it is unwise to make any major decision for the first year following bereavement; this includes the selling of property and making investments.

If you receive a lump sum settlement from the death of a spouse, you should keep in mind that this can be depleted very quickly if you decide you are going to use it "only when you need it" or "on a monthly basis." This is a sum which needs to be viewed in the context of the *rest of your life*. Deposit it into an insured savings account with the highest interest possible until you have the emotional and mental resources to make informed, intelligent investments.

Eventually, if you have a considerable sum to invest, you will investigate (1) mutual funds, (2) stocks and bonds, (3) trusts, (4) money market certificates, (5) treasury bills, (6) real estate, and (7) annuities.

When you are ready to make major decisions, don't be reticent about seeking the help of a professional. Be cautious about following the advice of any person who may gain from your investment. You may like to seek the advice of a lawyer, a CPA, or a professional financial advisor. Be discriminating about your resource person so you can avoid dealing with someone who makes choices for you which can result in his or her own financial benefit.

Being Alert to Inadvisable or Illegitimate Schemes

As dismal as this fact is, there are those in our society who can develop a self-serving scheme to take advantage of any crisis; sadly, the death of a loved one is no exception. In fact, your new financial status, independent state, and emotional vulnerability can turn you into a prime target for a disreputable schemer. Acquaintances, even strangers, can suggest that you invest in their "sure fire" project that they are kindly "letting you in on." Too often, this person is looking for easy capital to sink into a personal venture which doesn't qualify as a sound risk to lending institutions.

There are real estate brokers who "guarantee" you an enormous profit from your home and promise you that your house, once they list it, will sell immediately. And it may indeed sell immediately because the broker buys it below cost and resells it to make a quick and sizeable profit.

Anyone who tries to manipulate you emotionally is suspect. If, for example, an agent, broker, or investment counselor calls saying he or she was a friend of your husband's and you have never heard of the person, be cautious.

Another popular "con artist" procedure operates like this: You receive merchandise in the mail (COD) addressed to your deceased spouse. You assume the article, such as a Bible or collector's item (coin, stamp, etc.), was ordered by your loved one, and you feel that you should pay for it. The price you pay, however, is disproportionate to the cost of the item. The result is you get something you don't want or need and the bogus mail order company gets rich.

There are "life insurance agents" who require a "delinquent" payment from you in order to issue payment to you of a large life insurance policy that does not exist.

There are phony charities which suggest a memorial fund be set up in your spouse's name, and companies which try to sell you items with your loved one's name engraved on them.

If you are suspicious about any proposed transaction, check out the company or person who approaches you. Ask for references. Suggest that the person talk over the matter with you in the presence of your friend who is a successful business person, or ask the individual to explain the proposal to your attorney or accountant. See how the person reacts to such a suggestion, and then, if you are genuinely interested in what is being offered, follow up and check it out thoroughly.

If you suspect an illegitimate scheme, contact the police. Many con artists have been deprived of their impressive incomes by alert and wary survivors.

Transforming the Mourning Process into the Nurturing Process

During the mourning period, your moods will fluctuate. You will have some days of complete despair, and other days when you convince yourself that you will be able to function again. This moody unpredictability is both tedious and draining. During this period, you will benefit by being aware of your own self-acceptance. Ask yourself: Am I treating myself better or worse than I would treat a friend? The point is that as you grieve you may be much too hard on yourself. You may berate yourself for not being more in control, more capable, or for not improving faster. Instead, you need to befriend yourself. You can do this by (1) improving your physical health, (2) redefining yourself, and (3) enhancing your physical and social environment.

These suggestions may sound excessively ambitious, perhaps even unrealistic for a grieving spouse, and indeed they are if tackled all at once. You will, however, enjoy personal benefits if you consider each of the suggestions and integrate into your life those which meet your current needs and energy level. Some suggestions which have no appeal to you now may prove interesting and helpful later.

Improving Your Physical Health

It has already been pointed out that suppressed emotion contributes to physiological symptoms and can, ultimately, produce serious disorders. When you have to conduct yourself through your daily life while imposing constraints on your strong emotions, your body will bear the consequences. As stressed earlier, it is necessary to discuss your concerns and vent those emotions, keeping in mind that those which are buried or denied can inhibit healing.

Drugs and grief. If you have been given tranquilizers or perscriptive drugs to "calm you down," "block the grief," or "relieve the hurt" you may never have had an opportunity to experience a natural purging of your feelings. If you suffer from insomnia, one of the common conditions during the grieving period, you may have resorted to sleeping pills. It is important not to operate "on automatic" where drugs are concerned. Be aware of *what* drugs you are taking and *how long* you have been taking them. Monitor your usage so it doesn't become dependency. If you feel mentally or emotionally unable to do this, ask someone else to keep track of your prescriptions for you. The aim is for your body to be able to function independently of drugs.

Maintaining awareness of your general health. Following the death of a spouse, *you can't just let your health happen*; you have to exercise control over it. It is tempting to resort to an excessive intake of coffee, tea, and other stimulants during the grieving period. Some survivors live on liquids or snacks and rarely eat a balanced meal.

> The last thing in the world I wanted to do was eat. Everyone kept urging me to eat something, so I only ate to please other people and when someone was watching me. When I was alone, I ate nothing. In the first month following my husband's death I lost twenty pounds. I was already thin before his death. A neighbor convinced me to take a daily walk with her. After about a week of walking two miles a day, I had a normal appetite again. *(Sixty-three-year-old widow)*

Exercise is an aid to physical, mental and emotional health, but you are not likely to have the energy nor the desire to engage in extensive exercise. You should, however, remember that it is vital for you to be mobile, to get up and move around, get things for yourself and, if at all possible, to take at least a short walk of a few blocks several times a week. You might be thinking, "But I can't do that. I'm too tired to walk across the room." Or, "I don't want to go outside where I may have to talk to other people." Or even, "What does it matter whether I move around or not? The person I loved is gone. That is all that matters." Each of these reactions is legitimate and is one with which a survivor of *any* death would empathize. The point here, though, is that you are among the living and it will be easier in the future if you get your blood circulating, your heart working, and stretch your muscles.

Those are the obvious physiological benefits, but there are other benefits as well. First, insomnia, which is among the top three symptoms resulting during conjugal bereavement, can often be counteracted by exercise. Many surviving spouses who were insomniacs, report they were able to get to sleep more easily if they had some exercise during the day. Second, physical exercise helps reduce emotional stress. As bodily tension is released, emotional relief is achieved as well.

Redefining Yourself

It has been pointed out that the loss of your spouse creates a change in your identity. The degree of this change depends on the extent to which you were defined as a couple, your reliance on that bond, and the various roles you fill in all areas of your life—home, work, and play. In general, the more dependency you had on your role as wife or husband, the greater the void is now that the role is no longer necessary.

During the first six months or so, you will mourn the loss of that role. As time goes by, you will find yourself in different roles; some of them an inevitable outgrowth of your loss. The young widowed father, for example, will naturally assume some aspects and responsibilities of the deceased's role. The widow will assume the role of head of household. Other new roles may be deliberately activated.

This is illustrated by the fifty-year-old widow who found that during her thirty-year marriage she had given the best parts of herself—her potential, her talent, capability, love, and sensitivity—to her spouse.

> I invested it in him. It was all focused in one spot. When he died, I realized I needed to get all that I *was* back inside myself so I could use it. I needed it to get through life. I had to think, "I didn't give him all I had, I loaned it to him. Now I need it again."

When you find yourself with increasing physical energy, when you are able to spend days free from emotional pain, you will be able to think about yourself without feeling as if you are being selfish or overindulgent. Try taking a look at your *total self*. A forty-two-year-old widower talked about how he viewed himself after his wife's death.

> For almost a year after Linda's death, I thought of myself *only* as Linda's husband and Karen's father. One day I was driving home from work. I heard a woman on a talk show using the term "reclaiming yourself." It didn't seem selfish. It seemed sensible.

Reclaiming yourself can only be possible when you know who your self *is*; that is, before you reclaim, you must *identify*. Think about these four aspects of yourself: (1) your physical body, (2) your mental self, (3) your emotional self, and (4) your abilities, skills and talents. You may even try a simple exercise. Write down each of these four categories. Then, ask yourself two questions about each one: What am I today in this category? (Your identity.) In what way do I need and want to change?

Nurturing natural interests and expanding experiences. Redefinition is inextricably linked with your interests and experiences. Your new identity will grow from them. Widows and widowers have reported developing a variety of interests when they found themselves alone. They work in senior citizen centers or stores, are docents at the art or science museums, volunteer in hospitals or political organizations, instruct music, or write for a small local paper such as a weekly shopping news. The list is endless.

Most communities have organizations especially for participating senior citizens, such as teacher's aids in elementary schools, foster grandparent programs, or a senior citizen's employment placement center where retirees work on an individual call basis utilizing their years of skill in such areas as carpentry, plumbing, electrical work, · or gardening.

A widow who had been aided immeasurably by Hospice during her husband's terminal illness gained an appreciation for, and interest in, the Hospice program. A year and a half after her husband's death, she trained as a lay counselor for the Hospice program. She made the transformation from "helped" to "helper." The woman's identity gained an added dimension. The fringe benefits to her were increased self-esteem and renewed energy.

A widower who admitted to not having been "much of a grand-parent" because he preferred spending all of his private time with his wife, began engaging in the role of grandfather after his wife died. He became teacher, storyteller and fishing companion. In reflecting on the pleasure generated by his new identity as grandfather, he realized, "I had been selfish. I hadn't wanted to share my wife with anyone. When our grandchildren came over I was always jealous that they were getting my wife's attention."

When thinking about your interests and needs, you may like to consider what the local schools have to offer. Adult school programs at high schools offer courses in crafts, arts, languages, introduction to computers, and mechanical training, as well as instruction in the basic subjects.

There is no age limit for a community college student and the wide variety of courses at this level would accommodate the interests of any prospective student.

Again, new roles can come in any area of life and will occur from your personal interests, experiences, and needs.

Enhancing Your Social Environment

Though it is grossly unfair, the widower is viewed as more "acceptable" as the single dinner guest than is the widow. Because the percentage of widows greatly exceeds that of widowers, the man is seen as an eligible partner. He doesn't pose a threat to the hostess. His social invitations, therefore, are usually much more frequent.

If, however, the man is very reserved, he may always have relied on his wife to arrange the social activities and may, after her death, feel "outside of society," and "cut off." He will find it difficult, if not impossible, to go out without her and will have to develop his social skills and put forth effort if he is to enjoy the pleasure of other people's company.

Elder widowers and widows find interaction with others requires less effort when it takes place in church, senior citizen's centers, or political organizations. Through affiliations with community recreational groups, they enjoy activities such as theater, lawn bowling, chess, or swimming.

Elderhostel programs are offered in over 800 colleges and universities in the United States and Canada. In these programs people in their sixties or older live on a college campus for a week or more and take non-credit courses on a variety of liberal arts and sciences subjects taught by the regular faculty of the institution. A participant does not need to have prior knowledge about, or training in, the subject he or she chooses to study.

Groups of twenty to forty *Elderhostel* classmates live in the dormitory, have their meals on campus, attend campus cultural activities and enjoy recreational resources. The *Elderhostel* program, with headquarters in Boston, also offers scholarships to those who require financial assistance.

Enhancing Your Physical Environment

A glance at your immediate environment — your bedroom, living-room, kitchen, backyard — wherever you spend the most time, can often reflect your emotional state. If, for example, your clothes have not been put away, the newspapers have piled up, or mail remains unopened, you are probably feeling depressed, despairing, exhausted, or, as one widow put it, "convinced that everything is futile."

Ordinarily, one does not make any changes from the *outside* in; changes usually work best when they generate from the *inside* out. An exception is the environment in which you spend most of your time. You will find that exerting the effort to enhance your environment, make it more pleasant and more cheerful, will have an impact on your emotional health. Look around you. Think about giving yourself a *present* in the form of an addition or change in the room where you spend most of your time. The change can be extremely simple or very extensive. It may cost nothing, or be expensive. The change, of course, depends on your desire, energy, and financial capability.

Add color where there is none. Put a plant in the living room, a pair of colorful pillows in the den, or a new bright comforter in your bedroom.

Have a skylight installed in your study, make a terrarium for your kitchen or livingroom, hang a new print or poster in your bedroom.

Go through some "stowed away" family pictures and have them framed for the hallway. Buy yourself a new comfortable chair. Make a list of all the little things that need repair and have them fixed, one by one (the dripping faucet, the broken light switch, the frayed drapery pulls, the loose drawer handle).

The ways to make your daily living more pleasant are innumerable. By being aware of the positive influence your environment can have on your feelings and then implementing change, you are gaining additional control over your emotional and psychological state.

Looking Ahead

There is no definite point in time which signals the completion of your grieving process, no point at which you can be expected to say, unequivocally, "I have successfully healed after the loss of my husband or wife." Instead, a series of positive phases will enrich your life as your physical energy increases, your old roles are relinquished and new ones established, your social environment satisfies your personal needs and coincides with your interests, and your physical environment improves. These phases may occur so gradually they are barely discernible, or you may experience significant changes fairly soon after your loss.

You will be assured that your healing is being reaffirmed every time you are able to enjoy a full and peaceful night's rest, talk about your loss with a feeling of control and relative ease, become involved in an activity without being plagued by painful memories and images, meet a challenge using your own resources, take care with your appearance, reach out to help someone, and do not feel afraid to laugh. Most of all, this healing is substantive when you no longer regard your life as various increments to be *gotten through* a day or week at a time, but as *your future over which you have control* and in which you are confident to experience pleasure and personal reward.

> A year was a big event for me. It was a clearinghouse I was through that year and didn't have to look back. I was coming back to the human race. I was going to have love and joy and humor. *(Widow whose husband died of a heart attack)*

4

Surviving the Loss of a Parent

My father said, "Well, I'm not going to live forever," but I didn't believe him. He wasn't going to die. He was never going to die.
MAN WHOSE FATHER DIED AT AGE 56,
WHEN THE SON WAS 28

Some way I had been conditioned when I was young to think that I would be grown up when I was forty. You don't need your mother. But after my mother died, I collapsed. I kept thinking, "I'm forty years old and yet I feel like a child." My sister and I said, "Now we're half orphans."
WOMAN WHOSE MOTHER DIED AT THE AGE
OF 69, WHEN HER DAUGHTER WAS 40

Even if you are in your adult years when your parent dies, you respond to that death as the child of your parent. At age thirty, forty, or even seventy, your reactions will be similar to those of other adults who lose a parent. In addition to feeling angry or guilty, the most commonly expressed reactions are

- I feel like an orphan.
- Now I am closer to death.
- I feel vulnerable.
- I'm frustrated because there was something more I needed to say or do.
- I am released from a burden.

Special Factors Which Influence Your Grief Reactions

Several major factors help to produce each of the above reactions. Examining these factors will make it possible for you to gain a more thorough understanding of *the entire context* of your grief's effects. You will be better able to recognize *what* is happening to you after the loss of a parent, and *why* it is happening. (See *Coping with Your Loss* below.)

Believing That Your Parent Is Immortal

The belief that a parent could live forever seems, on the surface, to be so ludicrous that it does not deserve any serious attention. No rational being could possibly have such a belief, you may think.

Yet, underneath your conscious awareness that immortality is impossible, you may have nurtured the subconscious belief that your parent's death would not actually occur. For some offspring, the denial is deeply and firmly entrenched.

Equally as strong may be your conviction that if your parent's death does occur, it will not be from disease; your parent will not be the victim of any demoralizing, debilitating illness. This person whom you love will—if he or she must absolutely die someday—have a death that is painless, uncomplicated, or possibly even "romantic."

> He had been hospitalized a couple of times in his life but in my mind he was still immortal. What he did pass on to me was the concept that my family was immortal. It was an attitude more than it was any kind of conversation. He wasn't going to die. He was never going to die. *(Thirty-two-year-old man reflecting on his father's death)*

Feeling Closer To Death

When your parent is gone, there is the realization that you are next in line for death. You become acutely aware of the quantity and quality of your remaining life.

I had the feeling, "I'm the next to die. There's nothing between me and death now." My mother was going to protect me from death. Her life was going to protect me from death. *(Forty-year-old daughter survivor)*

Losing Your Protection

When you lose the buffer between yourself and death, you may feel extraordinarily vulnerable to the world in general. This feeling is reflected in the statement at the beginning of the chapter, "I feel like an orphan." The adult who loses a parent often feels like a forsaken child. At the same time, he or she steps into the generational position previously held by the parent:

I remember one of the worst things when my mother died... the first voice to come into my head was, *"I'm* the mommy now, *forever." (Woman who lost her mother during middle-age)*

When your parent dies, you view yourself as the "older generation." This oldness brings with it new responsibilities, that of presiding over the younger generation, and reconciling yourself to meeting death head-on with no intermediary.

At the same time you feel the protection of your own life dissolve, you may also feel that your other loved ones are more vulnerable. Any one of them might die. If one of your parents is still living, you more acutely recognize the imminence of his or her death. Your increased awareness of death may reflect itself in new resolutions regarding your own behavior.

I have a consciousness about saying good-bye now that I didn't have before my mother's death. Even when my husband and I have real arguments I still say good-bye now. I am going to see my father who is eighty-five this summer, and I really want to make sure I get a sense of completeness with him. *(Woman whose mother died after a short-term illness)*

Losing Your Home

Everything a parent represents to a surviving offspring can be fully understood only by that daughter or son. For that reason, survivors' descriptions generally vary regarding what they feel is especially lost following a parent's death.

Losing your parents takes away your home, your place to go. *(Middle-aged man whose mother died)*

The hardest thing for me to deal with was the loss of the hub. He was like the hub of the wheel out of which I was maybe the rim of the tire. I wasn't just the spoke, but he was the hub and without him there in a very real and physical way, I had to transfer all that information into a spiritual sense. Not to say that he cannot still be a hub, but it's *a spiritual hub instead of a physical hub.* It was a really difficult thing to do, to shift from the physical to the non-physical. *(Man whose father died when the son was in his late twenties)*

I lost my place of retreat, my defender, my home base where I could always know I was accepted. *(Young woman whose fifty-year-old mother died of cancer)*

Regardless of what the loss is called or how it is described it represents a *void* in the life of each survivor. How that void is perceived and experienced depends on the surviving individual's beliefs and predilections.

Longing

When the parent-child relationship ends, there is a sense of discontinuity. A daughter may long for her parent to see how the rest of her life turned out, or to participate in important life events. She may miss her parents most severely when experiences are extraordinarily good or bad. The survivor thinks "If only my father or mother could *see me* now and be proud of me," or "*help me* now," or "*advise me* now."

Many public figures, when asked what their regrets are or what is missing from their lives, will express the desire for a parent to have known about their recognition or to have benefited from it. The survivors compare their own lives to their dead parents' lives, wishing their mother or father could have been touched in some way by their success.

A woman survivor, the single parent of two high school students said, "When experiences are really good, you long to share them. When experiences are very bad, you long for help."

There is also the longing that occurs in the course of normal, everyday life. You may find yourself feeling empty and despairing because you cannot pick up the phone and call your parent, run by to see how he or she is, or join your parent in an ordinary activity the way you used to. You long more than anything to have your parent there to enjoy a favorite TV program, share a favorite food, play a game of cards, or take a walk in the neighborhood.

Needing To Blame

As a surviving son or daughter you may experience great surges of anger, guilt — or both. You may be angry at God for taking your parents, be angry at the doctors, or a brother or sister for not taking better care of your parent. You may feel hatred toward what you consider to be an unfair world. All of this gives you someone or something to blame.

Guilt serves the same purpose. As long as you think there is someone to blame, even if it has to be yourself, you can assume your parent's death was controllable. (*Understanding and Dispelling Your Guilt* in Section I explains this in greater detail.)

Upon the death of your parent, you may even call forth a whole host of factors to support your belief that your parent could have lived much longer. One woman confided at length about how her own waning energy and inattention to her mother contributed to her mother's premature death. The neighbors, however, reported the situation entirely differently. The woman had, in fact, carried her mother from room to room, stayed in the same room with her throughout the day, talked and visited with her (even though her mother was totally deaf), cooked her favorite foods, and devotedly administered her medication.

After this survivor told how her own defects had caused her mother's death, and that her mother should have "lived another five years," the interviewer inquired, "How old did you say your mother was when she died?" "Ninety-eight," was the reply.

Death as a Catalytic Agent for Unfinished Business

Your parent's death may bring on regrets or self-recriminations similar to these.

- My father never told me he loved me.

- My mother never said, "You're all right."

- I was never able to discuss some specific important part of my parent's live such as why my mother divorced my father, how my father's behavior was affected by his alcoholic parents, why my parents never wanted another child, or why my father never grieved after my brother's death.

- I was never able to discuss some important aspect of my *own* life. I always intended to talk about some action I took or belief I held that had caused my parent unhappiness. I needed to talk over the fact that I felt inadequate in my mother's eyes, that I wished I could be more of the person she wanted me to be. There were goals I wanted to talk over, but never did. I never told my parent that I appreciated him or her. I never revealed to my parents that I was gay.

Unfinished aspects of the parent-offspring relationship can be tormenting and may take on added importance as each day passes. If you have found yourself reviewing similar unfinished business, you may also be wishing, "If only I had another chance, I would ask the unasked question, make the admission that was too painful, or venture to initiate discussion into forbidden or ignored territory."

The parent's personal unfinished business. Sometimes an adult survivor's emotional pain originates from a disturbing or shocking confession made by a parent during the final days. The parent may have expressed deep regrets about past behavior, or may even have perceived his or her life as having been worthless. Witnessing the emotional distress of a father or mother during the parent's physical decline in the face of death may leave the survivor with disturbing and haunting images.

In a young man's journal which chronicled his father's final days, this entry stood out:

A new day, in theory. In fact, still the night he died. I've been manic, fazed. I haven't cried yet.

Yesterday morning, saying good-bye after sitting the night beside the hospital bed, I said, "I'll bring Mama back in a little while."

I leaned down and kissed his stubbled, sunken cheek. He reached up and patted my cheek with his right hand. I stood up, holding his hand, looking him in the eye.

"You're quite a guy," he said. I leaned down and kissed him again, his forehead. I cradled his head in my arm and spoke into his ear.

"You too, Papa, you're quite a guy yourself." I stood up.

"No," he said, looking away through the rail, raised now because I was leaving, "no, I'm not. I haven't been much good."

He looked through the stainless steel bars at the wall.

He gave me his blessing. He couldn't give himself forgiveness.

When I cry, a lot of the tears will be trying to wash out that particular chunk of grit.

In such cases, death mandates that the survivor needs to become the forgiver of the parent's guilt as well as their own, if he or she is to heal.

As one woman survivor expressed, "There is the hope that I can forgive my father's perceived misdeed, not only for my sake, but for *him* too."

Role Reversal

Toward the end of your parent's life you may have experienced a role reversal; that is, your father or mother became your child and you assumed the role of parent. This most typically occurs when a parent has a terminal illness or is the victim of senility. In such a situation, you may have had to attend to your parent's physical and emotional needs, and to have met many demands a child would have made. Though you did not want to take the parenting role, it was imperative for you to do so in order to maintain your parent's safety, and to administer or monitor his or her health care.

The memories of your own actions in such a situation may now cause some emotional distress.

> He said, "Don't put me in the hospital. Don't do it." I was on his couch and I could hear him in his room, groaning and moaning and in pain. He said, "I want to die at home." Finally, about two or three in the morning I did call the hospital. He couldn't walk and the ulcer was very, very painful so I had to make that decision. You go against his wishes to call the ambulance but you have to make that choice. *(Thirty-two-year-ole man reflecting on his father's final days)*

> I criticized dad for drinking. I was pretty hard on him. I shouldn't have been so judgmental. He had lived his life, raised his children, conducted his business. What difference did it make if he wanted to drink once a week? He was eighty-three years old. *(Fifty-year-old man reflecting on the last year of his father's life)*

> I scolded Mama for not eating, not cleaning her plate. I always tried to make her eat as if she were a baby. Now I realize she had no appetite and she had probably decided she wanted to die at home. I made too much fuss over her meals. I didn't have any respect for her wishes. *(Sixty-eight-year-old woman reflecting on the last months of her mother's life)*

The role you assumed before your parent's death not only affected you and your parent, it may now be determining the present role you play within your family. During your parent's terminal illness, for example, you may have assumed a role which thrust you into the position of overseer and caretaker in the family. You were closest to your parent's daily experience. You may have made the necessary decisions or administered the funds needed for proper care. When a position such as this becomes established within the family, the balance of power changes among remaining family members. After the death, you may find yourself remaining in the position of caretaker with one or more family members expecting to be cared for. While this expectation is rarely voiced by a surviving family member, it is made evident by his or her actions. These actions indicate that the survivor considers himself or herself to be *more severely affected by the death* than other members of the family. In fact, several family members may jostle for the position of "most bereaved."

A caregiving individual will often contribute to this dynamic because of his or her own emotional needs and patterns of coping.

Because a surviving adult child needs to avoid overt grief, he or she may step into the more comfortable and familiar role of solicitor-caretaker.

> I asked what would happen to dad. Worrying about my father would have postponed my grief. It's easier for me to take care of others than to show my own feelings. *(Woman reflecting on her actions when her mother died)*

Compounded Stress

If your parent was hospitalized for an extended period of time or was steadily declining at home, you may have been subjected to a variety of stresses arising from one or more of these situations.

1. You were emotionally torn between the demands of your job or your home and your devotion to your parent.

2. You were physically exhausted by the added responsibility of medical arrangements, hospital visits, and providing emotional support to other family members.

3. You were financially drained by your contribution to medical care services.

4. You were solely responsible for decisions and preparations related to the funeral, and perhaps for the cost of funeral services as well.

When any of these circumstances are present and then the death occurs, you may experience a great sense of relief. This relief may compound your stress. Even though you feel released from an overwhelming burden, you may also feel guilty for experiencing relief. Although you are freed to return to a more normal, less demanding existence, you will still need to regain your footing, clear up neglected work, get physically rested, or replenish your exhausted funds.

If you do not receive the support from others that you require, even deeper stresses are produced. To complicate matters, because you are an *adult survivor* experiencing the loss of an adult of an *older generation*, you may not feel it is legitimate or proper for you to seek external support.

Coping with Your Loss

There are several guidelines for dealing with your loss. First, consider what you are doing with your feelings. As an adult survivor of a parental death you may try to hide your grief responses. A grown son or daughter, you may think, is supposed to accept a parent's death within the normal cycle of life's events. Though the loss is extremely traumatic, you may feel that exhibiting emotional devastation is not "grown-up":

> I collapsed and felt so silly. I kept thinking, "I'm forty years old and I feel like a child."

Your grief, if suppressed, will last longer and be poorly resolved. In addition to finding comfort in expressing your feelings, you will find it helpful to (1) memorialize your parent in some way, (2) enjoy a healthy identification with your mother or father, which includes keeping a few personal possessions of your parent, and (3) develop an awareness of the final destination of your parent's presence.

Allowing and Expressing Your Feelings

> I would urge a person who is grieving to allow yourself to feel whatever comes. Allow yourself a physical space if you can, go away to a place where you can really experience what you need to feel. Allow yourself to feel. *It is a graceful state! (Forty-year-old woman survivor)*

Survivors who give themselves permission to feel are facilitating their own healing process. One woman stated, "In the first few days following my mother's death, I might be in the grocery store and I'd suddenly lean against the wall and start crying. I didn't care and that was wonderful. I just allowed myself to do that."

Releasing surges of feeling is extremely beneficial, but it is not always possible, especially if you must maintain a specific image on the job — if you must be the person who is reliable, competent and in control.

A fifty-year-old engineer reported that for the first few months after his mother's death he would find a legitimate reason to leave his desk and walk across the landscaped grounds of his plant to the opposite building.

> Whenever my sorrow welled up, I wanted to be outside. I felt closer to her, almost as if I could commune with her as I walked along the path and under the trees. Also, in retrospect, I think the walk, even though it was short, released inner physical tension which eased my emotions. *(Forty-seven-year-old engineer, reflecting on his grief following the death of his mother six months before)*

If you are expected to display a modulated demeanor, you may need to seek a place where you will have privacy, and where you can allow yourself a good cry when you feel like it.

Many survivors tell of being in social situations when they are suddenly overcome with their sense of loss. They go off to the bathroom, shed a few tears, and return to the group.

In addition to allowing feelings to flow, it helps to talk them through with an understanding friend or relative who has also lost a parent.

The two friends who lost their mothers were especially helpful to me because they were talkers. They would come and talk. They'd go over what happened when their mothers died and that was very helpful to me. *(Middle-aged woman who lost her mother)*

As you talk, it will be beneficial not only to express your sadness, but to talk about several areas within the broad scope of your loss:

Your relationship with your parent. What kind of relationship did you have? What were the most important aspects of the relationship?

Your parent's perception of you. How would your parent have described your personality, character, capability, success and appearance? How does this differ from the way you see yourself?

Your strongest emotional responses to the death. Why do you feel angry, guilty, vulnerable, afraid, or relieved? *Who* or *what* is it that is provoking that response in you?

Your regrets. What more did you want to say or do? If your parent were still alive how would you take care of this unfinished business?

What specifically do you miss? Do you miss knowing you can go home and talk over problems, making the telephone call on Sunday, having your parent be a grandparent to your children, sharing your parent's sense of humor? (What you miss does not necessarily have to be positive. You may, for example, miss having someone to take care of, having someone structure your life, or giving unsolicited help or advice.)

If you find that you want to *talk* more than anyone wants to *listen,* make arrangements to share your loss and your reactions to it with a minister, priest or rabbi, or set up an appointment with a counselor. You might also like to participate in a support group for survivors. If so, contact the pastoral care office of your local hospital, or call a local Hospice and ask them for information regarding groups that are active in your area.

Men in particular often feel their grief is inappropriate or disproportionate to what is expected. Or they are perceived by others as needing little, if any, emotional support. A young man described the reaction of his woman friend following the loss of his mother.

When my mother was dying, Lynn wouldn't go up there with me. I felt like when you're in a relationship with somebody and this is their time of need, you better damn well support them. She refused to do that. I went up there by myself and saw her.

When primary attachment figures do not provide support, the stress produced by the death is intensified. The survivor has even greater feelings of isolation, vulnerability, and abandonment. In cases such as this the survivor benefits from sharing with a professional. Doing so does not indicate weakness or inability to cope; quite the contrary, it proves that the survivor is taking control of the situation and being responsible for getting what he or she needs.

Men who lose a parent often seem more inclined to express themselves on paper, rather than orally. For some, writing about feelings is easier or more necessary than talking about them. Also, writing following a death has more than a single purpose. On one level, it is expression and, in the case of some survivors, an act which fits within a life that was already inclined toward literature or art. At another level, writing memorializes the person who has died and records the final stage—the week, hour, or moment of death—and tries to put the death in perspective, to make sense of it.

A thirty-two-year-old man tells of sitting down in the hospital room where his father lay after his death, and beginning to write immediately. "It was not more than five minutes after my father died." The surviving son wrote a poem to his father which begins, "Peaceful, unhooked, your white hair wild at last..." And the poem continues, "You, my dream of America, joining your own father on the last stageline/your body glows an instant on this earth..." And it ends, "I thought for a moment I lost you/but no, I don't lose you. Your soul runs free."

Writing can also take care of unfinished business, all those things which still remain to be said. The anxiety produced by this state is illustrated by the excerpt from a young woman's poem following the death of her mother.

> I try to call you back so we can talk again
> maybe in a dream so I can say
> something more, make something clearer,
> let you know how much I still hope to wake up.
> When will this be over?
> I've chopped the bitter ending of your life
> from the good part
> and kept the wrong piece.
>
> *(LETTER TO MY MOTHER SOON AFTER HER DEATH, JO WALZ)*

Thomas Mallon, author of *A Book of One's Own,* described his use of a diary after his parent's death.

> I wrote a lot about my father when he died five years ago. I had a very happy relationship with my father, but there were gaps in it, and I used my diary to fill in some of these gaps. Losing my father was terrible, but it became almost a good thing that there were things to wonder about, to get confused and regretful about. It

gave me work to do, things to think about with an eye toward solving them or being content to let them rest, instead of just wishing he were still here.

(PEOPLE MAGAZINE, MAY 21, 1985)

In addition to talking to others or writing about loss, some survivors have found it helpful to record their thoughts or feelings on tape, particularly during the period when they were dealing with the last stages of their parent's terminal illness.

A fifty-two-year-old man whose mother was dying of cancer tells of taping the facts, his feelings and reactions every day as he drove from the hospital to his job. It was his way of allowing himself to say what he needed to say in a safe and private place. And it provided the method for preserving his last conversations with his mother.

Your physical environment is directly related to your ability to adequately express yourself, but finding a quiet space where you will be free from interruption can sometimes be very difficult, especially if you have young children at home. Among the "safe havens" sought out by survivors, where they could think and feel in relative solitude, were a nearby church or synagogue, a quiet corner in the library, their own basement or attic, a local or state park, a museum cafe, and the vacant apartment of a friend.

A woman survivor and mother of three children describes the importance of her selected quiet space.

I went to a kind of church where they believe that you can make everything happen. My friend suggested that I might feel okay going there. I went and sat there. I'd never been to a church like that. I cried through the ceremony and they all looked at me so sympathetically. I would sit and listen and quietly cry through the service. At the end, everyone held hands and swayed. I didn't talk to them. I didn't want to talk to them. I didn't feel the need to. I was a bit embarrassed that I was crying, but I loved going and sitting there. The minute the music started, I cried. It was very helpful to me.

An older woman told of going to a nearby state park and discovering a hiker's trail which led to the top of a small mountain.

I would hike on that trail a mile or two and then turn around. And I made a pact with myself: While I was on the trail I could think or feel anything I wanted to about my mother. I missed her so. One day I became aware that each time I hiked, I went farther. Then I realized that by the time I was able to hike all the way up the mountain it would be a big event for me, a sort of celebration of feeling all the raw feelings I needed to feel, and crying all the tears I needed to cry at the time. It doesn't mean I don't still miss her. I do.

But I think that we made it up that mountain together, my mother and I, and the grief peaked, just as the mountain did.

The Memorialization Process

The importance of a final ceremony, most particularly a personalized service, was emphasized in Section I. A service facilitates the healing process because it helps you fully recognize the end of your loved one's life on earth, say good-bye, express the feelings and review the memories that are most closely associated with your parent, and it makes it easier to integrate your loss into your present life.

In addition to the public service, there are other ways you can memorialize your parent. Two of them have already been discussed — writing and tape recording. Still other individualized approaches have proven helpful to mourners.

> My aunt and I went away. At night, we'd lie down in our beds and talk about how wonderful my mother was. And I wouldn't cheat. My aunt thought my mother was perfection. I didn't tell her that mother could be very angry. We talked about how wonderful she was and how she was good at tennis. That was lovely. *It was like going to church every night when we talked about how wonderful mother was.*

> My friend gave me tapes of Elizabeth Kubler-Ross. That was important. I would listen to them and cry. Listening to them gave me a formality. I would sit down and listen to them and it took about an hour. *It was a kind of ceremonial.* I listened to them a lot.

Often a private ceremony or memorial is not something that is planned; it happens when it needs to happen. Other times, memorializing is more complex and requires conscious planning and skill on the part of the survivor. A young actor tells how he dealt with the memory of his father.

> After my father's death, I wrote a play, a one-man show about his life, his thoughts, his dreams and my relationship to him. I performed it in local theater and then was invited to perform it at theater festivals abroad. It was my tribute to his life.

The process of finalizing a parent's death and commemorating his or her life helps the survivor begin the process of *letting go* of old roles and *relinquishing sources of gratification* that came from the very specific nature of the parent-offspring relationship.

Identifying With The Parent

I got to the hospital and he had died. As my poem about him says, "His white hair was wild at last." His mouth was open and he was unshaven. He was very untypical of anything he'd ever been in life. He was untypical of himself but at the same time, he was very typical of me. I had always been unshaven and my hair was wild. He became much more like me after he died and I became much more like him after he died. So we merged and we've been merging ever since. *(Thirty-two- year-old man reflecting on the death of his father when the son was twenty-eight)*

An identification with another person can be manifested mentally, emotionally, socially, physically, or materially. Often the survivor becomes acutely aware of identification with a mother or father during the mental review process that takes place after the parent's death. The silent questions are asked: *Are* we alike? In what *way* are we alike?

Some survivors make a conscious selection of the qualities, traits, skills, interests, mannerisms, eccentricities, or goals to be perpetuated. Other survivors have a subconscious identification process; with still others, it is completely absent.

For example, identification may mean that the survivor uses a manner of speech that was unique to the parent, emulates a gesture, has the same habit, or seeks out the same kinds of friends the parent had. He or she may dress similarly, carry out a parent's dream or wish, or participate in an organization or work for a cause in which the parent was interested. This type of identification, which is not harmful, may offer a great deal of satisfaction.

If, however, the grieving person feels the compulsion to follow in the parent's footsteps or emulate the parent's behavior when *the son or daughter does not genuinely want to do so, or does not have the required skills or abilities,* the identification process will not facilitate grieving, but distort it.

The importance of personal effects. Having an object to keep as a physical reminder of your parent is helpful. A possession, which may mean nothing at all to someone else, can serve two major functions. It is a treasure for you to cherish, and second, it is visible proof of your parent's earthly life. Survivors who find themselves without such effects may experience despair, regret, remorse and distress as a result. They feel bereft, left without something they *want to hold, look at,* and *own,* something they need as tangible evidence of their parent's individuality and former presence.

A woman survivor told of her extreme distress after finding out that one of her mother's rings, the one she had considered to be hers (because it was her birthstone) had been given to her niece.

A voice inside my head said, "That ring is mine." Then I told myself, "Let it go, let it go." That was about six weeks after her death. I thought I was going insane. I wondered how I could write to my brother and say, "That ring is mine. I must have it." I would rationalize, "Let it go. I have something of mothers. I have the *memory* of her." Then I would want the ring again. My husband thought I was going crazy. I would wake him up in the middle of the night and discuss how I could ask for the ring. I became obsessed with having it. I consulted psychics about it. I mean, I was crazy. I couldn't stop thinking about it. I would even wake up thinking about it in the morning. Finally, I was talking to someone about the ring and the person said, "You'd better do something about that." I realized I couldn't go on like that any longer. I went home. I really thought my mother wanted me to have that ring. I went out and bought a very beautiful ring and sent it to my niece who had been given my mother's ring. I wrote a long letter, a huge rationale about wanting the ring back. I felt guilty about writing the letter. The ring was sent back to me immediately. When I received it I felt as if something had dropped off me. The ring was the first material thing in my life that I had really fought for. I am not a material person, but I just couldn't let it go.

The importance of having something to hold onto is clearly illustrated by the case of a poet who lost his mother when he was eight years of age, and his father when he was twenty-eight. He had never been given any of his mother's possessions. In contrast, when the man's father died, he was able to retain articles, clothing and keepsakes.

Now I have the paintings of him, his shirts, different artifacts. I can smell him, feel his presence, I know who he was and what he was doing. As a kid, I had no artifacts from my mother, very few memories. I didn't have a whole lot of tangible information. My poetry about her says, "A scarecrow brought me into this world" ...things like that because I *have no memory, nothing to tag it to.*

Survivors often feel distraught when they sense that a memory they once had is fading. This situation is relieved when they have a personal possession. It is as if the article can always be depended upon to stimulate the memory and to bring back the parent more clearly.

The Destination of Your Parent's Presence

It may sound quite strange but many survivors have a drive to achieve a personal understanding of their parent's presence after death. There is, of course, no way any survivor can verify his or her belief in this regard; it is based on a wholly private and usually comforting conviction.

A survivor who is religiously oriented will usually be inclined to state definite beliefs. Without hesitation, the survivor will specify the destination of the parent's presence as being one which corresponds to accepted religious teachings. This type of statement is typical: "When my father died, there was a sense of a life accomplished, of going home to the Lord."

Other survivors may tend to be more spiritual in a general way, or to be more cerebral in their judgments. Such a survivor feels the parent's presence as a spiritual presence, but one which retains the quality that was such an essential part of the physical person; in other words, a force or essence transformed from the physical to the non-physical.

Closely related is the idea that the parent is part of the universe in some way:

> I looked up at the sky and I saw all the clouds moving high up. It's very interesting but I did immediately feel a connection with the heavens, that my mother was up there. *(Woman whose mother died in her late sixties)*

The locations arrived at are varied and intriguing, but they all have one thing in common: they provide for closure and allow for a personal interpretation of the mysterious aspects of death. In the minority are those survivors who fix on inappropriate destinations for their parent's presence. They may believe the dead parent is living in another person, in an object, within the survivor, or in an animal. Though this is uncommon, a survivor who places a parent in this way would benefit from discussing with a professional the nature of the loss and the survivor's emotional relationship with the deceased parent. An exception to this would be the survivor whose beliefs are within the tenets of his or her religion.

Subconscious coping. Often a sense of the parent's invisible presence eases the survivor's emotional pain, temporarily relieves loneliness, provides comfort or help, or underscores the survivor's belief that he or she is being watched over.

There may also be a recurrence of the parent's presence in vivid dreams. Here important and realistic conversational exchanges take place, feelings are conveyed, or tasks undertaken, the purposes of which are usually to relieve anxieties or fulfill wishes. Many of these dreams are evocations of positive past experiences or pleasant fantasies.

> In the dreams I'll be on a cruise ship or on an airplane and I'm taking control of the helm and I want to make sure that we're going to take off okay and that he's comfortable. He's a passenger. He doesn't take an active part in the control mechanism of the dream. I take a great control and he's there and we try to please him. *(Man whose father died in his eighties)*

As you heal, you reconcile yourself to several aspects of your parent's death, as well as to your present role in relation to the loss. This son's recurring dream summarizes some of the simplest and most helpful realizations any survivor can have. Specifically, you are in control now and you have taken over the helm, knowing your mother or father is in a comfortable place. As you continue the voyage, your parent's presence is with you.

A fifty-three-year-old woman survivor states, "I recognized that it is within my private realm of power to go forward, taking with me the gifts that come from my relationship with my mother—the good things I learned from her, her values, compassion, her quiet humor. I can leave the rest, the less valuable behind me and go forward with the certainty that she's there. She knows. I'm not as alone as I thought I was."

5

Surviving the Loss of a Child

Nobody knows what they can handle until they have to. If someone had told me that my child was going to die, and I was going to survive it, I would have said, "You're absolutely crazy. I could never handle that.
MOTHER OF A STILLBORN DAUGHTER

The death of a child is perhaps the ultimate shock, one which seems too horrendous to fathom. As you try to cope with what has happened, one of the most disturbing issues to deal with is the *wrongness* of your child's death. Because the natural order is for you to precede your child in death, you must, when your child dies, readjust to a new and seemingly illogical reality. This reality says that even though you are older, have been the caretaker, and have a shorter future, you have survived while your child, who had the *right* to survive, has not.

This unique individual you loved so deeply has been taken away from you. Nothing nor no one can remedy your loss. Having other children or being able to have another baby does not diminish your grief over your child's death. Researchers have found, for example, that mothers who lose one baby in a set of twins grieve just as much as mothers who lose a single newborn baby.

Losing What Your Child Represents

In addition to coping with the loss of a particular and unique individual, you are also being seriously affected by the absence of what your child represented to you.

He or she represented several, or even all, of the following:

- Part of your self; part of your physical body.
- Your own connection to the future.
- Your love source.
- Some of your treasured qualities and talents.
- Your missed expectations.
- A loss of your own power.

It helps to examine each of these briefly, in order to fully understand its impact.

Part of your self; part of your physical body. As you mourn, you reminisce as far back as your child's very beginnings, to his or her conception. You consider the physical characteristics of your child and focus particularly on those which bear resemblance to you or your spouse.

Your own connection to the future. Your personal continuity was embodied in your child. The two of you were bound together and moving forward into the upcoming years.

> Why am I bothering with life? How can I go on with my life when my son is dead? A child is so much a part of your future that when person *(Mother of a teenaged son who was killed in an accident)*

Your love source. You have other love sources, but none is the same as your child's love for you. This love was based on need, dependence, admiration, and appreciation. You were the model for your child, and your child's love was expressed by emulating your behavior. Also, depending upon your child's personality, you were loved with naivete, tenderness, reluctance, stubborn determination, joy, or even humor.

Some of your own treasured qualities and talents. You saw in your child some of the qualities and talents you most value in yourself. These attributes may have seemed to be magnified and more highly developed in your child. For example, you may always have thought that, given some encouragement or training, you would have been a successful soccer player, ballet dancer, or jazz musician. As your child developed, you saw those same talents emerging effortlessly or to a greater degree in your son or daughter. Similarly, you may always have valued your own capacity, however meager, for exhibiting empathy, courage, or wit. You saw those qualities reflected strongly in your child. As you watched your child grow, each positive attribute became a deeper source of pride.

Missed expectations. The experiences that you had anticipated sharing with your child never happened. The promised years of your child's daily life and activities are thrown away. It was as if these years had been allotted to you and your child, and then they were suddenly retrieved. The younger your child was at the time of death, the more you anticipated and the more expectations you had about his or her behavior, goals, accomplishments and pleasures. In this respect, the longer your child's life expectancy was, the greater your loss.

A loss of your own power. To some degree, you may see your child's death as a failure on your part. You feel anger and frustration at not being able to have exerted some control over your child's fate. You live with the idea that society expects you to protect your child, but you didn't protect him from pain; you didn't protect her from death. You feel impotent. For a long time after the death, there may be no "fight" left in you, no strength for the most ordinary of tasks, and no mental capacity for, nor interest in, complex thinking.

Miscarriages, Stillbirths, and Neonatal Death

Some common issues are raised as a result of miscarriages, stillbirths, and neonatal death. All of these deaths involve babies who have not yet been recognized by others and who have not yet been designated a "place" in society. Generally, unless the child had a personality and a presence that was *observed* by other people, the survivor's grief is considered to be less important than it would be with the loss of an older child, a spouse, parent, or friend. In fact, death due to miscarriage or the death of a newborn infant may be virtually ignored.

> In this type of loss [infant death] it is particularly difficult because most people don't even realize that a loss has occurred. Most of our babies are classified as nonpersons. Are we crazy because we're grieving for somebody who *wasn't*? *(Workshop facilitator for women who have survived the death of an infant)*

This lack of acknowledgement and sympathy from others deprives the parents of much-needed support, understanding and affection.

Unless people are directly involved, they are not likely to talk about a death which occurs during early infancy. These silent friends and relatives simply do not know what to say, or if they *should* say anything. They do not express the appropriate sympathy because they do not understand how deeply felt the loss is. They may even view the baby's death as an accident, a misfortunate circumstance that can be "righted" by the birth of another child.

People are also confused about what to *do*. They do not know if they should send flowers or a donation. The gift they had already given the expectant parents may cause them embarrassment and distress.

Further, they may be struck by the realization that if this type of death can claim the life of their friend's or relative's infant, it is also possible for it to claim their baby's life.

> I remember being real aware of the fact that even my closest friends were out there going, "Whew, I still have my kids." *(Mother of a stillborn baby)*

People who do try to comfort a grieving parent often make awkward statements that add to the parent's despair. "You're better off," they say, "because something would have been wrong with the baby, anyway. Think how hard that would have been." Or they assert, "If it had to happen to anybody, it's okay that it happened to you because you're really strong and you're the kind of person who can handle it. *I* could never handle it."

If you have lost a baby during pregnancy, or in the baby's first months of life, regardless of how well you seem to be handling it, you will experience some deep and consuming feelings which may continue for more than a year. These could include anger, anxiety, sadness, despair, confusion, guilt, and low self-esteem. Many of these negative feelings arise from a lack of understanding regarding your baby's death.

The Search for a Cause

As you seek to identify the cause of your child's death, you may realize you are angry at the medical community. The doctor may be perceived as having been rushed, indifferent, uncaring, unskilled, or temperamental. Sometimes parents who seek answers about their baby's death are told by the doctor that "this case is a rare one" and that there are, as yet, no identifiable causes for the death. Parents referred for genetic counseling may feel they are answering many provocative questions posed to them by professionals, but they are not receiving any pertinent or meaningful information from them in return.

> I was at my wit's end wanting to have all the studies done and have all the tests and take all the medicine so I could do it right another time. My doctor told me that even though I had lost two pregnancies, I hadn't lost enough to be statistically significant. *(Woman who had one miscarriage and one stillbirth)*

Fortunately, many doctors are sensitive to a patient's feeling of vulnerability following the unexplained death of a baby. The medical community, however, often fails to acknowledge the almost obsessive need you have to understand the *reason* for what has happened.

> You wonder how much control you have. Dope addicts have healthy babies. Alcoholics have healthy babies. There is so much emphasis now on taking care of yourself, not drinking coffee and

getting exercise. If you do all of those things and your pregnancy fails, it is extremely challenging to your beliefs about doing the right thing. *(Woman who had experienced a stillbirth)*

What makes it harder is the medical profession is never sure why. They will give you some information and then say, "Well, this is just a theory. *(Young mother whose son died at five weeks of age)*

A young woman who lost an infant son spoke for many women when she expressed her frustration:

All of us are dealing with the issue of the next pregnancy. What happened in my body that didn't go right? I go back, detail by detail, to see what I could have done differently. I want to be able to predict the future.

In addition to examining natural causes, there may be a question in your mind regarding the possibility of medical error. This question can be made even more anxiety-producing by your doctor's reaction to the baby's death. If your doctor's response to the loss is perceived by you as being one of acknowledged failure or obvious guilt, then you are almost certainly going to blame the doctor. (This will lessen any feelings you may have of personal failure, whether or not the failure is warranted.)

Even when you have been given a feasible medical explanation for the cause of your baby's death, you will still need to ask questions and have them answered. In a study conducted with parents who had suffered the death of a baby, this need for inquiry was underscored. Thirty-five families were interviewed and seventy-four percent of them understood the causes of death, as well as the degree to which the same condition could be expected to occur in the next baby, but the families still needed to question. They wanted to have statements reiterated and they wanted to analyze, in particular, the cause of death as it was identified on the autopsy reports.

Feeling Guilty

I spent months, even years, thinking it was the hot fudge sundae the night before. I had a hard time bringing it up with my doctor for fear it would be really true. *(Mother of a stillborn daughter)*

My mother-in-law suggested it was the diet I went on before I got pregnant. *(Woman who miscarried in her fourth month of pregnancy)*

The need to repeatedly review the circumstances is an inevitable outcome of your tragedy. As the mother of a deceased infant, you may *openly* ask questions like these, or you may find yourself *silently,* yet obsessively, reviewing them again and again.

Reviewing the pregnancy:
- What happened during my pregnancy that didn't happen to people with healthy babies? What did I do wrong?
- How many hours did I sleep each night? Did I sleep too much or too little? Should I have taken a nap in the afternoon?
- How many cigarettes did I have a day?
- How many cocktails did I have during my pregnancy?
- Did I run down the stairs or did I merely walk fast?
- Did I try to exercise too much? Didn't I get enough exercise?
- Should I have abstained from sexual intercourse?
- Did I *think* something that made the baby die?

Reviewing the birth:
- Did I select the wrong doctor?
- Did I go to the hospital too late in labor?
- Should I have refused an anesthetic?
- Should I not have attempted a natural childbirth?
- Didn't I try hard enough?

The questions are varied and many, depending on your individual circumstances. As you continue to review the pregnancy and birth, you define the boundaries of what you perceive as having been your personal responsibility. You release some of the guilt and begin the long, slow process of fully acknowledging your loss. As long as guilt is the major issue, the baby cannot be relinquished. The baby is held onto with *"If only's."* If only I hadn't run...or stayed up the night before...or eaten too much...or cried too much...or taken a diuretic...and on and on.

Along with the guilt you inflict on yourself, is the guilt you either assume or imagine coming from other people. For example, some husbands intentionally or inadvertently insinuate the child's life was in the wife's domain, thereby implying she should have prevented the death. Even the idle remarks of relatives or friends can reinforce existing guilt or produce new guilts. The father who says, "I told you to quit smoking!"; the sister who self-righteously proclaims, "My doctor told *me* not to drink at all during pregnancy, and I didn't"; the neighbor who asks, "Weren't you still going to work in your eighth month?" adds to your self-blame.

Guilt is even stronger if you had, at some point in your pregnancy, not genuinely wanted the baby, or if you had previously experienced an abortion. In these cases, you may view death as a personal punishment.

The Mother's Longing for the Baby

When your pregnancy was first in evidence, your body changed rapidly. Your breasts enlarged, your body structure changed, you felt movement and psychological responses began to occur. There was a feeling of duality, of living for two, and sharing. You fantasized about your role as parent in your child's life. (In research done with parents who received photographs of the infants in utero—the result of using sonograms for diagnosis—it was found that parental bonding was reinforced by an image.)

The physical longing for your baby is strong and instinctive. If you had been allowed to hold your baby prior to the death, or even at the death, you will have a sense of your son or daughter having been born and lived, regardless of how short the child's time on earth was. The baby's existence was made real. He or she was held, loved, and separated from you as a physical being. You are able to say, "This is how he or she looked. This is who my baby resembled." The baby is not now imagined as some damaged being, because the child was seen as a real person.

As explained by the mother of a baby who died at three weeks of age, never having left the intensive care unit, "I held the baby and touched her. I named the baby and helped to determine the kind of service we would have for her. I will remember holding her for as long as I live. I had her in my arms, if even for a few moments."

Sometimes holding is prohibited due to the critical nature of the child's condition, or contact is impossible due to the circumstances of the death. If you were prevented from having any physical contact with your baby, you may, to some degree, emotionally withdraw from the baby. You will experience some remorse about not having been able to hug, hold, and love the baby, if even for a few minutes. Further, your complete realization of the death will be more gradual, perhaps even delayed.

Facing the Empty Nursery and Your Other Children

If your baby was never released from the hospital, there will be several disturbing factors and procedures with which you will be forced to cope upon returning home.

If you have other young children at home, you may have to repeatedly answer their innocent remarks and questions. "I thought we were going to get a baby." "Will I have a brother some day?" "Did our baby die like Sally's baby died?"

Your milk-filled breasts are not only painful, they are an ever-present reminder that the natural order of things calls for you to be mothering.

Other aspects of your baby's absence will require your attention. You may need to pack the infant's clothes, blankets, and your shower gifts.

For years, your feelings of emptiness and sadness may surface without warning long after the physical reminders in your immediate environment have been carefully removed. Seeing other pregnant women and babies can be experienced as a personal assault on your emotions. Gradually, however, the severity of your reactions will lessen.

If I haven't learned anything else from losing this baby, I've learned that whatever is thrown at you, you can handle it. What else can you do? *(Mother of a stillborn baby)*

In some ways you never stop mourning the loss, you find a place for it, you integrate it. *(Woman who miscarried)*

The deaths discussed to this point have focused on those which occur as a result of miscarriage, stillbirth, and infant death due to illness within the first few months. Due to the unique circumstances of the Sudden Infant Death Syndrome (SIDS), this type of loss will be addressed separately.

The Sudden Infant Death Syndrome

The largest number of infant deaths is attributed to SIDS, or "crib death." More than 14,000 parents a year survive such a loss. Besides being the biggest killer, SIDS is perhaps the most baffling; even though research is intense and ongoing, the cause or causes still remain unknown.

There are three general conditions which precipitate extreme distress in parents of SIDS victims: attachment to the baby, perception of the baby as healthy, and assumption of guilt.

Attachment to the baby. Unlike stillbirth and infant death due to illness or accident, the SIDS baby is most often at home. As parents, you had the opportunity to bond with your child and to have experienced your child as a distinct individual who had his or her own unique personality.

The peak period for babies lost to SIDS is between two to four months of age. In this length of time you, as a mother, have been seriously involved in your baby's nurturing and well-being. As a father, you too may have spent considerable time with your infant and developed a strong parenting role. When your baby suddenly died, this major focus within your life was removed.

Because the death came with no warning, there is a tendency to deny the baby has died. For example, you may find yourself continuing with the parenting tasks, such as cleaning or arranging the nursery, preparing the formula, or tending to your baby's clothes.

When you begin to assimilate your loss, you may withdraw and resist interacting with people outside your family. You might, for a time, even withdraw from your family itself.

Your baby may frequently be the subject of dreams in which you are searching for, or caring for or playing with your baby.

As a father, you will likely suppress your feelings in your effort to carry on with a normal routine. While you may provide practical help around the home or become protective, you will generally not *appear* to be as emotionally affected as your wife. That does not mean that you do not need to talk about how you feel and to allow other outlets for your grief. (See *Easing Marital Stress* in this chapter.)

The perception of the baby as healthy. Initially there was shock and disbelief when your happy, healthy infant was suddenly found dead. There had been no indicators of your child's impending death. Your baby had never needed any diagnostic tests; nor had there ever been any thought of your baby's life being endangered.

This typical SIDS situation makes it extremely difficult for you to cope. Your loss seems impossible.

- The day (or the last few hours) before your baby being put to bed were spent in normal acitvity. Your baby's movements and expressions gave no indication of internal problems.

- Your baby did not cry nor make any sound which indicated discomfort of any kind.

- Your baby had been quietly sleeping in his or her familiar crib and was discovered dead during the night, or in the morning.

- Your baby was put down for a nap at the babysitter's and never awakened.

Because there was no warning before the death, you may now attempt to pinpoint an "indicator" you think you overlooked. This quest generates your own guilt.

The guilt factor. Because of the mysterious circumstances of the death, you may immediately blame yourself. If your baby had died while in your care, the seeds of self-accusation are further provoked by the required police investigation. Within hours of your baby's death, you are requested to answer questions aimed at helping the authorities make a diagnosis. The questions either increase your self-doubts and give you opportunities to blame yourself or, less frequently, they put you in a position to defend yourself. For example, when infants have died several hours prior to their discovery, they will likely be "black and blue," as if they had been severely bruised. The investigation, then, could pursue child abuse as a possible cause of death. Inservice education for investigating officers and other personnel helps to allay this suspicion. In some instances, however, where education has not taken place in regard to SIDS, the investigation may focus on what appears to be evidence of physical battery.

The extended interrogation. When the legally required inquiry and documents have been completed, you continue to put yourself through a silent grilling as you search for a cause. Your logic is that something or someone *must* be responsible, and you want to identify any reason for death, however implausible it may be.

You rehearse everything you did prior to the baby's death. You consider the clothing of the baby, the way the crib was prepared, the temperature of the room, what the baby ate or didn't eat. Was there a sigh, a cough, a cry, an irritability or dullness that escaped your notice? You may recall a gesture or a sound that, upon reflection, you decide was a signal of your baby's distress when, in fact, it is only a product of your desperate imagination.

You may also assume blame that you imagine is being directed toward you by relatives, friends, or even your spouse. As a wife you may feel your husband is not significantly sympathetic or reassuring. He may even seem to be implying that you did not know how to carry out your "mothering" tasks.

As a husband, you may feel that your wife is blaming you for not handling the baby correctly, not putting the right blanket in the crib, or turning up the thermostat too high. An unfeeling relative may inquire, "Well, how did you *know* the baby didn't cry if you were down the hall?"

If you left the baby with a babysitter you have still another set of guilts. Why did I leave her there? Why didn't I just stay home? Why didn't I call the babysitter to check on her? Why did I ever get a job and go to work in the first place?

> If I hadn't gone to work maybe he wouldn't have died. I took my next baby to work with me for two months. I stayed up with her all night if she had a cold.
>
> I kept her in the bedroom with us longer than I did with any of the other children. *(Mother whose baby was a victim of SIDS at two months of age)*

If you cannot find a cause, or if someone in the medical community cannot sufficiently explain this tragedy, then you feel there is a possibility that it can happen again — *that* you cannot bear.

Sometimes, grandparents overtly blame the daughter-in-law or son-in-law. If this is your case, the support you seek and need from your spouse's parents is unavailable. You feel increasingly frustrated and make attempts to identify *some* reason for this tragedy, regardless of how nonsensical or minute the reason is.

The benefits of an autopsy. As you try to pinpoint a concrete cause, an autopsy will help you to eliminate any blame you may have assumed for some real or imagined "carelessness." If you think the baby choked, hemorrhaged internally, had a heart attack, or "cried to death," you can investigate the plausibility of this occurrence by discussing the autopsy report with your doctor. Excluding the rarest of circumstances, you will have proof that the baby did not die because you did not feed him something else, pick him up, look into his room more often, and so on. You will find that your greatest fears have no factual relevance.

In *The Bereaved Parent*, Harriet Schiff relates the story of a woman who claimed she killed her baby by smothering it with a pillow. The young woman actually appeared in court and testified that she had been responsible for her infant's death. The autopsy report, however, showed that the baby had not died as a result of smothering, and the court dismissed the case against the mother. While most parents do not find themselves in a courtroom attesting to their own guilt or innocence, they are still inclined to question whether the death was, in any way, their fault.

Childhood Death Due to Malignant Disease

As a parent of a child who died with a malignant disease, you may have experienced one or more of four common reactions.

First, *you may not have accepted the fatal prognosis when it was first related to you.* Instead, you assimilated it gradually, or even denied it until your child was in the last stages of dying.

> It wasn't until a certain visit to the hospital that it became obvious that the disease was terminal. It would have been totally unfair for us to have the attitude that he was terminally ill. And that if we did, no matter how we attempted to cover it up, it would show. So beyond our own need of not really wanting to accept it, we felt it wasn't fair. His condition wasn't really driven home until five days before the death. *Death was nothing more than one of the possibilities. (Parents of a four-year-old boy who died of cancer)*

Second, *you may have fantasized either consciously or subconsciously, about your child experiencing a miraculous recovery.*

> We didn't accept that he was going to die. We accepted it on one level, and on another level we expected that a so-called miracle would occur and then he wouldn't die. *(Father of a young leukemia victim)*

Third, *you may have tried various healing techniques yourself,* such as visualization, administering a special diet to your child, changing your religious affiliation, engaging in certain activities that should bring "good luck," or bargaining with an omnipotent power, with God.

Fourth, *you may have felt your child's illness was an indirect punishment to you* for some past behavior for which you feel ashamed or guilty. (This feeling is not limited to parents of children with malignant disease, but also occurs among parents of children who have died from other causes, such as SIDS, accidental death, and suicide.)

Because of the nature of your child's illness you had some advance warning of the death. However, the idea that anticipatory grief reduces the need to mourn after the death or diminishes the impact of the death, is not valid. Before the death you are grieving about the fact that your child is going to die; afterwards, you are grieving about the actual death. These are two distinctly different experiences. The fact that your child is gone is overwhelming, even when you knew it was going to happen, even when you may have wished it to occur quickly to spare your child from having to endure any more fear or pain.

At a time when you are dealing with your own strong emotions, and during a period when you are most likely to be in a rundown physical condition, you also have to cope with various kinds of unexpected reactions from others.

> When the loss of my child comes up I hear, "Oh, you poor thing. How awful. Can you talk about it?" I am continually having to make it okay for other people and I don't like having to do that. *(Mother of a young cancer victim)*

Grandparents often are struggling with their own grief and are unable to offer you emotional support or understanding. You, in turn, have difficulty comforting them. As a result, you may feel emotionally isolated or abandoned by your own mother or father in your time of need.

Experiencing the Loss of an Adult Child

The loss of a child is *still* the loss of a child, regardless of the child's age. A parent can feel deep grief even if the child is an adult of fifty or sixty years of age. If you are an elder parent, there are several factors which distinguish your experience from those of other surviving parents.

You had the expectation that you would die first. This is true of any parent who loses a child, but the older the parent, the more pronounced the belief. You think your own death should have been given priority, that it should be more desirable than the death of your son or daughter, regardless of your child's age. You may even feel guilty for being alive.

You feel unduly punished at this late stage of your life. You assumed that the major traumas of your life would occur when you were younger, when you were out in the world in a more visible and vulnerable position. Even though you may have anticipated that your own life might lead to illness or accident, you did not think you would have to endure this shock caused by your child's death.

You may feel guilty for not preventing your child's death. After all, you may think, you are supposed to be the one who can control what happens, who can help make things right, and who can exert some power in your child's life.

You may be required to assume the role of parent to your grandchildren. In your advanced years, years that were supposed to be less pressured and more restful, you are required to begin your life all over again. It becomes necessary for you to have habits, schedules and goals you had in your younger years. While you may welcome your grandchildren into your home with great love and devotion, you may still feel taxed physically, emotionally, mentally, or financially.

You may feel that you are expected to suppress your own grief in your concern for your child's surviving spouse or children.

You may inherit money from your child. This inheritance adds to your guilt and unhappiness because you do not want to profit from the loss. If this occurs you may quickly find ways to dispose of the money through channels which are considered admirable, or at least socially valuable. You give it to the child's surviving brother or sister. You donate it to fund medical research, to finance a living memorial for your child, or to set up a scholarship fund in your child's name.

As an outcome of a child's death, an elder parent may even *will* his or her own death in order to be with the child. As despairing and dismal as it sounds, this desire is not uncommon. Fortunately perhaps, no scientific research exists to gauge how many deaths of senior citizens can be attributed to these precipitative circumstances.

Duration of the Grieving Process

The loss of your child elicits the most profound bereavement. It cannot be measured in the number of days or months since the death, but only in the *way* you have spent those days and months.

As previously discussed, the grieving person lives with any number of conditions following a death. These may be even more complicated and pronounced if the deceased person is a child. Anger, frustration, guilt, anxiety, despair, sadness, or withdrawal may be part of your life for two or three years. Additionally, you may have your own particular obsessions. Two years after the death of his child, one father said, "The thing I had the hardest time with after my son died was the pain. *Why* did he have to have the pain?" A divorced mother confided that she had great difficulty dealing with her own guilt. After her daughter's death, she explored, again and again, why she had not spent more time with her child and how she could have gone out on a date when her child was terminally ill. A grandfather expressed his anger at the diagnostic procedures which did not identify his grandson's lymphoma until it was too far advanced.

Regardless of your personal issues, you will feel vulnerable during the grieving period. As a parent you were supposed to have a certain kind of power which you have discovered you did not have. You were not able to exert any control over this tragedy.

Now you find that the things you need desperately to control are your memories of your child. You must remember what he said at a certain time, what she wore, where she sat, what he ate, how she smiled, and what his favorite activities were. You want the details to stay with you. They will be small comforts for the lonely stretch ahead.

> It's harder for us now than it was at the time of his death. When you have to accept death is when you can't remember things so well, exactly how his voice sounded, how he looked. The loss is more obvious as you remember less of the details. I find the grieving experience to be the opposite of what I had been led to believe. The easier part was when he died, because you're so involved in it. *Now* is more tragic. *(Parents of a four-year-old cancer victim who had died two years previously)*

Sibling Reaction

As you cope with your own feelings, you may have to deal with the disturbing reactions or conditions of surviving siblings as well. Poor health is a common problem among siblings of a deceased child. Colds, flus, rashes, sore throats, asthma, and accident proneness represent some of the most prevalent symptoms you may have to cope with when your *own* physical stamina is extremely deficient.

Emotional states intensify if your children begin to participate in one-upmanship; that is, if they compete for the dead child's love and assert that he or she loved one of them more than another. As disturbing as it is, it is their only way of "claiming" their sibling for their own, getting a bigger share of their brother or sister to keep for themselves.

Visits to the cemetery may provoke conflicting behavior among your family members. One child may be reluctant to go; another may be eager to be included as a part of the family unit which pays tribute to the brother or sister.

On your deceased child's birthday or the anniversary of his or her death, emotions that you and your family members had been successfully suppressing may surface.

In some cases, when a child dies, the bereaved parents try to "fix" the family by "replacing" the lost child, either by having another baby or adopting one. In still other cases, the family unit may break up.

Divorce After the Death of a Child

Following the death of a child, marriages commonly begin to flounder. It is as if the harmony of the marriage is being assaulted from all sides.

- Partners are undergoing the stress produced from grief and its accompanying conditions.

- Partners become mediators as conflicts arise among siblings.

- One or both spouses may be coping with job pressures which have magnified because of absence from work.

- One or both spouses may find that responsibilities which once seemed routine now seem monumental.

- Parents often have a heavy financial burden resulting from their child's illness or accident.

It is estimated that ninety percent of all couples who lose a child are confronted by some serious marital problems within the first year after the child's death. Further, the divorce rate is exceptionally high among couples who have lost an only child. In many cases, the marriage which ends in divorce appears not to have been one which worked well before the death. The tragedy put damaging strains on an already exacerbated relationship.

> Our son's death had a lot to do with our divorce. It wasn't a wonderful marriage. After the death everything that had been bad got much worse. *(Mother of a teenaged accident victim)*

> Whether or not the marriage survives depends on how much the parents can communicate and depend on one another. It depends on how they accept each other. They are two people grieving in different ways, with different intensities, and they can't give to each other. Relationship problems are inevitable. How the couple survives has a great deal to do with how they have survived other kinds of clashes in the past. If you are used to forgiving, accepting and talking, you weather the storms. But if you bottle up and don't talk, you won't have much of a chance to have your marriage survive. *(Support group facilitator for the bereaved)*

The couples who have a great deal of trouble coping may have had parenting roles that were much more intense and focused than their spousal roles. They may be more likely to say, "I did my part. Why weren't you doing *your* part?" The unspoken accusation is, "If you had done what you were supposed to do, the death would not have occurred."

As a result of this type of conflict, one partner assumes a big load of guilt which his or her spouse is quite willing to repeatedly inflict. When this happens, the blamed parent attempts to cope with three traumas simultaneously: the death, the general stress of the marriage, and the spouse's charges which turn him or her into "the accused." It is true, however, that this situation seems to arise less frequently among parental survivors of miscarriage, stillbirth, SIDS, and infant illness, than it does among parents who are surviving the accidental death of a child.

The information which follows covers specific perspectives, processes and strategies which implement healing after the loss of a child.

Working Through Your Loss

One of the major residual effects of your loss is the feeling of having been, and perhaps still being, ineffectual in the face of tragedy. You may find yourself frequently tormented by the strong visual images and unpleasant memories which were a part of your child's last months, days or hours. You may recall the father, mentioned previously, who said the hardest thing he had to cope with was, "the pain; why my son had to have such pain."

If only an explanation existed which could provide some kind of reassuring information about your child's experiences. Unfortunately, there is no way any expert or philosopher can successfully legitimize pain. In dealing with the anguish-producing memories, however, it may help to be aware of what it is in you that you are grappling with, and why The struggle is so very difficult.

Emotional pain and anguish produce feelings of helplessness. One father said, "My hands were tied. I may as well have been dead myself for all the good I did." A twenty-eight-year-old sister said, "I used to gaze at my little brother and think, 'Why can't I go into surgery and give him this heart of mine so he can stop suffering.' " She added, "I would willingly, gladly have died, but I was not given that option."

Examining Helplessness

To understand exactly what makes your help*less*ness so devastating, it is first necesary to take a look at your help*ful*ness. Let's say your ten-year-old son is "helping" you build a sundeck. As he hammers, he bangs his finger. He yells. Then, as the pain increases, he begins to cry. You take him into the house and run cold water on his finger to relieve the pulsing. Maybe you give him some ice to hold against his finger to reduce the swelling. The pain continues. He cries and complains. You become concerned that his finger may be broken so you decide to take him to the doctor. You tell him the doctor will help and that he will feel better after he gets some treatment for his finger. Within an hour, everything you told him has become a fact. He leaves the office feeling better.

Your three-year-old daughter is riding in a wagon that is being pulled by an older neighborhood child. The wagon tips and your three-year-old spills out onto the sidewalk where she sits, screaming. You run to her, pick her up, and examine her scrapes and bumps. To make her laugh, you give the "mean old wagon" a kick. You clean off her minor wounds, put on band-aids, wipe off her face with a cool washcloth and tell her she's fine. In a few minutes she is playing with the neighbor child again.

In instances such as these, you had tremendous power. You assessed the injury. You administered some aid. You gave verbal reassurance. If necessary, you got professional help.

Compare this to the degree of power you had prior to your child's death. When the accident or illness occurred, you tried to help, but your help didn't work. You were not able to get professional treatment which would make your son or daughter well again. You were not able to say with certainty—or maybe not at all—that "You will be better," or "Everything will be okay." You could not abolish your child's hurt, fear, or pain. Your help*ful*ness turned to help*less*ness.

As your child endured a terminal illness or the devastating effects of an accident, you were ineffective. In severe contrast to your past experience, there were three major areas over which you had no control: onset, duration and severity. You could not prevent the illness or accident. You could not control how long it would last, and you could not reduce its intensity.

Most likely, it was not only clear to you that you had no control, you were also *told* there was nothing you could do. Hearing it, made it even more stressful. For example, your son was ill with a cancer or a heart ailment which was completely unfamiliar to you. You knew nothing about the illness and you knew no one who had ever contracted it. You listened to your doctor's diagnosis, then you solicited a second diagnosis. It confirmed the first. When you sought further help or solutions, you were told there was no other hospital or staff better qualified to handle your child's condition. No new research foretold of new treatment which would reduce the likelihood of your child's death. At every turn, your control diminished. When the death occurred, you were its victim, along with your child.

You may now see yourself as weak. You may think that because you did not modify or eradicate your child's pain or fear, it means you are an ineffective person, or even that you are not a "good" person.

You may look back now on your child's death, certain that it was filled only with agony and that the agony was, at least in part, due to your own failing. *Consider that what you perceived may not necessarily be accurate.*

> I have learned from the dying children I have worked with that children tend to die with greater softness and ease than adults. Perhaps because they have not been so involved themselves with attempting to control the universe, there is not so much tension in their minds. They are more open to how things are. They don't have a solid concept about life or death, and so are less attached to name or fame, to reputation, even to their body...I have noticed that usually the younger the child, the less fear of death. The fear that I do see is often the reflection of the dread that their parents feel.
>
> *(WHO DIES?, STEPHEN LEVINE)*

It is time to relinquish the torment you have been carrying around with you. Allow yourself to be fallible. It is true, you were unable to make the world fair, but as a survivor you have power to improve the tiny corner of the globe on which you live. Be aware that *you are not only punishing yourself for what you could not do, you are punishing yourself for what no one on this earth could do.* Look realistically at what you are able to do and what you will do in the future. You will begin to feel less helpless as you exert a healthy degree of control over your domestic scene, work activities, and recreational choices. Remember, you have skills, desires, and proclivities which are strong and which can be utilized.

Reestablishing Your Emotional Foundation

The grieving process is an emotional rollercoaster. The emotions run high, then low, and often seem to be circling back on themselves. If your child was terminally ill or lived laboriously through post-accident treatment and surgery, your emotional rollercoaster may have been operating at full force for months, or even years. Your child's condition appeared to improve, then to worsen. Medications were prescribed, then withdrawn, then prescribed again. The unpredictability of events produced in you a shaky emotional foundation. It was as if your feelings had been played with, batted about, and volleyed back and forth. Just when you thought you knew what to expect, the expected was transformed into the unexpected. Now, as you struggle to gain control over your emotions, you find that grieving is still *another* up-and-down process.

The guilt connection. To reestablish your emotional foundation after the loss of your child, you will invest both time and energy in purging your negative feelings. It is important to deal with guilt as soon after the death as possible. If ignored, the emptiness and torment which arise from self-blame can be long-lasting and debilitating. (See *Diffusing Guilt* in Section I.)

If you are a parent plagued by guilt (substantiated or not) the behavior of others is often contributory. This is what happens. You feel guilt for something—a specific action, characteristic, or wish. Then the people with whom you are in contact don't talk about your loss. Friends and relatives are silent. This silence on the part of others can be viewed as an implication of your guilt. The death is so off limits, it cannot be discussed. Your self-blame then compounds.

Breaking the silence. You can change this situation by actively breaking the silence surrounding the death. When *you* talk about your child, you let others know it is an acceptable topic of conversation. You can even talk about your longing and the many memories occupying your thoughts.

Bringing up the subject is a tactic some parents have perfected. When they feel they are being avoided or treated as if nothing has happened, they make it a point to speak to others. They make it clear they are still real people and that they will not accept being ignored. They initiate social interaction which appears more normal and which does not endorse their child's death as "unspeakable."

The need for idealization. During the time when you may be dealing with guilt and reflecting on what a *poor* parent you were (or *are*), you are likely to focus on how *perfect* your loved one was. All of your child's remembered qualities, traits, and habits are more than positive; they are exalted. The child is not viewed as a real personality, but as a kind of perfected persona.

This idealization has its purpose. It provides comfort when you are experiencing emotional pain. As you idealize your child, you say, "all of this agony (caused by the death) is worth it." The guilt, anger, longing, despair, are worth it. Gradually, *idea/ization* becomes *realization* as the loved one's whole self is recalled and incorporated into your current life. When son or daughter is remembered as human, the loss of a *total, real* person, can begin to take a place in your life.

Clarifying your values. If you try to operate in accordance with values that you think you are supposed to have, or ones which served you well before your loss, you may find your current feelings in a tug-of-war. Instinct tells you one thing; habit or social convention dictates something different.

> After our son's death we were very tight as a family. We did not have time for anybody who wasn't contributing to the goodness of living. We never felt obligated to do anything. *One of the lessons we learned was there wasn't time to deal with people with negative emotions who bring gloom into your life.* You see how fragile life is and you understand that it is to be as joyful as it can be. The priorities established because of the death remained as a major underpinning in our lives. *(Parents of a five-year-old cancer victim)*

Your values will clarify themselves as you sort out your experience, reflect on your loss, and understand what it means in relation to your life now.

Identifying Your Sources of Support

Following the loss of your child, you may have one or more individuals whose company you prefer, or you may be comfortable only when you can withdraw entirely from interaction with others. If you are withdrawing you need to realize that complete withdrawal often retards the healing process. Support *can* be obtained from others. A friend, relative, or neighbor who can offer you valuable support, will meet certain criteria.

Selecting supportive individuals. First, *a supportive person must be accessible and available.* He or she must have time and energy to give.

Second, *the person should have some experiences with a loss similar to yours.* Though no two losses are ever exactly the same, they can resemble one another in terms of *type* (cancer, heart disease, accident, suicide) and *age* (infant, preadolescent, teenager).

Third, *the person will take an active interest in the continuation of your life after your loss.* He or she will encourage you to undertake daily tasks and activities but not push you into social participation when you are expressing the need for solitude. This successful interaction between the support person and yourself will occur naturally if you maintain mutual respect.

Fourth, *the person will assume tasks and run errands which are beyond your capabilities during the grieving period.* Typically, this might include 1) providing child care to allow you important time to yourself, 2) assuming some aspect of your job that is particularly stressful, or 3) intervening with relatives, friends, or neighbors whose expectancies or questions have become a personal burden.

Essentially, these four criteria describe the *ideal* support person. The qualities and characteristics put forth here may be used as a basis for your evaluation of support that is available. They allow you to identify the strengths and weaknesses of your support person and, therefore, to be able to clearly see the areas in which you can expect the most response. Also, by recognizing the person's deficiencies in regard to your special needs, you can save yourself the frustration or disappointment that results from unfulfilled expectations. You will recognize when your own requests may be misdirected.

The requirements on your side of this relationship are perhaps more easily spelled out.

First, don't feel as if you have to mask your feelings. Talk to your support person. *Understand that you will need to repeat yourself and don't be embarrassed by this need. Reviewing your situation and your feelings is an important part of your grieving process.*

Be aware of how often you turn down help in areas which are difficult for you. *Allow yourself to accept offers of assistance—even though you may do it infrequently.*

It would be unfair and irresponsible to treat this subject of support without acknowledging that every survivor will *not* have a support person, or persons within the family, neighborhood, or work place. Due to the nature of the survivor's living arrangements, family dynamics, age, or personality characteristics, it is quite possible that he or she will feel completely isolated and alone. A woman artist who had survived three family deaths put it this way: "All this stuff about caregivers and supportive friends sounds great. But what if you have no support? I mean *none!*" The answer to this is, "It is never *none!*" The support is there for every survivor, but it may be a bit further removed. It may not come from a neighbor, or brother, or best friend, and it may not come from an aunt, or lover, or co-worker, but it may be found in a *group*. *Regardless of where you are, who you are, or what type of loss you have had, there are others who can help.*

Locating a supportive group. A wealth of support groups flourish in this country. They can be located by contacting your local mental health agencies, or the social services department or pastoral care office of the largest hospital in your region. Five major organizations will be briefly introduced here: Hospice, Compassionate Friends, Candlelighters, the National SIDS Foundation, and SHARE.

The Hospice organization was formed in Connecticut in 1974. Since then, it has grown to approximately 1,200 Hospices throughout the nation.

The activities of local Hospices vary, depending upon their location and the community they serve. Their major emphasis is on the provision of home health aid, support and assistance to the dying, support for the bereaved person, and assistance in identifying other helping agencies which will meet the individual's needs. Some Hospices may offer support for survivors of accidental death. Some may offer groups for parents of children who were cancer victims.

> In our support group, we shared our fears and one of the fears is that you'll lose this child, too. If you have a child who has been ill and died, or injured in a car accident, the fears are more real because you've already been through the experience. *(Mother of a cancer victim)*

There are Hospices that develop support groups for widows and widowers. Others put survivors of various types of loss in contact with each other so that they may form their own independent group. In a few areas, Hospice may not offer support services for the mourner, but the local agency will make referrals to other groups which will meet the needs of the survivor.

Hospice also provides assessment of a survivor's coping potential and emotional condition. This assessment is helpful in pinpointing any preventive intervention which may be needed by the mourner.

The *Compassionate Friends, Inc.* is a voluntary, self-help organization for bereaved parents. Support is obtained through affiliation or contact with a local chapter. At present, there are approximately 496 chapters throughout the United States. Each chapter develops its own resources, newsletters, libraries and community of caring people.

Local chapters provide sharing groups that create an atmosphere of openness and honesty. The members have a mutual understanding of the special issues faced by the parental survivors of a child's death. The feelings and opinions expressed at meetings are treated with complete confidentiality.

Any bereaved parent contacting the national office will be responded to individually and, whenever possible, will be provided with the name, address and telephone number of the leader of the closest local chapter, (The *Compassionate Friends, Inc.* National Office, P.O. Box 3696, Oak Brook, Illinois 60522. (312) 990-0010)

Compassionate Friends' newsletters, which offer insight and aware-ness into the feelings experienced by a parent survivor, can be requested from a local chapter.

> When Lauren was killed, I felt so alone. I felt afraid to say what I was feeling and thinking. At first it was nearly impossible for me to have any kind of a conversation, so I literally lived for the monthly newsletters of *Compassionate Friends*. They pulled me through. Later, I was able to go to a group. *(Mother of a twelve-year-old accident victim)*

Candlelighters is an international parent support network for parents who have, or have had, children with cancer. The organization, which was begun in 1970, now has approximately 200 chapters in the United States, 24 groups in Canada, and 19 groups in other countries throughout the world.

Local chapters offer individual parent contact, self-help support groups, and referrals to local caregivers when a family is in need of professional counseling. Candlelighters parents share the shock of diagnosis, the questions about treatment, the despair at relapse, the hope of remission, and the uncertainty as treatment ends. If cure is impossible, they share the grief at death. Group members act as an emotional support system of "second families" for each other.

The many additional services of the organization include advocacy, supplying information and providing educational opportunities.

The *Candlelighters Foundation,* in Washington, D.C., serves as the educational division of the parents' group and assists parents who wish to form a group within their area. The educational and communication services, as well as the publications, are free. The foundation operates on funds from the American Cancer Society and from tax-exempt dona-tions.

Among the many publications of the *Candlelighters Childhood Cancer Foundation* is an excellent quarterly newsletter. Referrals to local chapters and requests for publications will be answered by the national office. (The *Candlelighters, Childhood Cancer Foundation,* 2025 Eye Street, N.W., Suite 1011, Washington, D.C. 20006)

The *National Sudden Infant Death Syndrome Foundation* (NSID) was organized in 1962 for SIDS survivors. The foundation has approx-imately 80 chapters nationwide. Their goals are to promote research on sudden infant death syndrome and to provide peer support to SIDS families. They offer self-help groups, telephone exchanges or one-to-one talks. They also educate SIDS extended families, the general public, and involved professionals.

For a referral to a local support group, any parent surviving a SIDS death may call the National Foundation who will identify the chapter nearest you. Requests can also be made to receive the foundation's newsletter by calling 800-221-SIDS.

Other SIDS organizations include the *National Clearinghouse For SIDS* (8201 Greensboro Drive, Suite 600, McLean, Virginia 22102), which offers fact sheets and educational materials; the *Council of Guilds for Infant Survival,* headquartered in Davenport, Iowa, which has a national network of support chapters for parents; and the *American SIDS Institute,* headquartered in Atlanta, Georgia, which is dedicated to advancing medical research into the cause and prevention of SIDS.

SHARE (Sources of Help in Airing and Resolving Experiences) is a support group for parents whose infants have died from any cause. The organization has 138 chapters in the United States, 1 in South Africa and 1 in West Germany.

Within the support groups, members are free to share their feelings and experiences but are not required to do so. It is understood that the parents may feel more comfortable listening and being in the presence of others who can empathize. Tears, fears, confusion, and other feelings which arise upon the death of a child are shared.

Anyone seeking referral to a local SHARE chapter, or wishing to request their monthly newsletter, may contact the founding headquarters. Sister Jane Marie Lamb, the founder of the organization who works in the Pastoral Care Department of St. John's Hospital, encourages parents to inquire about support services in their area. (SHARE, St. John's Hospital, 800 East Carpenter, Springfield, Illinois 62769. Telephone (217) 544-6464.)

Writing It Out

For some survivors, writing about the loss can be as beneficial as talking about it. Most often, writing that is done during the grieving process takes one of two forms — the journal entry or the poem.

> When I write about the stress, I am immediately more calm. I kept a journal the last year before my daughter's death and it is mostly feelings. The strange and sad thing is I didn't write anything the last two months of her life and I'm sorry I didn't. I want to sit down and reconstruct it. I know it will help. *(Mother of a cancer victim)*

(For specific suggestions on structuring your journal to facilitate your needs, see "Writing About How You Feel" in *Surviving an Accidental Death.*)

A mother whose son was killed in a mountain-climbing accident was able to give written expression to her feelings about her loss. In a series of poems, she explored the various aspects of her relationship with her son, her son's relationship to others, and her reflections on her own grief. Here is an excerpt from one of the poems in the series.

> They sent back the things
> he left at base camp,
> the leather belt he always wore
> the levis shaped to his knees
> his old Adidas with knotted laces
> a tube of rumpled lip-balm
> with dirt stuck in the creases,
> a heap to hold
> smaller than a baby boy.

REQUIEM FOR MATTHEW, LUCY DIGGS

It is not uncommon for a surviving parent to discover that writing is not only a valuable emotional outlet and one that helps put things in perspective, but it is a challenging discipline in which one becomes increasingly interested. At first, the loss may produce a poem or two, a short story, or a piece for a support group newsletter. Then the parent may find himself or herself joining a writer's group, or taking a night class at a high school or community college. Writing, begun as therapy, ends as avocation.

Easing Marital Stress

As previously discussed, marital stress arises or increases after the death of a child. Except for a small minority of survivors, the exacerbation of the marital relationship is inevitable. It need not, however, be long-lasting, nor damaging.

One of the key causes of disharmony is the way in which people grieve: no two people grieve in exactly the same way. In addition, as a general rule, women and men grieve differently. Our culture assumes that after a family death the man will be steadfast and he will be leaned on by the immediate family members. People inquire how his wife is "feeling" and "taking it," or "holding up." At the same time, he is expected not to show his *feeling*. He is supposed to *take it* like a man and *hold down* the fort. An objective observer may find it difficult indeed to figure out if such a man is grieving and, if he is, *how*.

Some men express their grief through anger or through demanding, energy-consuming activity. They lead a search party on a rigorous expedition when there is no hope of finding their child alive. They undertake an exhausting project at home — building something, or chopping something down, or making major repairs on the house or car. They work longer hours on the job, or begin to take more business trips.

A man after the first few months is usually silent about his loss. His habits may change. He goes for a drive alone, goes to the store when it is not necessary, or visits the cemetery by himself. Usually, however, in one way or another, the male tries to disguise his grief from those around him.

In contrast, a woman is expected to discuss her feelings with her husband, children, friends, and relatives. It is not extraordinarily difficult for her to arrange coffee with a friend for the sole purpose of talking about her loss; for a man to do the same with one of his peers, would not be as easy. Even though he may join a sympathetic co-worker on his coffee break, or meet a close friend for a beer after work, if the surviving father mentions his child's death, it will be most likely to relate a *fact,* not a *feeling.* For example, he may say, "The car Brent was in skidded forty feet before going over the cliff." But he would not be apt to confide, "I was looking forward to all the things Brent and I could do together now that he was getting older." He would probably not say, "Sometimes when I see a boy who closely resembles my son, my heart nearly stops beating."

Considering the differences in grieving, no wonder there are tensions in the household. Two people who are in daily contact with each other are handling their feelings in dissimilar ways. Further, grieving tends to be a solitary experience much of the time.

But there are positive steps which can be taken to reduce these normal tensions. Following, are several procedures which couples have found helpful:

- *Set aside a time each day to discuss the events that have taken place, and to share thoughts and feelings.* It should be a time when interruptions from other family members will not be possible. .

- *Be an attentive listener who listens beyond words.* Hear what your partner is sharing about the way he or she feels, and what his or her individual needs are.

- *Agree on the family activities which will always be shared by both of you,* regardless of how much one of you would like to thrust the responsibility on the other. (school conferences, soccer games, church functions, certain kinds of shopping, visits to other family members, etc.)

- *Agree on activities which can be done by one of you* without the support or attention of your spouse. (helping your child with a certain type of homework, visiting certain relatives, participating at a health club or in a sport, etc.)

- *Express affection throughout the day.* Hugs, pats, and hand-holdings are needed now more than ever. Physical touching not only provides assurance and displays love, it gives energy to your partner.

- *Recognize the need for solitary time, during which rest and reflection can take place.* Do not take it as a rejection if your partner feels the need to go off and be alone. It has more to do with what is inside a person than what is outside. Inner needs often have nothing to do with the immediate environment or available companionship.

Pleasure and Intimacy During Mourning

During the grieving period, you and your spouse may have differing views and needs regarding sex. It is not uncommon for the wife to comment that her husband wanted to have sex "right away," while she had no interest in it whatsoever. There are two major factors at work here: energy and morality. That is, the wife may be too emotionally empty, too preoccupied, or not yet physically recuperated from the devastation of the loss. On the other hand, she may actually *want* to participate in sex but thinks it is wrong. In such a case, she will want to wait until she feels sex is appropriate.

If both of you are feeling responsive, then the need for physical contact should not be denied. Even during the grieving period, the actual act of making love can be rejuvenating. It affirms love, aliveness, closeness, and your ability to reciprocate through gestures, caresses, and words.

It is important to understand that experiencing pleasure is not the same thing as renouncing your dead child. Pleasure must not be associated with disloyalty. If you are enjoying yourself in any way, it does not mean you are forgetting your loss. It means you are first learning to integrate *pleasure* into a *life devastated by loss*. Then, much later, this situation will reverse itself and you will have integrated the *loss* into the *pleasures of your life*.

Pregnancy After the Loss of a Child

Depending upon the circumstances of your child's death, you may feel fear, confusion, uncertainty, or abhorence in regard to pregnancy. The emotion most often expressed among young mothers is fear — fear that the baby will be stillborn, or die during infancy, or be the victim of accidental death. In some types of infant death, an autopsy can often allay fears regarding genetic hereditary factors.

Understanding the cause of your baby's death will help reduce your fear. By becoming as informed as possible, you decrease the aspects of mystery which have been a painful part of your situation. Consider the possible resources you have for information. The most obvious is, of course, your pediatrician. In addition, you can get information in the following ways:

- *Contact a support group or foundation related to your loss,* such as NSIDF, Candlelighters, etc. Most support groups have educational materials, fact sheets, and newsletters that contain valuable and current information. In addition, many groups sponsor public education lectures and seminars.

- *Visit a hospital to gain access to, or obtain, educational materials designed for parents.* (For example, a sampling from a list of educational tapes in one hospital includes these titles: *Childhood Cancers, Sudden Infant Death Syndrome, Sickle-Cell Anemia, Heart Failure, Warning Signs in Pregnancy, Nutrition in Pregnancy, What Causes Miscarriages,* and *Hodgkin's Disease.*)

- *Visit your local library to obtain reading material relevant to your loss.* If you are unsure about the most efficient way to locate resources, the reference librarians are most helpful.

- *Request genetic counseling* for you and your spouse, if appropriate.

As you explore below the surface of your loss and increase your storehouse of information, you will feel less apprehensive about pregnancy.

If there seems to be no cause for your child's death, your first step will be to pursue your individual case with the doctor who attended your child. Remember, *the physician will not be likely to seek you out and supply you with information.* When you have organized your thoughts, prepare a list of questions based on your concerns. Schedule an appointment with the physician and take your list with you. After your doctor has discussed your questions, ask to be referred to specific agencies or hospitals which have access to the most current research. You have every right to pursue as many answers as may be available, but you will have to take the initiative.

The replacement baby. In contrast to the couples who are fearful of having other children, there are the couples who set out immediately to fill the void left by the child who died.

Of course, *when* one should have another baby is not a question which has an answer that is applicable to all surviving parents. It would be presumptuous to suggest any time requirements, based on months or years. There are, however, some *guidelines* for evaluating when the time is right for you. Take into consideration the following:

Your childrearing capabilities are influenced in a major way by your emotional state. Ask yourself, are you still experiencing frequent fluctuations in your emotional state, such as from calm to despair, pleasure to deep sadness, patience to extreme irritability?

Your physical condition determines, to a large degree, the ease of the birth and the extent to which you will withstand increased demands on your energy and endurance. Ask yourself, are you still feeling the residual effects of stress such as rapid heartbeat, insomnia, dietary disorders, or muscle spasms?

The loss of your child needs to have been incorporated into your life. When the loss of your child remains as a void to be filled, the new baby will be destined to try to fill that void. The child will never be able to *be* his dead brother or sister and, ultimately, you will recognize that there is no magic way to substitute one individual for another.

> We went right out and bought (adopted) another baby. She wasn't a personality, she was the "lost baby." My arms were empty and I wanted to hold that baby again. *(Mother of an infant who died at six months)*

Having a child too soon may essentially interrupt your grieving process. This would be detrimental to you, your spouse, and the new baby. When the emotional climate in your home is healthy and nurturing, and when you feel you can wholeheartedly reinvest your energy in a different personality, not the persona of your dead child, then you may be ready for a new family member.

Reaching Out to Other Children

Some surviving parents are interested in devoting their time, skill and affection to assisting or comforting children who are not their own. There are numerous ways to enhance the life of a child in need.

The Big Brother, Big Sister program provides companionship to children who need the attention of an adult. Homes for retarded children need volunteers. There are volunteer teacher's aid programs in public schools, foster care programs, and halfway houses for adolescent boys and girls.

This country has a multitude of children whose emotional, physical, social and intellectual needs are not being met. If you choose to help, be assured your contribution of time and energy will do more good than you can believe possible.

In *On Children and Death,* Elizabeth Kubler-Ross points out how a tragic experience can eventually be transformed into something positive: "...understand that all my work with dying children came out of the memory of the horrors of the concentration camps of Nazi Germany, where 96,000 children were put in gas chambers. Out of every tragedy can come a blessing or a curse, compassion or bitterness...the choice is *yours!*"

6

Surviving Loss During Childhood

After my mother died when I was five years old, I felt as if I was getting smaller and smaller and that I was insignificant — so unimportant that I might disappear...I felt as if everyone else knew secrets that I didn't know and would never be able to find out because I was too different...It's very hard to explain but I believed that I was wrong, somehow. That wrongness was both deep and agonizing. For many years I felt I was on the outside of things, even though I'm sure others didn't think that I was.

THIRTY-FIVE-YEAR-OLD WOMAN WHO
WAS A CHILD SURVIVOR

A child's feelings resulting from the death of a parent or sibling may not be obvious to others. For that reason, it is extremely important for surviving family and friends to realize that besides easily recognized feelings and reactions there are others which a child survivor may be having to cope with alone. These are the "invisible" reactions to death.

As reflected in the above survivor's recollection, death can produce an anxiety that translates into the *fear of the loss of oneself.* The five-year-old felt as if she was "getting smaller and smaller" and that she "might disappear." A thirty-six-year-old architect who also lost his parents during childhood summed it up this way: "When you lose your parents, you lose yourself. You die somehow."

This fear of being lost, and the related anxieties about being on the outside of things, of not knowing the secret, and not feeling as if he or she belongs, are not experiences which are limited to the very young child. A survivor who is struck by parental death during middle childhood or adolescence can experience the same reactions.

> I can remember not even having enough guts to go to my locker. I carried all my textbooks around with me all day and I still have dreams about not being able to find my locker and I can't remember the combination to my lock. I'm still walking the halls. The school was so big I didn't think I could find my way to my locker and get around. It was all I could do to get from class to class, to physically locate myself in the building. *(Woman who lost both parents by the time she was twelve years old)*

The words "locate myself" are important here. A survivor of any age feels lost and made smaller by death; but for a child or adolescent, this sense of being *disoriented* and *reduced in the world* can be particularly strong and long-lasting.

Even though these feelings are intense, they are not made known; that is, they are not overtly stated by the child. It would be a rare child who would verbalize, "I feel as if I cannot locate myself," "I feel as if I do not belong in this world," or "I feel as if I am shrinking." Yet, more often than not, the child-survivor turned adult will understand such statements at once. There is no need for amplification.

In contrast to the invisible responses are overt responses such as noticeable sadness, rage, timidity, or withdrawal. These are visible. It is this *extensive range* of feelings and reactions which must be considered by any caretaking adult who is hoping to facilitate the child's emotional and psychological development after the death of a loved one.

To put a child's various responses to death in some kind of meaningful context, it helps to recognize that a child's understanding of death varies, depending on his or her age. *At each developmental stage, the child's perceptions and concepts of death change because he or she reaches a different level of cognitive development, possesses a greater storehouse of experience, and has new ideas about the world.*

A Child's Understanding of Death

Infancy. An infant's awareness of the world is very narrow. First, the child is aware of mother. Next, the infant is conscious of his or her own physical being, and finally, of existing as a separate being. The death of the mother is perceived as an unavailability, an *absence.*

This lack of availability is not perceived as permanent or impermanent because the infant has no concept of time. The infant's needs are for physical contact, warmth, and consistency. The child's fears during infancy are only those which pose a threat to his or her survival, such as the fear of separation from the nurturer, the fear of being left alone, or the fear that comes from seeing an unfamiliar face. Up to the age of two, there is no concept of death.

Preschool age. From about two to four years of age, a child's fears are more numerous. In addition to having feelings which arise from fear of abandonment, the child begins to understand, more clearly, external threats. This child can go away from home under his or her own power—on foot, or riding a tricycle on a "trip" down the sidewalk. The child sees things happen in the world outside and begins to learn from them. A small person can get bumped or tipped over. Other things can pose a threat to the youngster's body.

A preschool child is interested in the physical functions and characteristics of his or her body. This interest causes the preschooler to speculate about the person who died: "How does he play now?" "How will she get out of the box and up through the ground when she wakes up?" "Can he still eat cookies and spaghetti?" "Does she cry?" "Is he warm?"

At this stage, the child does not understand the possibility of permanent destruction. *Death is impermanent and reversible.* For example, the child whose pet has died may continue to act as if the dead pet is still alive. This preschooler will ask to feed it, may call it to come home, or look under the table or bed for it. Just as cartoon characters can endure being smashed, run over, or blown up, and can then survive to go miraculously about their business, so it seems to be with real people.

Because most preschool children are not able to make a clear distinction between life and death, they see death as a deep but temporary sleep. Often, the terminology associated with death reinforces this view: He closed his eyes and "didn't wake up." Now the person is "resting." The loved one is placed in a "slumber room" at the funeral home.

Ages five to nine. Between the approximate ages of five to nine, a child's understanding of death will undergo another change.

In a study of children whose ages fell within this range, it was found that fifteen percent of the youngsters thought about death at night and believed that people usually died at night, as opposed to during the day.

One of the major perceptions that occurs within (or near) this age range is that of death coming from an external source. Death is a bogeyman, a monster, a ghost, a skeleton, or an angel who comes to take people away. It comes from the outside, and in that sense it is not a person. Children think that by being clever and trying hard, they can escape personified death as they could escape an assailant.

While some children at this level may understand that death is a permanent passage into another realm, the majority of children think that death can be reversed or outwitted.

Children in this age group also show an interest in burial, as exemplified by the "final rites" they often arrange for deceased pets.

Ages nine to twelve. At this stage, the majority of children understand that death is the end of life, that it is irreversible and that all things die eventually—even they will die someday. *Death is no longer a bogeyman, but a biologocal process.*

They may also think that dying may be painful, and they begin to fathom the idea of death as obliteration. Some will consider abstract concepts, such as death as a vast darkness, or a spiritual world.

There is also serious concern with the *consequences* of death—what changes, they wonder, will be necessary as a result of death. For example, schoolchildren told of the death of a classmate's parent will ask such questions as, "Will Jane have to move?" "What will Tommy's mother do now?" "Who will take care of Ann?"

Teenagers. Death is understood as an abstract concept by teenagers. At this stage, youngsters begin to exercise philosophical capability, to consider those things which are universal: life, love, death, and society.

Often, the first personal exposure the adolescent will have with death is through the loss of a grandparent. Though the teenager understands that death is irreversible, it is also supposed to be distant. In fact, all of the changes that are occurring in the teenager's body and mind reinforce the idea of death being distant; the adolescent experiences powerful sexual drives, pronounced moodiness, and strong thought processes. The teenager's life is so intense and full of energy that death could not possibly touch it in any way. Yet, when a grandparent dies, or there is the untimely loss of a parent or sibling, the teenager can no longer regard death as distant.

At the same time that teenagers desperately try to set themselves apart from death, they also *fear* death. Because of this fear, they may try to prove themselves more powerful than death. This proving takes the form of reckless driving, accepting life-threatening dares, and putting themselves in positions in which they must triumph over great odds. They test their mortality, as if doing so will allow them to gain control over it, to make them immortal.

It is important to understand that every child will not experience these developmental stages at the ages specified here. *The age ranges are all approximate.* There are no age limits which can be homogeneously applied to every child's understanding of death. Some children's cognitive development, experiences, and perceptions of events in the world differ greatly from those of their peers. In summary, a child understands death when he or she knows

• Death is not temporary, but permanent.

- Death is not magical nor personified, but a biological process.

- Death cannot be outsmarted; it is inevitable.

- Death is not something which occurs to a selective few; it is universal.

A child's understanding (or lack of understanding) of these facts will vary. The way in which the death of a loved one is explained to the child is extremely important because the explanation can augment the child's information and clarify misconceptions. Specific guidelines for talking with a child about death are presented later in this chapter.

The Child's Reaction to Death

Most commonly, the child's major reactions to death are fear, guilt, anger, and confusion. It helps if the caretaking adult has a general understanding of the motivation for each reaction. By examining the various layers of feeling, as well as the variety of influential experiences that are a part of the child's world following a death, the caretaker can cope better with the child survivor's needs.

Fear Resulting from Loss During Childhood

The child who has been personally affected by death will have multiple fears. Among them will be any number of the following:

- Fear of losing the other parent.
- Fear that he or she too will die.
- Fear of going to sleep.
- Fear of being separated from a parent or sibling.
- Fear of being unprotected.
- Fear of sharing his or her feelings with others.

Fear of losing the other parent. If death has taken a parent, the child then sees the remaining parent as a candidate for death, also, for if one parent can be powerless against death, so can two.

Fear that he or she too will die. If a child has lost a sibling, he or she may identify very closely with that death, having feelings that range from vulnerability to complete helplessness. When the child is younger than the sibling who died, the survivor commonly fears (even expects) his or her death to occur at the same age.

I was very afraid I would die when I reached the age when my brother died, but I didn't tell anybody. Then I woke up one morning and said, "Now, I'm older than he was." *(Teenaged girl whose brother died at eighteen years of age)*

As an extreme reaction to the death of a brother or sister, a surviving child may become physically ill, manifesting symptoms which are identical or similar to those of the dead loved one. In such a case, the symptoms reinforce the child survivor's belief that he is doomed to suffer the same fate.

Fear of going to sleep. A child may be fearful of going to sleep because he or she equates sleep with death. This concept is strengthened when the child hears adults refer to death as "sleep," or "a long rest." (The prayer which suggests "If I should die before I wake," adds to the existing anxiety.)

In addition, sleep actually separates the functioning people from those who are not functioning. The child is sent to bed, but the lights are on in the rest of the house, activity continues, and anything can happen to the remaining family members when the child is not watching them. The awake, mobile family members can desert the child who is in the dark and is subdued in an isolated environment.

Sleep may also be made less desirable by the prevalence of nightmares or night terrors, usually having to do with separation, desertion, or the surviving child's threatened destruction by an outside force. A child may also begin bedwetting, which adds another obstacle to a full night's rest.

Fear of being separated. As pointed out, sleep is a form of separation and the child fears separation in general. He or she may be afraid of going to school, being left with a baby sitter, or being required to go some place unaccompanied by an older brother or sister. The fear of separation can be overwhelming and long-lasting. It is linked with the idea that when the security of the parent, the home, or the sibling is not available, *anything* is likely to happen.

Fear of being unprotected. Coupled with the child's inevitable sense of desertion when his or her parent dies is the feeling that the child is no longer protected. Perceiving oneself as unprotected is frightening for any child, regardless of age; for a young child it can be especially terrifying.

Fear of sharing feelings. Less noticeable is the child's fear of sharing feelings with others, a fear which may be particularly pronounced in the adolescent. If feelings are shared, the status quo may be upset, the teenager thinks. A family member may cry—or worse yet, may not understand.

An older child may realize that a memory which produces in him a longing or sweet sadness may have the opposite effect on another family member. The brother survivor may gain great pleasure from remembering when he and his brother went bike riding to the canal. His sister, however, may remember with sharp bitterness that she had never been allowed to accompany them.

Not able to risk the possible outcomes or repercussions of his or her feelings, the child survivor keeps those feelings private.

I was afraid to talk about how I felt to my mother because I knew she would start crying. Then my brother would get mad at me for upsetting mom. So I kept my feelings to myself, and eventually I was afraid to say much of anything. *(Teenager whose father died when he was ten)*

Guilt After Loss During Childhood

Because guilt can arise from virtually any thought or act, it is impossible to enumerate all of the reasons a child survivor may feel guilty. There are, however, some major motivations for guilt. These grow from any of four beliefs commonly held by the child survivor:

- The death is a punishment to me for misbehaving.

- I *wished* the other person dead.

- I did not love the other person enough.

- It is not right for me to live when the other person is dead; I should be dead in his place.

Guilt is one of those insidious invivible reactions; a child survivor can carry a huge burden of guilt without anyone else recognizing it. Even if the surviving child or adolescent exhibits changes in behavior, these behavioral symptoms will not necessarily be linked to guilt. It helps, then, to consider that any child could be living with any one—or more—of the disturbing beliefs cited above.

"The death is a punishment to me for misbehaving." Children can experience harsh self-blame for actions they view as bad. These actions may include making inadvertent mistakes, refusing to share, or accidentally breaking something. To make matters worse, children often have a remarkable memory for their own unfortunate or disruptive acts. Even though, in retrospect, they now cause the child emotional pain, these same acts may have gone entirely unnoticed by others or have been dismissed as insignificant. *It is important to be aware of the great storehouse of potential misery that the child may use for self-condemnation.*

I remember thinking that maybe his dying was some kind of punishment. I broke his typewriter in the office one time, and another time I broke his swivel chair and I thought it was as if I'd done all this bad stuff so, you know, his dying was like a punishment. *(Girl whose father died of cancer when she was eight years oldWHEN A PARENT DIES, BY JILL KREMENTZ)*

Death-as-punishment is a theme often related by children who are surviving the loss of a parent or sibling. *Helping the Child Heal* in this chapter contains guidelines for counteracting this and other debilitating beliefs.

"I wished the other person dead." A child is, by nature, egocentric. This allows the youngster to think that it is possible for his or her thoughts or wishes to produce external events. It is common, therefore, for a child to think he or she caused a death by *wishing* the parent or sibling to be dead. In such a case, the child survivor unfortunately does not make any distinction between the *wish* and the *deed.*

A thirteen-year-old girl whose younger sister died with cancer, after a long period of hospitalization and invalidism, expressed her feelings in regard to her terminally ill sibling.

> Part of me wanted her to die because she was getting everything she wanted. I thought if she died, I'd be the most important one, but it didn't work out that way.

When a child survivor is aggressive toward a sibling or parent and that parent dies, often the child considers the death to be a direct result of the aggression. For example, a child may push little brother, talk back to mother, take dad's credit card without permission, or borrow a sibling's favorite item of clothing without asking. In addition to the survivor feeling guilty, the child very often lives with the expectation of having to endure some retribution in the future.

"I did not love my brother (sister, mother or father) enough." Children often think that if you exhibit enough love, warmth, attention, or affection toward the other person, he or she will not die. This belief does not necessarily manifest itself in the child's behavior *prior* to the death; but, in retrospect the child thinks that such loving attention would have saved the loved one. The survivor suffers self-recrimination and longs for a second chance.

> My little brother was always asking me to play with him, begging me all the time. I brushed him off. I thought I could always play with him later when I felt like it. Well, now I feel like it and he isn't here, you know? He's dead. I really don't think he ever knew I loved him at all. *(Fifteen-year-old brother of eleven-year-old accident victim)*

> It seems like every time my mother hugged me, I squirmed out of her reach. I was always wanting to be on my own, to go with my friends outside. If I would have hugged her back, she would have felt better. She needed to be shown affection but I didn't show her I cared. *(Eighteen-year-old reflecting on her mother's death when the girl was thirteen)*

"It is not right for me to live when my brother (father, sister or mother) is dead; I should be dead instead." This thinking reflects the idea that death is some kind of exchange, that one life can be substituted for another.

A child who believes this idea thinks he or she is living *at the expense of* the dead sibling (or, less often, the parent), and that the parents preferred the sibling to the surviving child. The mother of a teenaged boy whose older brother was killed in an automobile accident said, "He thinks his father would be happy if he (the younger son) were dead and the other child were still alive. He says it. He thinks the family would prefer the brother's life to his."

Feeling this way can lead a child to any number of behavioral reactions; among them are temper tantrums, fights with siblings, a lack of interest in school, or a dissatisfaction with surroundings in general.

Anger After Loss During Childhood

The child who thinks he is unworthy of being alive may exhibit aggressive, disruptive behavior at home and school. This is because, as has been noted before, guilt and anger are closely linked.

In addition to anger growing from guilt, it can grow from any of the four following beliefs which may be held by the child survivor.

- I have been abandoned. Now I must cope with life on my own, and with little help.

- I am unimportant. That is why my loved one could leave me.

- My future has been taken away from me. I was looking forward to interacting in a unique way with my sibling or parent. Now, I don't have anything to look forward to.

- I have to fight forces that are bigger than I am. They are very powerful and I am inadequate. I should have been able to prevent the death and I didn't. I am powerless.

Often, a brother or sister who survives a sibling's death will direct his or her anger at parents, teachers, classmates — or even God. The child survivor will feel mistreated, victimized by a higher force, and will challenge or lash out at a particular target. The child vents the rage which arises from the impotence he or she experiences in the face of death.

The survivor's anger may exhibit itself in obvious ways, such as verbal outbursts, irrational accusations, temper tantrums, physical fights, or the destruction of property. It is important for the caretaking adult to recognize that anger which is just as severe can be turned inward, resulting in withdrawal, depression, accident proneness, digestive disturbances, and abdominal pain, to name the most common symptoms.

Confusion Resulting from Loss During Childhood

Consider the task of the child who must try to sort out, among other things, 1) God's role in relation to death, 2) ambivalent personal feelings about the loved one who is dead, 3) mixed messages from surviving family members about the child's own behavior following the death, 4) conflicting social expectations, 5) confusion about his own perceptions and memories, and 6) dichotomous and volatile feelings of those closest to him. This task is indeed overwhelming.

Confusion about God and religion. If children have been raised in a home where religion and God are an integral part of family life, the God-is-Good principle may have been an accepted factor in their upbringing. When the death occurs, the child is told (or it is implied) that the loved one has gone to be with God. In a religiously oriented home, the child's indoctrinated faith may be a powerful source of solace and comfort. The intrinsic relationship to God allows for an acceptance of the death. In contrast, a child may also be confused by a loved one "going to be with God." Such a child who loses a parent, for example, may find the concept extremely difficult to understand. The child thinks, "But I need my mother and I loved her. She should be here with me so she can help me grow up. How can God be good?" The child may experience, for the first time, bewilderment about the role God played in the child's own deprivation and hurt.

Also, a young child does not have the capacity to think abstractly, and, though he or she may try to understand God's relationship to untimely death, the child will more likely be puzzled and frightened.

> We had a British governess. When mother died I was in third grade. The governess came to the school, took me down to the beach and said, "God took your mother away." I said, "Who is this God character?" I thought, "What kind of a character is going to take your mother away?" *(Thirty-two-year-old man reflecting on his mother's death0*

> Ever since Mommy died, it's been hard for me to go to church every Sunday—the way we used to. I still go on Christmas and Easter and sometimes I go and light a candle for her. But the one thing I can't understand is, if God's so terrific, how could He let my mother die? *(Child survivor, WHEN A PARENT DIES, JILL KREMENTZ)*

> As a child of six or seven I didn't believe in God and I had to reconcile that. If God was good why wasn't earth good? If God created the earth and was omnipotent and could control life, He wasn't doing a very good job. *(Male survivor reflecting on his thoughts after a parental loss occurred in childhood)*

The child survivor may have another type of reaction in regard to religion. In some families, prior to the death, religion had no role and was not part of everyday life. After the death occurs, the child hears religious references for the first time, and is given explanations within unfamiliar religious context. The child does not have any previous experience on which to base what he or she is being told.

In addition, the child may be hearing that mother is in heaven. Even though all statements imply that heaven is a wonderful place to be, people are crying. The child wonders, "If heaven is better than earth, why is everybody so sad?" Still another puzzle for the child survivor is, "If heaven is preferable to earth, why am I *here* instead of in heaven along with mom?" If the child is told that God wanted the loved one, then the child is also forced to wonder if God will want him or her, too. Will he be "taken away?" Will she be "called home?"

Confusion about others' expectations. Following the death of a parent or sibling, the child may be expected to "Act like a little man," "Be brave and help your little brother," "Come here and give me a hug." The messages here all have the same theme: be in control, grown-up, comforting to others (the surviving parent, or a brother or sister). *At the same time,* this child may feel very doubtful about being able to meet the expectations of others. The child survivor wants to feel that someone else is in control, grown-up and serving as a support person. As a result, the child may feel torn between childhood and adulthood. On one hand, he is supposed to be helpful and "manly"; on the other hand, experiences himself as the frightened "baby" he really is.

Adolescents, in particular, have difficulty figuring out what behavior is acceptable or unacceptable within their social environment. They may need to show how they feel, but be inhibited by what they perceive as disapproval from their peers. They don't know what is considered normal and natural.

> My friend kept saying, "Don't you care that your father died? Aren't you sad?" I said, "Yeah, I'm sad, but I can't cry all day." It was like she thought I didn't care, but I couldn't cry at school.
> *(Ten-year-old girl whose father died in an auto accident)*

The older child or teenager who loses an older brother or sister may have feelings of insecurity which are the result of having lost a role model. This older brother or sister was supposed to set the pace, figure out things for both of them, lead the way into the future, or be the protector. Now, suddenly, the surviving child may be the *only* child, or the "front runner" for younger siblings.

Confusion about perceptions and memories. Sometimes the death of a parent or sibling is followed by extensive and inordinate praise of the deceased person's character, personality, skill, and sensitivity. The child survivor who doesn't remember the dead loved one as perfect is confused. *Was* that person perfect? If dad was perfect, the child thinks, then I am bad for remembering that sometimes he called mom names, he didn't help out around the house, and he sold my dog without telling me. Nobody else seems to remember the things I remember. I must try to change because I am probably wrong.

Confusion which results from moodiness. Finally, in cases where the child has lost one parent, that child may be expected to deal with a father or mother who is smiling and helpful one minute, and morose and untalkative the next. When John comes home from junior high, dad calls from the office, sounds cheerful, and asks John about his day at school. Then dad comes home from work, gets dinner, and by the time the meal is completed, he isn't speaking a word. Moodiness and unpredictability of the surviving parent are a natural outcome of parental loss, but it can be most disturbing to the child who needs closeness and reassurance. The child is left to wonder, Did I do something wrong? Doesn't dad like me? Does dad wish he wasn't here? How can I turn things around?

There are definite practices and strategies which the adult survivor will find helpful when interacting with and assisting the child survivor. The groundwork for successful grieving and eventual healing begins as soon as the death occurs.

Telling the Child of the Loved One's Death

Even though this is not likely to be the first death the adult has experienced, it may quite likely be the first for the child. A special sensitivity and awareness are necessary when the child is being told of the loved one's death. The following guidelines may prove helpful:

- Use language that is appropriate to the age of the child.

- Use language that is free of philosophical, religious, or sentimental references.

- Tell the truth about death, identifying the cause of death without giving the details which are unnecessary or disturbing.

- Do not expect the child to respond in a way which is "acceptable" to adults; for example, with overt sadness.

- Observe how the child appears to be feeling.

- Allow the child to release strong immediate feelings, which may even include anger or bitterness.

- After sharing the most important and basic information about the death, allow the child to take the lead, to ask questions.

- Answer the child's questions readily and honestly. If the child asks a question for which there seems to be no answer, the child should be told that the answer is unclear or not available and as soon as there is more information it will be shared with the child.

- Reassure the child about his or her place within the family; emphasize that the family exists and the child is a part of it "just like always."

- Show affection, support, and acceptance of the child.

The caretaking adult needs to understand that the child is capable of talking about things within his or her own realm of experience or speculation. The child's questions deserve answers.

Sometimes, however, it is not possible to provide answers. This is particularly true in regard to an accidental death, suicide, SIDS death, or a death that appears to be a homicide. In these cases, frightening speculations should not be offered to the child in lieu of facts. Further, it is especially important not to offer contradictory information about the death. Death is hard enough for a child to grasp without having to wonder which piece of information to believe.

As pointed out previously, when the answers are not known, the child should be told that the adult will share any subsequent information that he or she receives.

When listening and responding to the child's initial questions, be on the alert for any misinterpretations or distorted perceptions the child may have regarding death, and try to clear them up before they become accepted as facts.

Following a death in the immediate family, children who are survivors are very concerned about their own physical and social welfare. This concern is made evident by the questions they commonly ask when they learn that a family member is gone. They want to know to what extent their well-being will be affected. Will we have to move? Will I still sleep in my bed? Can I still go to school? Can we keep our puppy? Unlike an adult, a child is helpless to make decisions about, or to exert control over, his or her own welfare. For that reason, the child survivor needs to be assured that the immediate world will stay put. Specifically, the child needs to know:

- The family will stay together.
- The child will not have to move.
- The child's daily routine will remain, for the most part, unchanged.
- The child can play with the same friends, go to the same school, and keep the family pet.

The caretaking adult needs to offer this reassurance repeatedly and consistently, whenever the child exhibits anxiety or insecurity regarding home, family, pets or routine.

Realistically, it will not always be possible to guarantee this kind of security. In such cases, the adult can make the imminent changes less foreboding by explaining that when any necessary change is going to occur, it will be discussed in advance. There will be no big surprises.

Talking to the child about the death will be an ongoing process. The child survivor may reopen the discussions at any time, asking the same questions again and again, or posing entirely new questions which have arisen out of new experiences and a changed level of cognitive development.

Besides talking about the death with the child, the adult needs to discuss the funeral and give the young survivor the option to attend.

The Child and the Funeral

Some adults believe that children do not belong at funerals because the sadness of the service will be too much to bear. To the contrary, researchers have found that children get a clearer sense of the finality of death when they witness evidence that the loved one's earthly life has ended.

It helps to be aware of the specific benefits to be gained by the child who attends the funeral.

- The child will be better able to understand the death and will usually have less difficulty integrating the death into the total life cycle.

- The child survivor is better able to differentiate himself from the dead loved one.

- The child's fantasies about death and burial, which can be far more disturbing than reality, are dispelled.

- The child feels equal to other family members because she has been included in a serious and profound family event. The child perceives herself as a vital part of the surviving family, an important member who has been accepted into the circle of deep intimacy created by the loss.

- The child is able to see that his or her deceased loved one is loved by others, respected, and will be missed by many people. This confirms the loved one's value and is a source of pride for the survivor.

We had a funeral in our church and all the benches were taken up and people even had to stand. So I knew my dad was important to other people. It made me feel good knowing that my parents had lots of friends. *(Child survivor, WHEN A PARENT DIES, BY JILL KREMENTZ)*

While attendance at the funeral should be allowed, no child should be *forced* to attend. A child may choose not to attend for a number of reasons. He may be afraid. She may feel guilty about her relationship with the loved one. He may feel embarrassment or shame because of the death. She may feel resentment toward her loved one, or toward surviving members of the family. Whatever the reason, the child's choice should be respected and he or she should not be coaxed, condemned or excluded from other family activities associated with the loss, such as the social gathering of family and friends afterwards.

I didn't go to the burial service because Mom thought it would be too sad, but I sort of wish I had. *(Child survivor, WHEN A PARENT DIES, JILL KREMENTZ)*

Daddy decided it would be better for all of us if we didn't go to the burial...I was ten and Henny was 8...I think it was nice of Daddy not to take us because I do think it would have been very hard for us, especially Henny. But I can't help thinking it was kind of rude of me not to be at my own mother's funeral. *(Child survivor, WHEN A PARENT DIES, JILL KREMENTZ)*

Preparation for the Funeral

When a child chooses to go to the funeral, an adult should then talk with the child beforehand about what to expect. Depending upon the child's age and maturity, he or she will need to be informed about several, or all, of the following:

- Where the funeral will be held.

- What kind of room the family will be seated in (small, quiet, with pews or chairs).

- Who will sit next to the child.

- What the child will hear (music, a talk that will be about the loved one, prayers).

- Where the person who has died will be (in a closet casket, open casket, in another location).

- What other people will be likely to do (sit quietly, cry, come up to the child and hug him or talk to him).

- What the child should do when people express their condolences.

- The reason for going to the cemetery and how the cemetery will look.

When events, sights, and expectations for the child's behavior are explained, the young survivor will be less anxious and frightened about the services. An informed child is better able to participate in the necessary customs and ceremonies when he or she feels aware and at least somewhat confident.

The child's participation is also made easier if he is allowed to ask questions, has physical contact with an adult (mother holding his hand, sitting on his big sister's lap, grandfather sitting with his arm around him). If there is an open casket the child may want to join the others who pass by. If passing the open casket is the child's choice, he or she can be permitted to write a loving note, draw a picture or give a sibling a toy or flower as a token of devotion. It is advisable for the child survivor be able to hold the hand of a parent or sibling, as the youngster passes the casket.

Other children will benefit by taking part in planning their sibling's funeral. They can discuss the place for the service, the type of service they prefer, who they would like to have as pallbearers, and who they want to participate in the memorial service. When children are old enough to participate in the planning, the activity unites them, gives them direction, and a sense of unity.

The Gathering After the Funeral

The time following the funeral can be quite unsettling, even threatening to the child, particularly if he or she is a preschooler.

When the final services are over, usually several things occur.

- Suddenly, the house is filled with people, many of them strangers who, with all good intentions, express affection to the bereaved child.

- There is no physical place for the child to be. His or her room may be filled with coats and handbags, leaving no room for the child to sit, and no area to use as a retreat.

- The child's parents (or parent) may seem to be neglecting the young survivor as they respond to the attention and concern of adult family members and friends.

A group of children who were asked about their feelings following the funeral of a parent or sibling said they felt ignored and crowded out, and they wanted the other people to leave so things could go back to normal. Children seem to understand that chaos does not contribute to their own emotional well-being.

Prerequisites to Mourning

As noted previously, a loss during childhood produces both visible and invisible responses. The more the child survivor is helped to cope with and integrate the death into his or her life, the more likely the child is to experience a successful adjustment.

It should be understood that a parental death is always part of a child's life, regardless of the apparent degree of adjustment. To suggest that the child will *not* be affected to some extent for the rest of his or her life is unrealistic. This does not mean, however, that personality or emotional disturbances are inevitable.

Though the loss of a loved one creates great stress in the child's life, there are concrete ways in which this stress can be reduced, and successful grieving can be facilitated. Following are guidelines for the caretaking adult:

- Do not act as if the parent or sibling did not die.

- Encourage the child to express feelings. Do not try to distract the child from what he or she is feeling.

- Do share your feelings and memories of the dead loved one. This proves that feelings are not bad or unnecessary and that they will not destroy the family.

- Maintain a physical and emotional closeness to your child and exhibit affection.

- Reassure the child that his or her basic needs will be met and whenever possible basic routines will not undergo major changes.

- Make sure you seek any necessary counseling for yourself, or join a support group, so you will be better able to cope with your own physical, emotional, and mental needs. You must have others to talk and share your feelings with.

- Be aware that you are serving as a model for *working through* grief successfully.

Some parents who are unable to get beyond their own feelings of personal deprivation and emotional pain cannot facilitate their child's mourning. In a survey conducted with teenage survivors, none of them remembered being able to interact positively with their parents during the grieving period. When a parent retreats, or withdraws silently for an extended period of time, the child survivor "loses" that parent; moreover, the child interprets the parent's behavior as a personal rejection.

The parent may consciously deny the child's feelings in the hope that denial will help suppress sadness, longing, and despair within the family. This, however, will complicate mourning, rather than make it easier. When the barrier is lifted between parent and child and both can express feelings to each other, they will feel better.

This does not mean, of course, that the parent collapses, sobbing, in front of the youngster or puts that child in the position of doing the "fathering" or "mothering." Such self-indulgence on the part of the parent would be unfair and damaging. On the other hand, a parent who offers steely responses and who withdraws will foster an emotionally unhealthy environment in the home. A parent who shows real feelings without being overindulgent will be appreciated by the child survivor.

It meant a lot to be able to cry with my mother and grandmother. I found there was no set pattern, that we had to feel and let things flow.

My dad felt like he had to support the whole family. I know he loved my brother, but I wanted him to be sad, to cry. *(Teenager whose older brother was killed in an auto accident)*

Mourning together provides consolation and mutual comfort, and it stimulates mutual physical affection. Also, at the death of a brother or sister, the surviving sibling needs to see the parent exhibit grief in order to validate that the child was loved and missed. The surviving child identifies with the dead one and draws conclusions about how the parent or parents would respond if he or she died, too. If the child knows that the parent would be sad, the child is then assured that he is cared for deeply — as is his dead brother or sister.

As memories and feelings are shared, not all family members feel the same way about a certain event or a certain aspect of the loved one's behavior or personality. A younger brother may remember with delight his older brother's penchant for playing harmless pranks. The older sister, who always felt victimized by those same pranks, may not like to have them recalled. A mother may remember with great longing the pleasure trips she took with her husband. The children, who almost never accompanied their parents, may remember those trips as unhappy times, during which they felt excluded.

When the memories and feelings of family members differ, it is necessary for the members to exercise mutual acceptance and respect for one another's experiences and perceptions in regard to the dead loved one. Communication and sharing are the keys to successful functioning.

Sometimes, the young survivor's sense of security is threatened. Due to the death of one parent, a change in the family's economic conditions or the nature of the loss, the family must move. In such cases, it is vital for the parent to consider what is happening from the child's perspective.

The "small deaths." A parental death may necessitate moving from one house to another, selling the family furniture or automobile, leaving friends at school, or saying good-bye to the neighborhood. The mother may have to work full-time outside the home, or go back to college. A grandparent, other relative, or roomer may move in to help with expenses or with child care. While these changes may be essential to survival, each change constitutes a loss. In fact, to the child, each change is often another small death. Another piece of the familiar world has gone away forever.

> One of the strong images that I remember is that our house was completely empty. All the furniture was sold to anybody who could take it. Then I went through culture shock when we had to move from a middle class neighborhood, to an elite, upper class neighborhood to live with my grandmother. I felt different from the other kids. *(Woman who lost her parents by the age of twelve)*

During the child's period of adaptation to a new environment it is helpful for the caretaking adult to provide as much consistency and security within that changed environment as possible. This is important at any time, but is especially necessary when the external world of the child may appear to be falling apart or dying off, bit by bit.

Consistency can be maintained by having specific times for meals, eating as a family and sharing experiences during meals, having definite chores for family members and maintaining bedtimes that do not fluctuate greatly from night to night.

Discipline. Closely related to the consistency factor is discipline. Allowing discipline to break down, to be negotiated or completely ignored is not helpful to the grieving child. This does not mean that the caretaking adult must yell, spank, threaten, or administer severe unwavering punishment. It does mean that the person needs to exhibit a calm firmness and order because both give the child a sense of security.

This is graphically illustrated in the case of the father whose wife had died and who was experiencing extreme difficulty handling his own grief. He denied the tragedy for many months. He never mentioned his wife's name nor exhibited overt sadness. Yet, his nervous, irritable and indecisive behavior rendered him unable to control his son, an only child. One night when the eight-year-old boy badgered his father to gain an inappropriate privilege (staying up past midnight on a school night) the situation reached a climax. The boy had been ranting on for several minutes, but his preoccupied father didn't respond. The son danced around him, again and again, whining, "Can I dad? Can I dad? Dad, dad, can I? Can I?"

The bewildered father could only reply, "Oh, I don't know, Paul, I just don't know." Finally the son stopped suddenly, lunged at his father and screamed, "Tell me NO, dad. Tell me NO!"

Desperate for boundaries, the son wanted his father to exhibit concern about him going to bed on time and getting enough rest. He wanted to be recognized as needing care.

By being aware of the child's need for order and structure, the caretaking adult can often prevent disciplinary problems before they arise. To summarize, the adult who implements these objectives will have a more positive experience with the grieving child.

1. Be consistent.
2. Be honest.
3. Don't be afraid to show your feelings within reasonable bounds.
4. Be a good listener and observer.
5. Be aware of the need to strike a balance between overprotection and overindulgence.

Helping the Child Heal

It has been stated previously that it is often difficult, if not impossible, for the observer to fully recognize the internal emotional battles of the child survivor. The observer may not realize the severity or extent of the child's sense of loss. For example, researchers who worked with youngsters during the first few weeks after a parental death found that the surviving children were intensely and consistently aware of their loss on a daily basis. Most commonly, the childrens' longing and frustration resulted in overwhelming despair or defensive behavior.

In interviews with another group of children who had experienced parental loss during childhood, the children reported feeling old, sad, unimportant, ugly, and, as noted at the beginning of the chapter, outside of things, or lost. These feelings and reactions represent only some of those experienced by surviving children. Clearly, the challenge to the caretaking adult is a big one. It may help to consider some ways in which an adult can help the child through the grieving process so that he or she can heal.

Verbal Healing

If a child questions or openly states feelings, the task of relieving them is made considerably easier. As one mother said, "Whan Daren started asking questions, I knew part of the battle had been won. I knew what was bothering him the most." As has been noted, there is a tremendous need on the part of the child to understand the death and to figure out his or her position within what now appears to be a frightening, insecure world.

These needs are not exclusively those of the young child. They affect the adolescent as well, and though the needs are very much the same, the inquiries come in different forms because they reflect various levels of development. The very young child will ask questions about where a dead person is, how he gets by, and when he will return. An older child who has a more highly developed concept of death will ask questions that cover a broader spectrum.

Besides answering questions, it is helpful to specify the cause of death (accident, cancer, heart attack, etc.). A child who does not know that a parent or sibling died as the result of a definite cause may expect to die at any moment.

It helps for the caretaking adult to be aware of situations which make possible more objective discussions about death. Such discussions can grow from an explanation of the bouquet of dead flowers in the living room (all living things die), the death of a pet fish (it is a biological process), or media coverage of a famous person's funeral (funerals are a way of giving thanks for the person's life, saying good-bye, meeting with others who have loved the same person, etc.). By using natural events which occur in the child's everyday life, the child's information can be augmented at a time when neither the adult nor the child is intensely involved or affected by the situation.

Immediately following the Challenger space shuttle disaster in 1986, young schoolchildren identified with the children of the astronauts who had died. They put themselves in the place of the child survivors. They expressed relief about their own parents being safe. They asked questions about the surviving families. "I wonder what will happen to that little girl now that her mommy is gone." "I felt like it was happening to me." "I felt like I was the person that lost my mother." The children's reactions were very personalized.

The older child who experiences the loss of a loved one knows that certain facts exist and he or she wants to know those facts.

> The other thing I'm kind of afraid to talk to her about is what really happened. They still haven't found out what made the plane crash. I have the feeling I want to ask her because she's been going into the city a lot and going to meetings and I think she might know something more that I'd like to know, but I'm afraid to ask her because I don't know what she'll do, or what she'll say. She'll start crying. Not knowing what happened is terrible. It's like you're in suspense all the time and you just want to get the facts so that you won't have to think about it again. *(Child survivor,* WHEN A PARENT DIES, JILL KREMENTZ)

> I wish I knew more details because it would help me get over it faster — I'd like to know just *what* happened and how it happened. It would help me to realize that it really did happen. I mean, I know he's dead because my mother had to send in certificates and stuff, but I'd like to know more. My mother thinks she's making things easier for me by not talking about it, but I want to know everything — even if it does make me cry. *(Child survivor,* WHEN A PARENT DIES, JILL KREMENTZ)

Obviously, children's questions deserve to be answered. The first child stated, "You just want to get the facts so you won't have to think about it again." Knowing the facts does not, of course, mean that this child will never think about the details of the death again, but it does mean the child will not be obsessed in regard to what he or she does *not* know, and will be able to focus on other concerns. The second child summed it up accurately in the statement, "I wish I knew more details because it would help me get over it faster."

Another major benefit to be gained by the child who gets answers to his or her questions is that the child is *released from the need to fantasize.* A child who does not know where mother went, or if sister knew that her death was imminent, or whether or not father killed himself, will make up a fantasy (or fantasies) to explain the unknown. Fantasies can be much more frightening and depressing than reality. In this regard, the truth — as grim as it may be — can be enormously comforting.

If the child does *not* ask questions, the caregiving adult's task of "reading" the child is made more difficult. Often, however, a child who does not formulate his or her concerns into questions, will indicate them through casual remarks or incidental actions. When the caretaking adult hears the limited remark or sees the smaller gesture, he or she can often facilitate expression by putting the child's feelings into words. This technique is illustrated in these examples:

Brent: I'm not going to play Little League. Jimmy's dad is the coach this year and Jimmy is always hanging around him.

Mother: I know you're probably wishing your dad were here like Jimmy's dad. I miss your dad very much, too. But you might like to try Little League for a while. Your brother and I will enjoy coming to your games this summer.

*   *   *

Karen: Dad never talks to me and so I'm not going to talk to him.

Mother: Since your brother died, Dad does seem more quiet. He is feeling sad because he loved your brother very much, *just as he loves you.* When he is quiet, it doesn't mean he doesn't care. It means he cares about his family a lot. Maybe giving him a hug will make your both feel better.

*   *   *

Jay: I never used to take out the garbage when Mom asked me to. I used to let it pile up until she got mad at me. I don't know why I was so mean.

Dad: I remember when you did that. Mom *did* get mad but she understood that kids don't always do what you want them to, *when* you want them to. She always knew how you felt about her and she certainly knew you weren't mean.

Not all feelings expressed by the child will be positive; instead of longing and love, there may be anger or guilt. The child needs to be able to vent the feelings, regardless of whether or not they seem appropriate. This will be possible if the caretaking adult can be trusted and accepting. The child who expects to be reprimanded, or who knows the adult listener will register shock, will not be inclined to share his or her feelings.

Guilts about parents and siblings are prevalent among child survivors. These guilts may be the result of unpleasant behavior that was exhibited toward the parent or sibling, cruel things that were said, even a wish for the person to die. For example, a surviving child who has been in a situation where a brother or sister was ill and getting all the attention may actually be glad when the sibling dies. *Then*, the surviving child feels guilty.

This is a situation which the child should talk through with the caretaking adult who can then acknowledge that the surviving child must have felt ignored, not as important as the brother or sister, and very lonely. As the child confirms these feelings and finds they are not indications of his or her inherent evil, the guilt is diffused. On the other hand, when the child survivor represses remorse and guilt, his or her successful emotional adjustment will be severely hindered.

Anger that is not expressed can be equally debilitating. It can be directed toward God, another parent, other siblings, or peers. It can be directed toward the self. In fact, anger can have as its target most anybody or anything. A child may feel anger at the parent's preoccupation following a death in the family. The child may become angry because of the increasing demands made on him or her.

A child can harbor great hostility toward the one who has died because of that person's deficiencies or problems. For example, a sister survivor is angry at her brother who was killed in an accident because he was reckless, drove too fast, and always bragged about it. A daughter is angry at an alcoholic father whom she perceived as a weakling who couldn't face up to reality. A brother is angry at his sister who he felt jeopardized her life by ignoring his warnings about "hanging out" with the wrong crowd.

A child cannot successfully mourn someone who is not human, who is faultless. The child needs to be able to see the total person, to recall the good and the bad, to understand that the loved one's behavior had both positive and negative aspects. The caregiving adult can help by confirming the accuracy of the child's recollections, and by further explaining that lavish praise comes from people remembering only the positive, wonderful aspects of the loved one's personality and character. These people, such as the mourners at a funeral, are also concerned that their remarks show complete respect for, and devotion to the surviving family members.

Though it is often difficult for a caretaking adult to hear anger directed at a loved one, it must be heard for what it is, recognized for its legitimacy, and accepted as valid. If the adult sets up a defense against the anger, the child will discover that only positive emotions are acceptable, and he or she will be inclined to become more angry. The skewed message from the adult can complicate bereavement.

Nonverbal Healing

Besides answering questions and discussing a child survivor's concerns, there are other ways the child's healing process can be augmented.

Identification with the loved one. Identification is one of the coping mechanisms employed by some surviving children to perserve a loved one and to integrate the loss of a parent or sibling into the present and future. A young child, for example, may use identification as a way to remember his or her relationship with the dead parent or sibling. The surviving seven-year-old son may insist on walking the dog after dinner as he and his father had done almost every evening for many months. The surviving six-year-old sister may repeatedly play the same game she played with her older sister. By repeatedly engaging in the activities associated with the loved one, the child is *recalling* the loved one, *fitting* *him or her into daily life,* and silently *asking other survivors to validate that experience* by acknowledging that it happened.

It is important for the caretaking adult to verify that the selected activity took place; to remark, for example, about how much dad enjoyed his walks after dinner, or what fun the girls had experienced when they played the remembered game.

An older child may make a more concerted conscious effort to identify with a lost parent or sibling. One young woman said, "My mother never got a chance to go to college and she wanted so much to be a professional, to attend med school. Now I'm pre-med. I don't see it as unhealthy. My own major genuine interest is medicine. But, as a wonderful bonus, I feel I am fulfilling my mother's unrealized goal."

A surviving sibling felt he was "acting on the best part of his brother's character" by working for his brother's political cause.

A woman reflecting on the loss of her mother talked about emulating her mother in order to gain temporary comfort.

> It was a refuge for me to iron. It was something tangible that I could do. I still do that with my anxiety. When I'm really threatened by something, I start cleaning house. There was a part of me that felt that what I was doing was right because I was imitating what I thought should happen, what a mother should do.

Sometimes identification with the loved one carries with it a threat or fear. For example, the threat might be, if you act like your father, you will meet the same fate. (You too will die.) There may also be identification that permeates so many aspects of the child survivor's life that the child is not able to maintain a separate identity or to develop independently.

It should be acknowledged, therefore, that identification with the loved one can be healing when it is not carried to the extreme, or distorted. A caretaking adult can help the child differentiate between behavior which is acceptable or beneficial to emulate, and behavior which will be destructive or debilitating. It is okay, for example, to be a good singer like mother was, but it will not help you feel better if you are domineering with people because your older brother was.

Besides behavioral identification, a child can identify with a loved one by keeping and cherishing a possession which belonged to the dead parent or sibling. The item is a comfort, a memory, a talisman for the future. The brother of a teenaged accident victim carries his brother's headband with him. The younger brother of a cancer victim wears his brother's clothes to school, even though they are oversized and inappropriate. The clothes and belongings help maintain the child survivor's identification with the loved one. It is not unhealthy for the articles to be treasured indefinitely. They are a part of the past to be carried into the future.

Ceremonies. A dead child may be commemorated at special times by the surviving members of the family. The family can plan a small private celebration for the child's birthday, show his or her picture, and share memories. This type of positive activity can turn a dreaded day into an observance of the lost loved one's worth, and a "thank-you" for the child having lived.

> On our daughter's birthday, we have a little celebration. We don't really tell anyone else about it; it's just for us. We look at her scrapbook and her pictures. We listen to a tape she made and we give thanks that we knew her, if just for thirteen years. It might be hard for an outsider to understand but it makes her birthday easier for us. If we all went around pretending that it wasn't her birthday, we would all be miserable. *(Mother of a teenaged cancer victim)*

Art. Children's drawings aren't reproductions of the world. Instead, they are illustrations composed of selected subjects, objects, or symbolic forms: ones which have special significance and meaning to the child. A youngster of kindergarten age will often use art to convey feelings and ideas—those which are *less* possible or *im*possible to verbalize. When a child isn't able to say what he or she knows or fears to be true, the child can sometimes draw it. A young child who is having difficulty— nightmares, fears for his own safety, or thinks the lives of those around him are threatened, may be helped by drawing the death he is so afraid of. The child can't deal with the abstraction of death, but he can deal with it if he draws it. First, he can see the way it looks to him. He can face it. Because it is on paper it is smaller than he is. Further, he controls it because he created it. He can cross it out, make it "talk," paint over it, talk to it, and no harm will come to him.

Friends of a teenaged accident victim were helped in their grieving by an imaginative high school teacher who proposed that the class make a memorial mural to honor the dead teenager. The students' painting reflected their personal associations with the accident victim as well as their personal view of death; for example, one student painted the teenager's football number, another a picture of a boy climbing a mountain, ascending beyond the line of trees in the distance.

By using art, a child (and an adult) at *any* age can gain control over emotional pain; indeed may even be able to eliminate it altogether as feelings are converted into products—drawing, painting, sculpture, or weaving.

Play. Play can be extraordinarily therapeutic for children, particularly young ones whose verbal skills are limited. There are three major benefits to be gained from play following a death: (1) play allows the child to exhibit painful emotions, fears, and confusions; (2) the child can fit feelings into a fantasy context, thereby exerting power over them; and (3) the child can establish himself or herself as an entity apart from any horror or shock generated by the personal tragedy.

Some Welsh children who had lost their father when a commuter train derailed killing eighty-three people, invented a game which involved the reenacting of the accident. Again and again, the children smashed the toy train into everything, knocking over objects and creating noise and chaos. A boy whose father died of cancer played war games for months after the death. Repeatedly, the boy was shot or blown up by a hand grenade. His sister recalled, "In the months following our father's death, my brother died a thousand times in the foxhole he had dug in an adjacent field."

As children play, they will use whatever materials seem relevant to their personal tragedy — war toys, miniature cars, a playhouse, a doctor's kit, toy planes, puppets, sheets (for ghosts), or scary monster masks (for death). The children may also conduct final rites or burials of dolls or other toys. As they play, the youngsters are affirming what they know to be true, giving themselves power over the event, and establishing themselves as *separate* from the event.

Writing. Children whose primary writing skills are developed may express their anxieties and death-related fictions or fantasies on paper. The caretaking adult can help by asking the child if he or she wants to read the story aloud. If the answer is "yes," the feelings that are implied or mentioned in the story can be discussed. The message of the story can be validated. For example, "In your story a monster comes and takes the boy to heaven. That must be very scary for the boy to think that could happen. The boy would probably like to scare the monster instead of having the monster scare him." The adult may then help the child through his fear: "How about writing or drawing something that tells or shows how the boy could scare the monster?" As the child carries out this activity, his helplessness is reduced. He is made more important. When he draws himself scaring the monster he may smile at his sweet revenge. He enjoys relieving his fear because doing so gives him a sense of power.

An older child may enjoy keeping a diary or journal and "talking out" his or her feelings on paper. While the caregiving adult can make the diary-keeping opportunity available, the adult should not *instruct* the child to do it.

The journal, notebook, or diary may be given as a surprise gift. The child who wants to use it will do so.

> One thing that does help me a lot is writing in my diary. It's really neat because it's like a friend who will listen to you. I loved reading *The Diary of Anne Frank* because she wrote a lot about her secret feelings. Just like me. *(Child survivor, WHEN A PARENT DIES, JILL KREMENTZ)*

Frequently, a child will begin to write poetry after the loss of a loved one. The child may share his or her offering in an appropriate class at school, or may keep the writing entirely private.

A junior high student who lost both of her parents when she was in fifth grade, wrote this poem for her creative writing class:

I waited
out in the middle of the street
for life to stop.

It didn't even honk.
It just
ran over me.

Whenever poetry is assigned in a high school or college class, death will emerge as one of the dominant themes.

Secrets and bonds. There is another healing phenomenon that occurs among children. It is not as commonly recognized as identification, play, art or writing might be. This is a secret or a bond that is completely private and usually quite imaginative. The bonding can be with an animate object, such as a pet; or an inanimate object, such as a pillow, light, or coat.

It can also be a dedication to—and bonding with—a kind of self-created ritual.

I still have dreams about my father—happy dreams. They make me feel good. And sometimes I see the light outside my window—and it's on our garage—shining into my window, and I think it's Dad—his spirit. It's a secret. My Mother doesn't know and my sisters don't know either. Nobody knows about it because the light only shines into my window. It makes me happy. *(Child survivor, WHEN A PARENT DIES, JILL KREMENTZ)*

There are special moments when I say, "Oh God, I wish Mom were here." Like last summer our neighbors had a horse who was really scared and skittish around people. After a while he got to know me and he knew I was gentle and wouldn't hurt him. He would walk up to me and I felt so happy when this happened. Sometimes at night I'd sit on his back and look up at the stars and the moon. That poor horse had so many cries on his back and so many secrets told to him. He was sort of like my diary because I would always go and talk to him about what had happened during the day. I remember one night in particular thinking how beautiful it was and telling him, "I wish Mom were here to see this." It's basically when I'm alone and happy with myself that I miss my mother the most. *(Child survivor, WHEN A PARENT DIES, JILL KREMENTZ)*

A girl whose father died when she was three years old confided to a friend that for years she had a secret. When she was eating hot cereal on a winter morning, she would look at the man on the Quaker Oats box and pretend it was her father.

Another girl whose father died when she was five lived with the unshared belief that one day she would go on a routine errand to the corner grocery store, just like she always did, and her father would be at the store waiting for her and they would go home together.

A woman who lost both of her parents during early childhood recalls her dedication to a self-made ritual.

> When I was about eleven, I started a ritual I performed every night. I believed that the ritual insured my good luck and gave me security. The procedure went like this: I *thought* one numeral; then, every night I *added* another numeral, repeating all the numerals in order to make a sequence. I did it every night for a very long time, remembering the sequence and saying it aloud, faultlessly. I never did forget but it became increasingly more difficult. On one night when I was too tired to say the sequence and fell asleep without doing it, I had a dream that I was away at camp. Both of my parents came driving up in an old car to take me home. I was overjoyed. They smiled at me and we all hugged. Then we walked toward the car with our arms around one another. It was the happiest moment of my life. When I woke up, I was emotionally devastated. It was the first time I really consciously realized my parents would never come to claim me.

Books. A variety of books are available which are designed to aid the child suffering the loss of a loved one. Books having constructive death-related themes have been written for children of all ages—from preschool through adolescence.

Such a book can serve one or more of the following purposes:

- Promotes physical closeness to the reader.
- Acts as a catalyst to stimulate discussion about the child survivor's feelings.
- Provides death-related information which can dispel some of death's mystery.
- Stimulates the development of important values.
- Illustrates death is universal.
- Motivates further expression by stimulating the child to write an original "spin-off" story.

Any children's librarian will be able to recommend library books which are appropriate for specific age levels. Many support groups provide categorized reading lists for their members, and book reviews are usually found in most support groups' newsletters.

There are two notes of caution about sharing a book with a death theme: First, before reading the book to the child, the adult should review it privately to know what to expect in terms of comments, questions and issues raised. Second, the book should not be used as a *substitute* for a direct exchange between the child and adult. One-to-one discussion about the child's particular loss is still necessary.

Maintaining Special Awareness

There are some areas of special concern to the surviving child or adolescent which may be minimized, or even overlooked by the caretaking adult. By being aware of these areas the adult will be in a better position to help the child achieve a successful adjustment to the loss and its aftereffects.

Disconcerting or Damaging Statements

A woman who was orphaned in early childhood stressed that she experienced a great degree of emotional pain as a result of what she heard the unthinking adults saying to one another. She overheard that she was "going to die just like her parents" that "nobody wanted to raise her," and that "her own grandparents did not want her." She made this point: "Please tell the caretaking adult that *children who are the victims of parental loss are not deaf.* Adults get caught up in their own needs and forget what they're doing to the child. The things people say in front of children are appalling."

Her case is certainly not an isolated one. A young man recalled what he heard one of his mother's relatives say after the death of his alcoholic father. "He just drank himself to death. He never was any good. His whole family was trash." Of course, the child of "trash" cannot help but classify himself in the same way. Such was the case of this preadolescent. With counseling, he was able to experience increased self-esteem and to understand that it was appropriate for him to have high personal expectations and to establish ambitious goals for himself.

Unfeeling remarks don't have to be this ruthless in order to have a pronounced effect on the child survivor's security. A widow talking on the telephone to her friend may express deep concern about her ability to make a living for the family. Her young son, who is playing in the adjacent room, hears the conversation. When his mother hangs up, he goes to her and with anguish says, "I know I need to get a job but I can't because nobody will hire a seven-year-old. How will we get food, Mama?"

Children who lose a loved one during childhood are already afraid, confused, and usually suffering from reduced self-esteem. Hearing thoughtless or dramatic remarks by adults can exacerbate the emotional struggle they are already experiencing as a natural outgrowth of the death.

The Difficulty of Peer Relationships

The child survivor's peers will have had little or no experience with death. As a result, a child who is particularly devastated by the loss will set himself apart from the group or have perhaps only one or two peers as trusted friends. The supportive peer will be the exception.

There was a drastic change in sociability after my father died. When my mother died, it sent me off to the introverted, reserved category. I was always real interested in what the lives of the popular kids were like. Was really curious to know. I'd make up fantasies about how everything was perfect for them. *(Woman whose parents died during her preadolescence)*

It cannot be emphasized enough that the surviving child feels different, in a world unto himself, and often feels wrong.

I felt as if I was too different. Since my Dad died I've had the belief that I've been really different from other people. I felt as if anybody should be able to see that. *(Woman orphaned at twelve)*

You feel different from the other kids. You structure an alternative world and have an active fantasy life. *(Man who lost his parents at an early age)*

A child who has a loss during early childhood may withdraw during elementary school and then "come out of his shell" later on. However, underneath the surface personality, the child still wrestles with feelings of social isolation and low self-esteem, regardless of what appears to be social success.

A woman who had been outside a circle of friends during elementary school when she lost her parents "came out of her shell" and gained popularity in high school.

I felt wrong, as if I just didn't fit. Even though I was popular and had a lot of friends and got chosen for offices and honors at high school, I felt as if I was just lucky, or that people felt sorry for me — or that it was all some sort of joke. It was as if the other kids went home to regular, normal homes, and I went home to the dog kennel.

The woman who was orphaned at twelve echoed these same feelings:

When somebody was attracted to me I wouldn't know why. I'd think they were just being really nice. For some reason this person picked me out of the people in the photography class and liked me, wanted to spend time with me and I could never understand why.

The important task here for the caretaking adult is to recognize the struggles and courage that are required of the child as he or she interacts with peers. The child survivor's self-image has drastically changed. The child often perceives himself or herself as shameful, damaged or unworthy. The child may feel stigmatized by loss. Again, talking through these feelings with a caring adult will help immensely.

The negative self-perceptions that the child has can also be reduced through a concerted effort to increase the child's self-esteem. A child survivor will benefit greatly from a compliment on an original or interesting idea or praise for a task well done.

When the child shows enthusiasm for, or fascination with, any constructive activity, that interest should be encouraged. For example, the child survivor may exhibit a curiosity about computers, some special scientific phenomenon, a specific animal or bird, or his or her own personal history. The child may simply express a desire to collect something. The interests can range from the very simple to the exceedingly sophisticated.

Many adults who experienced loss as a child tell of being involved in fantasies and self-generated activities, especially those which required a high degree of sustained imagination. A child survivor who shows a proclivity for drawing, singing, songwriting, storytelling, building, or dramatization will benefit from approval and encouragement. Too often, a young survivor who has a strong talent or compelling creative drive will hide his original work from other people because the work means so much to the child he cannot risk criticism.

The caretaking adult should be aware, as well, of the child survivor's need for encouragement and support as he tries to cope with social situations which may be easy for the average child, but are terrifying to the boy or girl who has suffered the loss of a loved one. Entering a new school, going to a scout's meeting, participating in a group sport, engaging in classroom discussions, joining the school orchestra, or inviting another child home can be enormous challenges to the child survivor.

The Altered Family Structure

The whole family unit is affected when a death occurs. Surviving adults may be so involved in meeting the challenges of the changed circumstances following death, they don't realize the degree to which a change may be affecting the child survivor. Among the major factors which can pose problems and present special burdens are:

- An increased stress level within the family; a chaotic environment.

- The family's changed economic status.

- The family's changed social status.

- The changed roles within the family.

Stress level. One of the most obvious changes affecting the family is the increased stress level. Often, this is the result of one or more family members trying to keep their feelings and concerns about the loss entirely to themselves. If they don't, they reason, they may provoke an uncomfortable response, such as crying, longing or despair, from another family member. To the cautious family members, exhibited grief is viewed as a threat to the survival of the entire family. Honest feelings are seen as being catalysts to family disintegration.

Further, sometimes each family member thinks *his* emotional pain is the most severe, and his observations and needs are more profound than those of any of the other members. There may also be a silent competition for the "most bereaved." The result is a family that operates with tension, fear, and resentment.

When anger, guilt, yearning or sadness are permitted, the stress level is reduced. The atmosphere within the home becomes one of openness, care and consolation.

Chaos. Families that are subject to the most chaos are those which have previously, and perhaps continuously, been affected by various traumas. These range from the chronic illness of a family member or members, parental depression, parental discord, alcoholism, drug abuse, a previous death or accident, to a suicide attempt. In such cases, the emotional and financial resources may be depleted, and it is wise for the caretaking adult to solicit outside support from a social service agency, professional worker, or therapist. There is no value in trying to function independently when family members have been heavily taxed beyond their capabilities. Through outside help and guidance the family can learn how to create new patterns of behavior, how to stabilize as a unit, and eventually how to provide personal support to one another.

Two adults, who, as child survivors, were affected by several of the factors cited above, described the long term effects of childhood chaos.

> I feel as if I need to control my environment more than other people. Chaos is hard to handle. I don't want things to look disorganized. Noise bothers me a lot.

> I cannot stand being in a house where there is a lot of noise, dogs barking, or commotion among the people. It is a form of torture. Even entering a home where there is a stereo, radio, or television blaring is disconcerting. The only controlled environment is the quiet environment.

Altered economic and social status. When a working father or mother dies and that person's income is no longer a resource, the economic status of the family is affected.

Often, there may be a change in what a surviving child can do, buy, eat and wear. He may no longer be able to play video games with his friends all Saturday afternoon. She may wear her sister's clothes to school. The family may no longer be able to go out to dinner every Friday night. While these changes certainly cannot be considered deprivations in the broad social context, they *do* affect the child's lifestyle.

In addition, if it is necessary to move to another neighborhood or city, the child may encounter students from different economic or sociological levels—ones to which the child has not previously been exposed. Moving usually reduces, at least temporarily, the level of social acceptance a child will experience.

By the time I was in sixth grade, I had gone to seven schools. I didn't have a name. I was "the new boy." The teacher and students always referred to me that way. It added to my low self-esteem and reinforced my feelings of being on the outside of things. Alone in a separate world. *(Middle-aged man reflecting on his childhood after the loss of his parents)*

These significant changes contribute to an altered self-image for the child. The "altered child" who has an "altered living situation" is faced with a heavy burden and, depending on his age and level of maturity, must deal with this burden. While the adult can sympathize with the child, the adult can also explain that changes are difficult for everyone involved and that by working together cooperatively, the family members will get through the depressed period as an intact family. In cases where finances pose a major threat the child should understand that if necessary, outside assistance is available.

Changed roles. In any family, there are various roles played unconsciously by its members; for example, a simple role would be that of the dependent younger brother who is doted on and assisted in accomplishing everyday personal tasks. A more complex role would be that of the older sister who is the scapegoat for father's drinking bouts, and his alcohol related suicide. One child may be more in charge than the others (the leader), or more talented and outgoing than the others (the entertainer) or more often controlled by the others (the follower).

Sometimes when a family member who had a specific functional role dies, the missing role leaves a void. Family members, without being aware of what they're doing, cooperatively "assign" that role to one of the survivors. This occurs in families in which members are not valued for the individual and unique personality characteristics, traits, or needs; they are valued, instead, for the roles they execute. The brother who gets the silent message to fulfill the dead brother's role gives himself up to maintain the family equilibrium. He also makes it possible for the family to pretend that things remain as they were. An older son may step into the role of father, serving as mother's attentive, helpful and loving partner. In so doing, the boy forfeits his own social needs and becomes subject to the psychological distress produced by his inappropriate position.

Scapegoating of a family member occurs as a result of displaced anger about the death, or from the guilt of family members. A family member who accepts the scapegoating role is the one most likely to feel guilty and think he or she should be punished. That survivor is then made responsible for the poor functioning of the family, the lack of success of other family members, and any number of frailities and failures which other members may need to displace.

When a death occurs, it helps for the caretaker to *be aware of the role that was filled by the deceased* and to recognize any aspects of that role which the family needs for its own fulfillment. Those aspects can be shared cooperatively, or they can be rotated among surviving family members.

Developmental Stages of Grieving

As the child survivors of parental death progress through successive developmental stages and gain maturity, they need additional knowledge about the dead parent. By obtaining new information, the survivors incorporate the lost parent into their own changing lives, and also distinguish themselves in important ways from the parent.

Children do not stop grieving until they have gone through all of the developmental stages. At each developmental stage, there is new learning about the old experience. Because there is such a high degree of valuable and rapid learning, there is a considerable amount of integration which is required in order to cope with the loss. In this regard, some experts believe that the grieving process is not concluded until the surviving child is somewhere between the ages of eighteen and twenty-five.

7

Surviving an Accidental Death

*I remember thinking I couldn't live through
something like this. But your options are
limited. You can kill yourself by drinking or
some other method, or you can cope as best
you can. After I chose to live, I didn't know
how complicated it would be.*
MOTHER OF A TEENAGED ACCIDENT VICTIM

Accidental death is the number one cause of death among people ranging
in age from fifteen to thirty-four years. Because this type of death is
sudden, unexpected, and usually premature, it places the survivor in a
particularly traumatic set of circumstances. As a survivor of this type of
tragedy, you are shocked, completely unprepared and you feel both
deprived and vulnerable.

Reactions

Being Unprepared

If you were not present when your loved one's accidental death
occurred, you were most likely notified of it in one of these ways: You

received a telephone call, a law enforcement officer came to your home and informed you, or you were told by a friend, relative, or neighbor. You may have received the news in so abrupt or brief a manner you had difficulty mentally processing what had actually occurred. Sometimes the message is conveyed abstractly or indirectly so you can't grasp its meaning immediately.

Hearing of the accident.

> When we went to the hospital, the doctor came in where we were sitting and said, "There was an accident and Michael didn't make it." I said, "What do you mean, didn't make it? Didn't make what?" *(Mother of a teenaged accident victim)*

There is no easy or simple way to deliver such devasting news, but there are some circumstances which would have made the situation a bit easier for you to bear. The announcement should have been made to you in a quiet private room somewhere within the hospital or in your own home. The physician should have spent some time with you to answer your immediate questions. Or perhaps another professional—a nurse, social worker, trained volunteer, or member of the clergy could have sat with you and talked with you during your first half hour or so of shock and disbelief. If you had an opportunity to ask questions of those in attendance you will have had at least some of your fears allayed.

If this was not the case, you may be asking yourself, "Did he know what happened to him?" "Was she conscious?" "Did he get any relief from the pain?" "Did he ask for me?" "Did he die thinking he was alone?"

If you did not have the opportunity to speak to a physician regarding the tragedy, you may now find it difficult to believe that any doctor was actually trying to save your loved one's life. You question: "Did they even try?" "Did they call in a specialist?" "Why couldn't they resuscitate him?" Or you speculate, "Maybe she was left unattended for too long a time in the emergency room." "Maybe the wrong procedure was used."

If at the hospital you requested to see your loved one and were prevented from doing so for any reason, you will now have a more difficult time assimilating what has happened. You have experienced no visible proof of the death. Without firsthand observation, it is less possible for you to integrate the realization of your loved one's death. The accident may seem to be something someone made up, a cruel fantasy.

In some circumstances the clothes of the accident victim are given to the survivors. These items of apparel and other personal effects—a wallet, comb, compact or cigarette lighter—may become cherished possessions after the death. Parents of a teenaged boy killed in an automobile accident talked about their preferences following their son's death.

> We wanted to hold him, be with him. We didn't get to keep his clothes and we really wanted them. The procedure where we live is for the coroner to keep them for three days. If you don't come and get them within that period of time, they throw them away.

As you endured the first few hours of your tragedy, you should have had an opportunity to express your feelings in a nonjudgmental and accepting environment. You should have been allowed to cry, pray, or rage as you felt the need.

The optimum conditions mentioned here are those which would have made your initial mourning slightly easier to bear. If you did not experience such concern or care, if you were informed of the fatal accident in the hallway of a hospital, outside the door of the emergency room, or by the telephone, you may have been deprived of the people and surroundings you needed to feel at least a minimal amount of initial support.

If you were unable to question the attending physician, if you were sedated as soon as you started to express your grief, or if you were not allowed to view your loved one, your recollections of this tragic event may leave you with a feeling not only of incredulity, but of frustration or humiliation. Your mourning will have begun in an atmosphere of confusion and inhibition. If, on the other hand, you were fortunate enough to experience a supportive situation which allowed for your needs and helped you to meet them, you will have had, at least, an opportunity to pose your questions, clear up some confusion about the accident, and express your immediate feelings about the loss.

Placing the Blame

> When you first hear about the death, all the negatives come to mind. Were they drinking or on drugs? *(Parents of a teenaged accident victim)*

When a sudden death occurs, an autopsy is required by law. In some cases, the autopsy's findings can eliminate certain causes of death or reasons for blame, specifically those related to drugs or alcohol. As you analyze or question the situation which preceded the death of your loved one, you review the investigator's questions to you, or the parties who were present at the time of death.

At the conclusion of the formal investigation, you continue to put yourself through your own torturous interrogation.

- Why didn't I insist on my wife wearing a life preserver?
- Why didn't I forbid my son to go out with that bunch of bikers?
- Why didn't I pick up my daughter from the airport myself?
- Why didn't I ask my husband to stay home from this business trip?
- Why didn't we wait for the next bus instead of taking that one?

If you were present when the accident occurred, you will feel even more compelled to assume some blame. You may have been the one who was driving the car, who was looking the other way when the door to the patio and pool was left open, or who went with your spouse to the event where his or her fatal accident took place. If you saw yourself as a direct participant in the death of your loved one, not only will you torment yourself with personal accusations, you may think those around you are blaming you for what has occurred.

When the cause of a child's death is due to an automobile accident, fire, drowning, or poisoning, the parents generally expect to be condemned by others. This expectation manifests itself in various types of defensive, self-punishing behavior or withdrawal (or both).

Feeling accused.

> Every time I set foot outside the house I had to answer questions that made me feel guilty. It was like people were blaming me because I didn't know how to swim. They didn't believe me or something. I just felt blamed all the time and wished I would have drowned too. *(Thirty-year-old father whose son drowned in a boating accident)*

A young couple with two sons was devastated when their house burned to the ground. Two weeks later the woman was driving the car in which her youngest son was killed. Following the accident, the couple's preexisting marital difficulties began to intensify. The wife, who was already stricken with guilt, also became "the accused." She reflected on her burden at that time, "My husband accused me of burning the house down and killing his son."

Feeling as if you are an outcast. This same mother told of feeling as if she were outside society after the death of her son. She felt that she was no longer part of the mainstream. In her mid-thirties, with her son, her home and her marriage gone, she returned to college. Reentering "society" required an inordinate amount of personal courage.

> I felt as if I had blood spattered all over me and I had to work to cover up the blood. I felt like I belonged to a naughty club of some sort.

This woman's statement reflects the feelings of many bereaved people. Regardless of the type of death experienced by survivors, many of them perceive themselves as being outside "regular, normal society." They are outcasts who can never fit in.

> Everyone is going somewhere urgently, doing things, talking about the football game or the stock market, or their wives and kids. I'm wandering around in my skin without the motivation to do anything more than go through the motions of living. *(Father whose son was killed in a bus crash)*

A man who was driving the car in which his son was killed expressed his thoughts about the way he was being perceived and judged by his friends.

> Nobody wants to be around me because they think I killed my son. They don't want to "catch it." They don't want to have what I have.

Stress on the Marriage

As noted in *Losing a Child*, the divorce rate is extremely high among couples who have lost a child, particularly an only child. Marriages which were already stressed, struggle to survive, or eventually collapse. (See *Easing Marital Stress,* in *Losing a Child*.)

> We realized after our daughter died that we had been so involved in being parents that we had ceased to be spouses. We had to get out of the mother and father role a little bit and start being marriage partners. We went to counseling which really helped a lot. *(A couple whose only child was killed in a sporting accident)*

If the divorced parent of an accident victim is living in another town, state, or country, he or she may experience even more intense feelings of self-blame than the custodial parent. Often the non-custodial parent will not have had the opportunity to be present when the child's body was returned, and sometimes, due to distance, illness or other causes, this parent was absent from the funeral or burial. In such cases, this mother of father is being deprived of one of the key ways in which to confront the reality of what has occurred. As a result, the tendency of the parent to deny what has happened may be quite acute.

Traumatic Memories

The details of your loved one's death may preoccupy you to such an extent that you can think of little else. You feel overwhelmed, confused, angry, helpless, or panicky. These details may not only invade your mind during your waking hours, but they often intrude into your dreams, presenting themselves in various forms and circumstances.

> I kept dreaming about the accident. Each time the dream was the same but I had never been there. I was dreaming what I made up. I would try to stop the accident, to call out a warning about the other car, but she didn't hear me. I woke up shaking and crying. I had that dream for months after the accident. I still have it but it is less and less often. *(Young woman whose mother was killed in an automobile accident)*

Whether or not you know the actual facts surrounding the accident, you will find yourself reviewing details which are either based on factual reports or are made up to go along with what you vividly imagine to have happened. This review of the final events of your loved one's life is important to you for two major reasons. First, you may have the need to determine exactly who or what was responsible for the accident. As you review what occurred (or what you are fairly certain occurred), you make decisions about the cause, even if your decision is to recognize that *there is no way* to determine who or what was responsible.

Second, you need to remember what happened, to keep it as a concrete memory. You need to *know* you *know* that the accident occurred and you need to remember the post-accident details. This realization makes it possible for you to process the death and incorporate it into your present life. This is a necessary step in the grieving process.

Inability to concentrate. A mother tells of her lack of concentration which continued for an extended period of time following her teenager's accident.

> I am a good cook, but for two years I could not put a meal on the table. I would get the table set, then I would cook rice but would forget to cook meat or make a salad. I just couldn't figure out how to do what I had previously done with no effort at all.

A father tells of losing his powers of concentration to such an extent that the loss prevented him from keeping his job, which depended on the acuteness of his memory. Without the paper and pencil he carried in his shirt pocket, he felt himself to be "without memory."

Vulnerability and Fear

When you have been the survivor of the accidental or violent death of a loved one, you begin to consider the possibilities of others close to you dying in the same way. If you lost a son or daughter you may now fear your other children are constantly in jeopardy. Every daily event or activity such as a trip to the local record store, a high school game or dance, becomes another opportunity for accidental death to strike your loved one. This fear ultimately lessens, but for many months it may seem overpowering and interminable. (See *Reducing Anxiety and Fear* in Section I.)

Any unexpected occurrence, even the most mundane, leaves you feeling vulnerable. A ticket for driving too fast makes you feel as if you're a "sitting duck" for the highway patrol. If you find that an associate at work has been "laid off," your own job appears to be less secure. Now, because you have experienced an unexpected and severe personal trauma, you instinctively feel vulnerable to its possible recurrence. Anyone, you know now, can die at any time. This realization may dominate your behavior and influence your attitudes. It may determine the activities in which you choose to participate. It may change or modify what you feel about your spouse, friends, or children.

A mother reflected on her attitudinal change regarding her surviving teenager, following the death of the girl's brother.

> I changed my attitude about my daughter. Suddenly, it became all right with me who she was, *exactly how* she was because I treasured her so much. It was so clear to me after her brother's death how much I treasured her. The death changed my whole focus.

Helping Yourself Heal

Because your loss was completely unanticipated, you had no psychological, spiritual or emotional preparation. The mother of a young cancer victim who had also lost her father in a sudden death said, "I've been through it both ways, and the sudden death has got to be the hardest."

There are some people who would disagree with this judgment or with *any* statement which asserts that one type of loss is worse than another. Studies have shown, however, that unexpected and untimely deaths do produce conditions which delay normal functioning in the bereaved. In addition, sudden death survivors have more intense health problems than the survivors of other losses. Sudden death, of course, applies to suicide and homicide as well as to accidental death.

There are five major ways in which you can assist in your own healing process. First, of course, you need to deal successfully with your anger, guilt, and other debilitating feelings. (See the discussion of coping strategies presented in Section I, *The Grief Experience*.)

In addition, you can benefit by facilitating a highly personalized memorial service for your loved one; by talking and writing about your experience and your feelings associated with the death; and when you have begun to regain your emotional strength, by finding a meaningful, productive direction for your grief.

Facilitating a Memorial Service

> I have seen the coffins go down
> Jerking on straps from concealed
> Mortician motors
> The mourners clutching hands
> At some distance
>
> I would like to find a better approach to death.

(EXCERPT FROM "AT SOME DISTANCE," STEVE TURNER)

There are two basic kinds of memorial services: The most immediate and conventional is the traditional funeral, with the arrangements being made through a mortuary. There is another type of service which may be substituted for the funeral, or take place in addition to it immediately after the death — or even weeks or months after the death. In this type of service or ritual which acknowledges the *uniqueness* of your loved one, friends and relatives actively participate and share their remembrances of the person. It is more than a sorrowful good-bye; it is an act of *appreciation* for, and *celebration* of, that person's life as each participant knew it.

A mother whose daughter could not be retrieved from the site of her accident told of the importance of having a memorial service even though the teenager's body had not been found.

> In a case such as ours we really didn't have to do anything. But we needed to have a ritual. Everyone does. I am so glad we did because it was good for other people. It allowed us to gather together, to talk about what happened, express our feelings, and begin to say good-bye.

John, a young riding instructor in Northern California, was killed when his horse reared and toppled over on him. The young man, who had lived in a small cabin deep in the woods, had been an immensely popular person in the community. Because he was known for his generous spirit and true compassion for others, his friends planned a memorial that would reflect his warmth, his reverence of, and love for life.

The crowd gathered together on a sunny hillside, adjacent to a grove of pine trees. Individuals who wished to express some way in which their lives had been affected by John's life related an anecdote. Speaking from their hearts, the friends and relatives told of personal experiences which illustrated the young man's unique personality and character.

After the sharing, each person was given a brightly colored helium-filled balloon. At a given signal, the balloons were released, and they floated in a great airborne mass high over the tops of the pine trees. As the multi-colored spectacle was carried away by the breeze, one large, pink balloon was prominently visible. On it, a survivor had painted, "Thank you, John."

A ninety-year-old friend of John's looked up at the sky, smiled, and exclaimed with delight, "Oh, John would have loved this so!"

Having a *personalized* memorial, one which reflects the personality and values of the one who died, can be enormously therapeutic.

Talking About the Accident and Your Feelings

As you mourn, you need to be able to talk about the accident and express how you feel about it. The more you talk about it, the more relief you will experience. First, identify a good listener. This person can be a relative or friend who will not be embarrassed to listen, not feel uncomfortable, and who will not tell you that you should "get over it" and "be through with all that by now."

By talking about your personal tragedy, you are acknowledging that it has actually occurred. You are expressing how you have been affected by it, and you are voicing important personal concerns and preoccupations. Reviewing your thoughts, voicing your fears, talking about your attitudes and the relationship you had with your loved one are vital steps in the grieving process. If you hold in all your thoughts and feelings and restrain expression of your concerns, you delay the mourning process that eventually leads you back to the mainstream of your life.

If you have lost a spouse, friend, sibling, or lover, and you feel there is no appropriate person in your life to act as a listener, Hospice can be an excellent source of help. There, you will find supportive individuals who are trained to understand and meet your needs. You may talk with an individual on a one-to-one basis, or you may participate in sharing sessions within a group of bereaved people. (There are a few Hospices which may not have their own bereavement support groups; in this case, they will put a survivor in touch with helping groups and agencies within the community.)

If you have lost a child, *Compassionate Friends* offers friendship and understanding to bereaved parents. (See "Locating a Support Group" in chapter five.)

You may know people within your area who have experienced a loss similar to your own. If so, you might like to consider starting a small, informal group that meets on a regular basis. With almost no exceptions, the survivor who participates in such a group finds it to be an invaluable source of help.

> Being in the support group helped me to know that I was normal, that what I was feeling was normal. And they helped me know what to expect as I grieved the loss of my daughter. I was prepared for the anniversary of her death. I had been warned it would be tough. One of the members called me on that day and it helped a lot. *(Middle-aged father whose daughter was killed in an automobile accident)*

One couple, who founded their own survivor group after the loss of a teenaged son in an automobile accident, started the group with three other couples. They identified potential members by contacting the local hospital and mortuary, and by reading news articles in the local paper.

A note was sent out inviting individuals or couples to the group. The group convened on "neutral ground" so as to not appear to be sponsored by or affiliated with any organization.

If you are considering starting a group of your own it would be wise to meet in a home or in a "neutral" public meeting room. Meeting in a church or synagogue may indicate to the potential participant that the group is religiously oriented. Meeting in a community room of a hospital is also difficult because the hospital may be directly associated with the survivor's tragedy.

It is advisable for the group to have at least two members whose loss occurred a year or more prior to the group's commencement; that is, the entire group should not be newly bereaved. A facilitator should be chosen to make sure everyone has an opportunity to talk, and that no one person dominates the group or distorts the group's purpose. "The more you say what is on your mind, the more you talk about it, the more healing it becomes," participating members affirm. (Chapter ten, *Getting Help,* contains detailed guidelines for starting your own support group.)

Writing About How You Feel

Some survivors find that talking about their feelings *and* writing about them are equally beneficial. Others prefer writing to talking because they are less comfortable with verbalizing their thoughts. "When you write what you need to say, nobody can judge you or talk back to you, or be uncomfortable," explained a male college student whose father and brother were killed in a private plane crash.

The young woman whose fiance was fatally injured in a car accident found that writing about her experience helped her work her way through grief:

> I wrote poems about death. It was a safety valve. I saw it as a way of honoring him in my life. I saw it as a way to have something that would live on, that would reflect my intense feelings for him. It took me six months. Finally, I reached a point where I was exhausted and wanting to get on with my life. I also felt that nothing in life really makes sense. So I had reached the bottom of the grief process and went on. It wasn't a conscious decision or a conscious process even; it just occurred over a period of time.

If you would like to try writing it out, here is a simple way to begin:

> List the emotions you feel on the day you begin writing. Use only one or two words to identify each emotion or state — stunned, sad, lonely, afraid, angry, regretful, depressed, weak, or vulnerable.

> Get a separate sheet of paper for each emotion or state you have listed. At the top of each sheet, write the word or words which describe that one emotion or state, such as *lonely* or *confused.*

> Next, write about *how* that feeling makes you act and think. You may also write about *why* you think you have the particular feeling.

One bereaved mother who followed this procedure used her journal as an outlet for two years, writing in it every day. On a typical Monday evening, she had one page with this heading: "angry." This is what followed below.

> For the first time since Lynda's death, I watched the other parents walking their children to the bus stop. They went past my window, holding their children's hands, not even knowing how lucky they are. They looked as if they were taking their children for granted. This afternoon when I went to the market, a woman outside the store was slapping her child. The child was crying and I wanted to scream at her, "Stop! Stop mistreating him! Give him a hug instead. Don't you realize how lucky you are? Don't you know your child could die?" Then tonight on television, there was a documentary on child abuse. I felt as if I could kill the parents of those children. How could they be so cruel? How could God let people like that have children?

If writing is a comfortable outlet for you, it could be more helpful in resolving personal issues than you would imagine.

Finding a Productive Direction for Your Grief

Finding a way for *bad* to become *good* is another way to facilitate your healing process. You can do this by looking at what is behind your loss, what caused it, helped it along, or made it possible. Then you consider what you can do to prevent the same type of situation from happening to someone else, or at least reduce the *possibility* that it could happen. For example, the mother of a girl killed by a drunk driver formed MADD, Mothers Against Drunk Drivers, a national organization.

This kind of action can take place on a much smaller scale, at the local level. You can even initiate some legal or political changes within your immediate neighborhood or community. Depending upon the specific nature of the accidental death, you can help implement changes in several different ways.

Consider these ways in which others have tried to make the *bad* become *good*. A couple whose son was killed on a winding stretch of highway, where more than one person had gone down the steep embankment, carried on a successful campaign to get abutments and reflector lights along that same portion of highway.

A mother whose daughter was killed in a busy residential intersection requested the city to install stop signs on the corners where the accident occurred. She also went to her daughter's school and proposed that crossing guards be stationed there before and after school. When her suggestion met with approval, she participated as a guard for the first year along with several other parents.

A father whose son was killed in a surfing accident pointed out the need for warning signs to alert surfers to the dangerous undertow. Another father went to the parks department about an unposted area where his son had fallen to his death during a climbing accident. Within a few months, both sites were posted, warning people of the potential dangers.

There is nothing you can do to bring your own loved one back, but you can prevent other families or individuals from undergoing an experience similar to yours. *Where there is a potential tragedy, there is work to be done.* You may find a special and rewarding direction for your own grief.

8

Surviving a Suicide

You never get over a suicide. You just learn to deal with it. Your friends get over it right away and it's something the survivors live with for the rest of their lives. The worst part is not knowing why. If I could just say, "Yeah, he had been seeing a psychiatrist" or something—anything like that—it might make it better, but I don't know why he did it.

YOUNG WOMAN WHOSE FATHER COMMITTED
SUICIDE AT THE AGE OF FORTY-EIGHT

If your loved one has committed suicide, your mourning process will differ in two ways: 1) You will have the added burden of understanding the motivation for the death, and 2) your grieving process will be of longer duration.

Before losing a loved one to suicide you may have held one of these views: You thought the incidence of suicide was relatively rare. You held the opinion that a potential suicide victim displayed obvious behavioral symptoms, therefore, self-destruction could be prevented. You believed that suicide was exclusively the act of an insane or physically ill person.

A political science professor and father of a son who committed suicide in his sophomore year of college asked, "What happened to him? What kind of people do this? *Who* commits suicide? I need to understand this if I can." *Who* commits suicide is much easier to document than *why* a suicide is committed.

There are some startling facts regarding suicide, particularly in the United States.

- Suicide is the third leading cause of death for young adults.
- Men commit suicide three times more often than women.
- White men over the age of 50 make up approximately 10 percent of the total population but constitute 28 percent of the suicide deaths.
- Approximately 30,000 people in the U.S. commit suicide annually.
- Suicide among alcoholics is much higher than in the general population.
- Every day throughout the world, over 1,000 people commit suicide.

These facts do not illuminate the reasons behind your loved one's death. They do, however, allow for a perspective which reduces, to some extent, the perception of suicide as a type of death that rarely occurs. There are, at this very moment, a significant number of people who are mourning the loss of a loved one who took his or her own life.

Suicide Is Not a Single Act

It is vital to understand that suicide is not solely the result of some sudden, bizarre impulse; nor is it one single act which can be isolated and analyzed without examining the whole life context in which it occurred. Further, the cause of suicide cannot be studied from any single perspective. *This final life-taking act is part of a process. It has at its base long-standing conditions which arise in varying degrees from psychic, social and cultural factors.*

Explanations of suicidal behavior have been offered by many reputed sources. No attempt will be made here to give detailed, scientific explanations of the many and varied theories, many of which are conflicting. As a survivor, however, you will have a persistent need to search for an answer and to try to understand how your loved one could have conceived of taking his or her own life. To this end, it may help you to get a general idea of some of the dynamics which are part of many suicides.

Examining the Forces Which Contribute to Suicide.

Your loved one's suicide cannot be categorized, but there are several perspectives related to the issue which are worthy of consideration. They may provide some insight into your loss and, by so doing, offer relief from your personal, silent inquiries.

Suicide is, of course, unavoidably linked with despair and unhappiness. These conditions do not necessarily arise from those sources which others consider obvious. For example, a teenager who shoots himself after being rejected by his girlfriend is not necessarily killing himself "because his girlfriend left him." Suicide is not that simple. It is more likely that the student ended his life because the rejection was one of a series of events that produced negative emotions. In addition, acting along with any one event in any person's life are certain social and cultural factors. Why a person is unhappy, how a person views himself, and why he or she chooses to die are issues that are directly influenced by multiple forces. Even the country in which a person lives, the city within that country, the period of time in which that individual is living are, to some degree, influential factors.

In addition, each individual has his or her own necessities and expectations. When those are not fulfilled, or when there seems to be no clear way to fulfill them, when efforts fail to live one's life according to individualized perceptions of what life should be—emotionally and culturally—the individual can experience feelings of chaos or despair. The act of suicide then becomes a release because it appears to be the way to restore order and balance; that is, to the suicidal person it is not the taking of one's life that becomes the focus, it is the *controlling* of one's life that is important. It is a way of getting rid of that part of the self which seems unable to produce, elicit, or receive what it needs. The suicide is perceived as a way of "setting right" the confusion.

Suicide occurs in all levels of society, among rich and poor alike, but suicidal motives differ for many reasons, two of which are *where* an individual is, and *who* he or she is. For example, a black teenager from the inner city does not kill himself for all of the same reasons as a fifty-year-old white male advertising executive. A forty-five-year-old secretary in San Francisco does not commit suicide for the same reasons as did Ernest Hemingway.

One of the suicide stereotypes concerns the college student who kills himself because he was "worried about his grades" or "thought he wasn't going to graduate." The conjecture is that for these reasons, he viewed himself as a disappointment to himself or his family (or both). In actuality, the suicidal college student does not as a rule come from a family whose expectations for their child's academic success are a major issue. The family, in fact, may not place much importance on academic endeavors or achievement. This student may have, instead, been seeking a refuge in school, using it as a way to distance himself from other aspects of his emotional or social life which had already caused him unhappiness or disappointment. When the refuge did not provide the shelter he needed, he experienced a feeling of despair and helplessness and an inability to conceive of a workable alternative to suicide.

Another stereotype concerns the suicide of an elderly person. This type of suicide may appear to be motivated by the senior citizen's severely limited economic resources. The explanation, therefore, may be,

"All he had was a small pension and his social security, and he just couldn't get by." Though this assessment of the situation may seem logical, it is, in fact, not necessarily accurate.

To the contrary, studies have shown that suicide among the elderly has other more significant factors at its base. Male suicide occurring after retirement, for example, may be precipitated by a reduction in the victim's capacity to work, to function independently of others and to exercise control. Such a person experiences a decline in usefulness, mobility, status and self-esteem. An elderly person who has always had difficulty with the way he viewed and judged his own performance may have a greater tendency to experience despair in later years.

The older person's emotional situation is accentuated largely by the physical and social limitations that exist because of age. Further, these limitations *increase* with age, so they are perceived as increasing as each day passes.

It is also true that an individual who has great difficulty accepting the death of a parent, even if the parent is 70 or 80, is more likely to be among those who are suicidal. In a study of senior citizens who had attempted suicide it was found that members of this group had experienced the recent loss or death of a loved one twice as often as members of a nonsuicidal control group.

In trying to pin down definite proclivities for suicides there are some major areas in which that is possible. There are, for example, four definite factors which predispose a person to suicide: alcohol, drugs, violence, and homosexuality. *Drugs or alcohol are involved in two out of three suicides.* Suicide by alcoholics far surpasses that of drug addicts and homosexuals.

In examining this phenomenon, there appears to be a strong relationship between one aspect of the suicidal victim's personal history and that of the alcoholic. Both of them share a common difficulty, which is the inability to maintain a rewarding and long-standing loving relationship, and to commit themselves to the accompanying personal responsibilities. Alcohol allows the individual to temporarily withdraw from a situation which could result in rejection. Suicide allows for permanent withdrawal.

The alcoholic may attempt suicide during, or as the result of, a quarrel. Though the act may appear to be an outgrowth of one specific incident, this is not the case. More likely the proclivity for the individual taking his or her own life has been developing since an early age. With each difficult relationship, the individual's reactions become more volatile.

Some alcoholics commit suicide after long periods of drinking during which they experienced self-blame and deep despair. In these cases, as in most others, suicide grows from the individual's emotional characteristics as well as from the individual's social and cultural integration. For instance, a person addicted to alcohol or drugs will be more inclined to commit suicide if he is unemployed, unmarried, or both.

In a study of homosexual students who were predisposed to suicide, there was a high incidence of trauma in their early lives, such as the loss of a parent. This separation, never fully resolved, caused the student to try to gain control over the pain of being "abandoned." At the same time, it is important to understand that the loss was not the only precipitating factor.

In examining a victim's personal and emotional history, it is common to find that the individual had one or more of the following: (1) a fear of having to cope with major change, (2) a highly self-critical personality, (3) low self-esteem, and, less often, (4) an unclear perception of death, a belief that somehow death is not really final. Again, along with personal history it is necessary to consider what is happening around the person in terms of social pressure and cultural expectations. There may be stress from outside sources on the job, at school, within the immediate community, and even from *all sources* at once.

Only by considering all the psychic, social, emotional, and cultural factors can a person get any idea of the necessities, expectations—even the obsessions—which have not been fulfilled or satisfied. While the above examples are limited in their number and scope, they illustrate that *it is a coalition of forces, both internal and external, which makes suicide possible.*

All of this is fine, you may say, but it does not appease my personal loss, nor does it give me definite answers to my questions. Just as the professor who lost his son implored, "I need to understand this if I can," you may be saying, "I want to know what my spouse, child, friend, or lover was *thinking*." As one mother, a middle-aged attorney, agonized to a counselor, "What was going on in my son's mind? What did he hope to accomplish?"

The State of The Suicidal Person

To a person about to take his or her own life, *death itself* is not the major factor. Death is, instead, conceived as an accompanying act to a painful state which has become both powerful and consuming.

Once the suicidal person has decided to end his or her life, the individual becomes closed to the outside, often described as being "uncommunicative," "withdrawn," or "preoccupied." It is as if the individual's thoughts and energies are being consumed as he or she plots a way out. When an individual reaches this state, *every small, disappointing incident can be viewed as supporting evidence for the conclusion that it is no longer possible nor desirable to live.* This "evidence" may be having to stand in line thirty minutes at the bank, burning the coffee pot, getting a spot on his tie, missing the bus, or answering the telephone and having the caller hang up before speaking. Each incident, regardless of how minor it is, reinforces suicide. It is as if the suicidal person were being given a message from some omnipotent force which is saying, "See, you have made the right decision. Your life is fouled up at every turn."

Many suicidal people have very high expectations for themselves which make perfection even more mandatory than it might be for the average person. The suicidal individual often makes unrealistic demands on himself or herself. The person wants more than actually exists or is possible to obtain. When the person's needs are not met, he or she feels an emptiness, a rejection. This produces mental anguish which, when it becomes intense enough, far outweighs the pain normally associated with suicide. By comparison, the pain is nothing to be feared.

In *A Savage God*, A. Alvarez speaks of his own mental state, prior to his suicide attempt.

> My life felt so cluttered and obstructed that I could scarcely breathe. I inhabited a closed, concentrated world, airless and without exits. I doubt if any of this was noticeable socially: I was simply more tense, more nervous than usual, and I drank more. But underneath I was going a bit mad. I had entered the closed world of suicide...

In this particular suicide, as in all others, *life stops before it stops*. The individual's world is shut off.

The Aftermath of Suicide

Rehearsing the Details

As a survivor, you try to reconstruct what happened, and as you do, you concentrate on the emotional, social, and physical aspects of the death. You think about what was said or done prior to the tragedy. You think about the way in which the act was committed, the preparations which were made. You may even try to mirror what your loved one was doing or feeling.

If your loved one left a suicide note it serves as still another piece of the puzzle. Depending on the note's content and the way in which you viewed it, it may cause you anger, confusion, guilt, or a number of other disturbing feelings. Generally, suicide notes tend to have one or more of the following purposes:

- To comment upon or explain the burden of the victim's poor health.

- To accuse someone of something which can be viewed as a contributing cause of death.

- To serve as a will; to dispose of property.

- To give practical instructions about tasks that need to be tended to.

- To alleviate any responsibility others may assume for the death.
- To say good-bye.

You feel anguish about receiving a note which you cannot answer. You may dissect the note's contents, giving multiple meanings to nearly every word. You may imagine the things your loved one intended to say, but did not say.

It is important to put the note in perspective. That is, it is one item which reflects your loved one's thinking along a whole continuum of thought. The note is not necessarily representational of the same mind which conceived the suicide and carried it out. The note only represents your loved one's state of mind when the note was written. It is a mistake to try to extract the essence of the tragedy from this one piece of communication, however lucid it proves to be.

Feeling Anger Toward Your Loved One

You saw your loved one's life as viable; but he or she saw it differently and chose to die. This choosing is not only difficult to understand, it is almost impossible to bear. Once you resolve your disbelief, your next reaction to the death may be one of outrage. You may feel that your loved one was acting with contempt toward someone or something. Or it may seem that he or she was seeking notoriety. You may think your son, daughter, wife, or friend was mistakenly perceiving himself or herself as unloved. Whatever reason you assign to the tragedy, it is likely to make you angry. Why didn't she see how much others would be hurt? Why didn't he understand how unfair this was? Why didn't she recognize that there were alternatives? Why didn't he get counseling?

These are a few of the questions you may be asking. In "Surviving the Suicide" in this chapter, your anger will be discussed from a perspective which facilitates healing.

Feeling Anger Toward Yourself

Your loved one may have said something, written something, or given some sign that things were not normal. Studies of successful suicides show that suicide victims have usually given some warning, either verbally or through some action. You may think, "If only I had done something...If only I had taken her seriously...If only I had understood his intentions." You are angry at yourself for not doing something to stop the death.

Feeling Guilty

Closely linked to this anger at yourself is guilt. When you experience a loss due to suicide, your guilt can be obsessive. *You may feel guilty because you think you contributed in some way to the despair which caused the suicide.*

I never said a kind word to my mother. I was only interested in myself and what I was thinking. I didn't help her at home. She would complain and I would just laugh it off. I would give anything in the world if I would have been kind, if I would have thought about how tired she was all the time, and how much she needed my help. *(Woman whose mother committed suicide when the young woman was in high school)*

You may feel guilty because your loved one was obviously suicidal, or because he or she actually reached out to you in the hours preceding the death and you were not there. Unlike death due to illness, natural causes, or accidents, there is more likely to have been behavior prior to the death which indicated unhappiness or confusion, or there may have been a situation at school, home, or work which was one of turmoil, one prone to produce despair, hopelessness or helplessness. Sometimes the suicidal person has been drinking heavily, taking more prescriptive drugs, acting depressed, or engaging in violent or withdrawn behavior. In retrospect, you may feel that the forthcoming suicide was "obvious" and because you did not prevent it, you see yourself as an accessory to the act.

You may have found out, after the suicide, that your loved one tried to contact you prior to his or her death and could not reach you. You may have returned home to find a note on your door, or a message on your answering machine. A middle-aged doctor who died from carbon monoxide poisoning left a message on his friend's answering machine asking the man to come over because "there is something I need to talk to you about." When the friend came home and got the message, he went directly to the victim's house, but the doctor had already closed himself in the gas-filled garage and could not be revived.

Prior to her death, a young woman graduate student who killed herself by an overdose in a hotel room was, as her fiance reflected, "reaching out all day long." She left three messages on her fiance's answering machine, a message on her brother's answering machine, and called her own psychiatrist as well as a co-worker who was a psychiatrist. When her calls were returned, she had already died. Each person who received a call was left with the disturbing possibility that his or her quick response could have made the difference.

Another forty-eight year old victim called home repeatedly from a telephone booth, stating that he was going to kill himself. His calls continued over a two-day period and he eventually carried out his threat, leaving members of the family with the belief that if they had earnestly searched for him and talked to him they could have prevented his death.

A junior high student hanged herself from a tree near her home in Morgan Hill, California. In the week following her death, six other students from her school attempted suicide. Guilt seemed to lay at the base of many of the attempts. Some of the friends felt they had failed the victim. On the Sunday following the girl's death, twelve of her friends planned a mass suicide. Fortunately, the plan was aborted when school officials learned of it and an intensive counseling program was instituted to help the survivors.

In reliving the suicidal person's thoughts, the survivor may begin to think the same way and to emulate the actions of the person whose death they mourn. In a sense, your loved one's suicide presents an alternative to your own grief and anguish.

You may feel guilty because you did not remove the instrument of suicide (gun, rope, pills), making it inaccessible to your loved one.

> I picked up the pills that my mother overdosed with. I went to the pharmacy and bought them and brought them to her. I didn't think anything about it. I just did it and then went out. When I came home I realized she had taken the whole bottle. *(Young man whose mother overdosed on sleeping pills)*

You may feel guilty because you believe that suicide is a sin. There is a reaction to suicide takes its impetus from the belief that because life is a gift from God, a rejection of life is the same thing as a rejection of God. The conclusion is that those who reject God, therefore, condemn themselves.

As a woman survivor explained, "When my father killed himself my family was deeply embarrassed and they felt guilty. They felt his death was a disgrace. It was as if they had done it themselves."

A survivor may feel guilty because he or she experienced relief when the death occurred. In some circumstances, the period prior to the death was so painful and disruptive to friends or family that the survivor experiences relief when the victim commits suicide. The survivor gains freedom from the agony to which he or she has been subjected, often over a prolonged period of time.

A woman whose husband had frequently attempted suicide and just as often had claimed an attempt which proved to be false (taking pills he had not taken), expressed some relief from the tyranny imposed on her by his behavior. Though this is not the typical case, some survivors do feel relieved from similar situations when interpersonal pressures, disputes, and abuses have been terminated.

Experiencing Ostracism and Feeling Shame

Until recently, suicide has not been openly discussed, nor dealt with as a problem which deserves the attention and requires the education of the community. As a consequence, a certain amount of erroneous assumption and unfortunate folklore thrives in association with suicide.

Among the most disturbing assumptions within this body of misinformation is: Anyone who commits suicide is insane. If you, as a survivor, discover that this is the accepted belief (stated or unstated) of the people with whom you interact, you may not only be faced with the stigma produced by this belief, but also by the *extension* of this belief which is that insanity always "runs in families." The claim is that because you are related to the suicide victim, you too are unbalanced mentally.

The result is you may find yourself avoided or shunned. Your family history may be called into question. Your social status may diminish. You may even feel as if your own behavior is under constant scrutiny to see if it is aberrant in any way.

A man whose wife committed suicide tells of feeling alienated by former friends. He was no longer a desirable guest. People who had been friends of the couple for years suddenly and permanently withdrew.

Many survivors of suicide have similar experiences, regardless of their relationship to the loved one—spouse, sibling, parent, or child. The daughter of a parent who died by carbon monoxide poisoning tells of her experience immediately following the funeral.

> It's funny, you know, to lose a friend because your father committed suicide. After the wake I went across the street from the funeral home. My friend lived right across the street but he acted as if, "What's your problem?" I guess he was having a hard time dealing with the death himself. He never called me anymore and we just went our separate ways. I couldn't deal with losing a friend. I think the whole thing just freaked him out. He couldn't believe it. I lost two friends because of this. The rest of my friends, they didn't want to hear about it. Maybe it isn't that they didn't want to hear about it, but that it was hard for them to deal with it too, so I don't feel as if I had a whole lot of support.

This lack of emotional and social support for suicide survivors is typical, and it is in direct contrast to the amount and quality of support received by survivors of many other types of death. Avoidance is sometimes preceded or accompanied by implied accusations, or even overt blame from relatives, friends or neighbors. There may be remarks which suggest the survivor "drove (the victim) to it."

Sometimes one's integrity and morality are also challenged when dealing with coroners, police and insurance representatives. Their questions can be painful. It is even possible that a survivor may have to defend himself or herself against the inference that the victim was assisted in carrying out the suicidal act. In these cases, instead of the survivor receiving compassion and understanding, he or she is forced to cope with accusations which *intensify* any preexisting sense of ostracism or shame.

In a death by disease, natural causes, or accidents, there is usually no implication that there were psychological factors involved. But the opposite is true of suicide. You cannot deny the existence of psychological factors as partial determinants of your loved one's death. Because you are at a loss to explain the factors, you are extraordinarily vulnerable to the questions and treatment of others. Feelings of shame may be unavoidable.

Moreover, shame may perpetuate your loss of self-esteem and lessen your sense of security. Additionally, you may be categorized by others at a time when you are mourning your loss, confused about your loved one, and overwhelmed by the shock and circumstances of the death.

To ease this type of situation, some survivors create a false "reason" for the suicide of their loved one; the most common of which is that the victim was terminally ill. Eventually, this deception only complicates the grieving process because the death itself becomes a fictional event around which a story grows. Consequently, the survivors' feelings and reactions are suppressed, any discussion of the tragedy is avoided and, often, the suicide victim becomes idealized. This idealization then masks anger, guilt, or shame, which must be explored in order for the survivor to move through the grieving process.

Suicide as Accidental or Natural Death

Authorities have estimated that *reported* suicides may constitute as little as one fourth of *actual* suicides. This discrepancy results from the misclassification of thousands of deaths each year as automobile or shooting accidents, heart attacks, accidental drug overdoses, or unintentionally fatal combinations of drugs and alcohol.

False classification may occur as a result of one or more of the following factors: (1) the family's desire to avoid guilt, blame and disgrace, (2) the survivor's subconscious desire which is so strong it overrides the obvious reality, and (3) a well-meaning and silent conspiracy of investigators and family or friends who call the suicide an accident in order to assure the survivor of insurance benefits.

> They did find alcohol in his blood and that's why the cause of death was termed accidental. Supposedly, they say he just drank too much and passed out while the car was still running. But, you know, the thing is that the reason I knew it was suicide is that it was the same day he threatened suicide and when I went into the garage every single window in the car was rolled down. I don't know why they said it was accidental. We all knew it was suicide. Then after it was termed accidental my mother said, "Oh it was an accident, an accident." ...We don't talk about it, even when we're just alone. We talk about my father but we don't talk about the suicide.

As previously noted, a cover-up produces other difficult reactions to be worked through, the most prominent of which is denial. Denial generates evasions and fantasies as well as guilt for concealing the truth. Instead of smoothing the way for successful grieving, denial places the mourner in a state of unreality. When the suicide is denied, the survivor also refuses to believe that the loved one *chose* to leave. To support this false claim, the survivor suppresses any negative feelings that accompany abandonment.

The Survivor's Resignation to the Same Fate

It is not at all uncommon for a suicide survivor to feel that he or she is now predestined to die by suicide. It is as if the bond between the survivor and loved one can only be maintained if they both "take the same path."

Also, because a loved one has committed the act, it is no longer viewed as forbidden. Instead, it becomes a viable alternative and, as such, a temptation. In some cases, a survivor may even consider it to be an inevitability to which he or she is resigned. One young man who survived the suicide of his father said he felt he could only "reunite" with his father by "following him in the same way." He meant using the same method for suicide and in the same location, the assumption being that doing so would take him to the same place as his father.

Self-destruction is not the answer to any survivor's pain. Instead, the survivor's healing process can be facilitated in a number of ways. Let's consider them.

Surviving the Suicide

The grieving process for survivors of suicide, as previously discussed, is of longer duration than for survivors of death due to accidents, natural causes, or illness. In addition, the suicide survivor bears a deep anguish which intensifies the other severe reactions, such as guilt, anger, confusion and depression.

As you work your way through the painful aftermath which is filled with debilitating feelings, unnerving repercussions generated by the nature of the death, and, most importantly, your unique sense of personal deprivation, the following perspectives and coping strategies can help lighten the burden.

Getting a New Perspective on Anger

Because anger is a logical outgrowth of suicide, it should not cause you embarrassment or shame. It is advisable, even mandatory, to talk about your anger with family members, a friend or counselor. When anger goes underground, it inhibits grieving.

Any anger you feel toward yourself or your loved one is likely to be complicated by one or more of the following:

- You feel rejected by your loved one. You see his or her suicide as an act of deliberate abandonment.

- Your own normalcy, perception, compassion, helpfulness, and effectiveness have been subject to speculation.

- You inherited your loved one's pain and confusion without any warning or preparation.

- You are expected to put a seemingly senseless act in some kind of context, to make some sense of it to others.

It helps, first, to consider certain aspects of your relationship to your loved one. You had a belief system regarding your loved one, as well as definite ideas about *your position* within that belief system. Now that system has been disrupted.

You feel that you misjudged the other person. Not only did you fail to recognize the possibility that your loved one could kill himself or herself, you may feel that you did not accurately assess the whole person. You did not thoroughly know your loved one. Let's examine one of the reasons this unfamiliarity is so disturbing.

When you care for another person you most often do so because of what you see in that other person. You recognize certain qualities, traits, tendencies, and sensitivities that you believe to be valuable, and therefore worthy of your devotion. After the death, you may feel deceived. You may question your love for, or affiliation with, the person. At the same time, you realize you are not as valuable nor as powerful as you thought you were in this particular relationship. The result is, you experience two major blows: Your self-image and the image of your loved one have been damaged.

Once you can recognize possible underlying motivations for anger, you can see more clearly how your personal experience is being affected. Further, you will be better able to pinpoint what you are feeling and to express it.

As mentioned previously, one of the most serious deterrents to expressed anger is the idealization of your loved one. By denying the possibility of any negative psychological or emotional factors being associated with your loved one, and by trying to permanently suppress any unpleasant memories, you do yourself a disservice. If you attempt to create a loved one who was without faults, weaknesses, or a single undesirable tendency, you construct an unrealistic fantasy around the suicide victim. Even though clinging to the fantasy may help you lessen your feelings of personal rejection or your idea of a devalued relationship, this kind of deception will prove harmful because it will deter your grieving process.

It should be noted that there are some survivors who genuinely experience only minimal anger. These are individuals who already possessed an in-depth understanding of the psychological, social, cultural, or physical factors which prevailed in their loved one's lives, and were, therefore, serious deterrents to survival.

As one such survivor explained, "After five months of being depressed, I tried to be angry at her (for killing herself) but I couldn't *stick to anger*." The victim in this case had been chronically depressed since early teenage years, had sought the help of five psychiatrists and one psychologist through the years, and had been treated with a variety of anti-depressants over an extended period of time. This is not to say there was no other way out of depression for this victim; it is, instead, to assert that based on the victim's experience up to the point of her death, there *seemed to be* no other way out.

In addition to seeing the suicide victim in his or her entire life context and recognizing the person's negative qualities as well as positive ones, it is enormously helpful to become educated about suicide.

Achieving these objectives will help you 1) reduce the possibility of becoming reverential in regard to the victim (grieving is delayed by reverence), 2) feel less chastened by society, 3) understand your relationship and *lack of relationship* to the tragedy, and 4) benefit by availing yourself of information whose purpose is to make sense of the "senseless act."

Getting a New Perspective on Guilt

In the preceding material, several seemingly legitimate reasons for your guilt were explored. At the base of most self-recrimination is the belief that the suicide was preventable and you did not prevent it. Moreover, you may even believe you caused it to happen.

It has been stated previously that suicide is not a single act, but *part of a process*. Because this is true, even the most knowledgeable researchers in this field have not agreed on the definite causes of suicide. *You cannot expect yourself to surpass the experts.* You must recognize, therefore, that you cannot assume the blame for such a complex issue as suicide.

It would be false to assert that there are no influencing factors over which you *may have had* some minimal control; but there are also major influencing factors over which you have no control whatsoever, such as a person's age, gender, physical condition, or addictive behavior. You had, for example, no control over the intensely personal perceptions your loved one had of his or her social limitations. You had no control over a significant death which may have seriously affected your loved one's emotional and psychological well-being.

Yet, regardless of how true all of this is, you may still fasten on some facet of your behavior or some action that you are convinced was a partial cause of the tragedy.

If your loved one indicated or even threatened suicide, you may now agonize that you did not heed the warning. There may be quite logical reasons why you did not. Suicidal threats seldom come forth in a cool, logical manner. They are often issued in the context of great ambivalence, or overt hostility. In teenage suicides, in particular, there is usually a chaotic background which obscures the warning. Prior to a suicide, the teenager is often exhibiting defiant, aggressive behavior toward his or her parents, siblings, and teachers, and sometimes even best friends. In this context of negative behavior, it is difficult to isolate one statement or action and assign it more credence than the rest; that would be like hearing a string of firecrackers go off, but *listening* only to the third "pop."

You may think hospitalization of your loved one would have been the answer. If only you had insisted upon it, things would have been different. Hospitalization is certainly no guarantee. Dr. Herbert Hendin, Professor of Psychiatry at New York Medical College and Director of the Center for Psychological Studies at the Veteran's Administration Center in Montrose, New York, makes the following statement in his book, *Suicide in America.*

> I do not believe it is wise to hospitalize someone who is depressed and suicidal but otherwise functioning and who does not want hospitalization. If I were persuaded that hospitalization in such cases was a lifesaving measure, I might feel otherwise. But coercive treatment is not simply a matter of violation of rights, it is usually ineffective.

Further, it may help you to know there is strong evidence to indicate that a suicide does not occur as the result of the availability of a *way* to commit suicide; that is, it is not determined by the availability of an instrument. To the contrary, suicide occurs at the same rate, regardless of what method is more readily available. In the United States, guns are used in approximately fifty-five percent of the suicides, but the suicide rate is no higher than it was before guns became available. In a country which legislated against the availability of toxic substances, the high incidence of suicide by poisoning *dropped* but the overall suicide rate *stayed the same* because more people hanged themselves.

One of the subconscious motivations for your guilt may be the need to see the death as *within the realm of your control or power.* The reason for this is simple: When you abdicate power, you have to accept the suicide as being in the victim's realm of control. Then you are forced to admit that you have been willfully deserted. In such a case it is a matter of selecting the provocation for your pain, regardless of which is the more logical choice.

Getting a New Perspective on Shame

Shame is usually experienced because of the social stigma — either real or perceived — by which you are affected. There is a fable which says that all suicidal individuals are insane and that suicide is the act of a psychotic person. To the contrary, researchers who studied hundreds of suicide notes found that the act had been committed by extremely unhappy individuals, but that the individuals were not necessarily mentally ill.

It is not up to you to contradict ancient folklore or to combat the attitudes of others. Instead, try accepting their sympathy when it is offered and don't feel you owe them an *explanation*. You have no responsibility to try to explain the suicidal act to others. Look at the situation this way: If you were able to call back your loved one and ask him or her to give the reason for the death, you would find that he or she would not be able to explain it to everyone's (if *anyone's*) satisfaction. You cannot, therefore, expect such an explanation from yourself.

Another cause for shame may be the religious, moral and ethical aspects of suicide. Some people believe the suicide victim is condemned. Some believe he or she is punished by God. At one time, for example, the Catholic Church taught that suicide was a mortal sin that was punishable in the hereafter. This is no longer true.

> The church takes the position that you don't know what someone's destiny is. Now all are given a Christian burial. The concept is the Lord knows the troubled mind and the Lord will take the person home. *(Catholic priest)*

Often, a survivor who feels God has punished or will punish his loved one is predisposed to be punishing himself; he tends to project his own personality onto God. If a survivor is an understanding, forgiving person, his or her God will most likely be forgiving and understanding. It will be helpful to hear another person's perspective on the suicide-related issues which are causing you difficulty. A minister, priest, rabbi, or counselor is often able to provide valuable assistance in this area.

Talking It Over

In Section I detailed coping strategies have been offered for venting, dispelling and resolving painful feelings. As stressed repeatedly, every negative emotional reaction can be eased by talking about it.

A woman whose mother-in-law committed suicide, reflected on it twelve years later, emphasizing the importance of talking it out.

> I won't try to kid you that I don't still beat myself with the "I should haves," but I do know from reading extensively and two years of counseling that the "should haves" would not have done much good. If she had not succeeded that time, she would have at another. What I do know now is that I "should have" spent time talking about it to the family and friends instead of hiding it in the closet...

It may take several months before you begin to make an effort to "readmit" yourself to your former life. As you resume your daily activity, going back to school, work, or parenting, you will find it beneficial, again, to talk (at least briefly) about what happened to you. A man surviving the loss of his fiance advised, "Avoid building your public identity around your loss, but do talk to people who are safe to talk to. It helps."

A young woman whose father committed suicide returned to her job, after deciding not to tell her employers of the tragedy. She was drinking more than usual at night, arriving late for work in the morning and being extremely moody. Simply put, her general behavior was self-destructive. One day, however, she decided to risk telling her employers what had happened. As a result, she gained unexpected relief by bringing the suicide out in the open.

> I told my employer. He said, "It was a decision that your father made and I'm sure he felt it was the right one." I can't tell you how much that helped me. It made so much sense to me. My father had made decisions all his life and I'm sure when he made this decision he felt it was right. That was all my employer said. He didn't say a lot, but that was enough.

Some survivors report that they find it easier to talk to people who were not acquainted with the suicide victim.

> It was so much easier to talk with friends who never knew my father. Maybe they're more distant. It's easier for them to deal with it. The friends who knew him had a real hard time dealing with it. *(Young woman whose father committed suicide)*

Support groups are an important and valuable source of help for survivors of suicide. You can benefit enormously by sharing your concerns and feelings within a group of individuals who have, like yourself, experienced guilt, anger, confusion, social ostracism, shame, fear or depression.

As you work your way through grief, do not rule out the tremendous relief you can experience as a result of counseling. If you are plagued by anger or guilt, if you can't quit reviewing the details of the tragedy and are trying to unravel the mystery, if your depression does not lessen, you will benefit by talking with a lay counselor or professional. Seek individual help regarding any persistent fears, thoughts, or beliefs that are causing you emotional or psychic pain.

Putting It on Paper

As you grapple with your feelings and try to regain your emotional balance, you will be moody. Your reactions to daily events will sometimes be inappropriate and unpredictable. Your performance may be erratic. Your emotions may be so mixed they make no sense at all.

> Immediately, there was guilt. But I went through a lot of denial but I didn't really want to admit it. I wasn't actually denying it, I just wasn't admitting it. I knew it on the inside, but I didn't admit it on the outside. *(Young woman suicide survivor, reflecting on her parent's death)*

When there are feelings that are sorting themselves out, when what you're feeling on the inside is not accepted on the "outside," you may find it helpful to put the conflicts on paper. Keep a journal of your thoughts, feelings, and reactions, remembering that admissions you make, fears you express, the rage or despair you write about are private. Writing what you think and feel will help you sort out contradictions, denied aspects of the relationship, fears, and anguish, and ultimately to work through some aspects of your grief.

You may wish you could tell your lost loved one of your torment and frustration in regard to the death. Some survivors who feel this urge to communicate write a letter to their loved one. By putting the anguish, passion, and hurt on paper, the survivors gain relief.

If you find yourself having obsessive thoughts about not having had a chance to discuss the subject matter included in your loved one's suicide note, write a note in reply. If you keep processing question after question, write out your questions and speculate on their answers. Once you have put down your thoughts, they will lose their intensity as well as their power to occupy your mind obsessively.

At first, you may consider letter writing to be an idle or even illogical thing to do (since you can't get it to your loved one), but give the process a try. You will find that aside from gaining a release from your obsessive thoughts, you will uncover feelings you didn't know were there. This will aid in your general understanding of your own condition during the grieving process.

Avoiding Remarriage as a Consequence of Guilt

Spouses of suicide victims find themselves in a particularly vulnerable emotional state. Some spouse survivors, for example, enter into marriages for the purpose of compensating for their guilt and other negative feelings which resulted from their spouse's suicide. The characteristics which the survivor is eager to exhibit are those of a sensitive, kind, nurturing, perceptive person. To achieve this, the survivor selects a new mate who requires someone especially "good" to care for him or her. The survivor may choose as a future spouse someone who has a drinking problem, is emotionally incapable of functioning normally, is chronically ill, or is severely physically challenged. Marriage which has as its goals redemption of the survivor and reparation of a tragedy, is not likely to have a positive outcome.

If and when you begin to interact with new companions, be aware of the need for objectivity. Consider your motives for selecting a particular individual as a partner. Openly examine the healthful aspects of the relationship before making a commitment. You need to insure that the driving forces behind the bond are not guilt and the need to make amends.

Aiding Children Who Are Suicide Survivors

When a family member commits suicide, the surviving adults are often treated as the major victims. As a result, the child's emotional, psychological, and social needs are given much less time and consideration than they require. The impact of suicide upon the child is tremendous. He or she needs to be talked to, listened to, and when appropriate, counseled by a professional.

From the time the tragedy occurs, the child may be excluded from important verbal communication. This sets the stage for confusion and despair. A child who is old enough to understand what the words mean should be told that the family member (parent, grandparent, or sibling) has ended his or her life. The act can be explained in a straightforward, general manner without the inclusion of details. If this recommendation seems harsh, consider the inevitable alternative: The child will hear it in the neighborhood or from another child at school. The child will hear it from another relative, possibly one who has little or no compassion for either the victim or the child. The child will overhear discussions among family members of the death but *know* that he or she is not *supposed* to know.

When a tragedy occurs within a family and the child is not told of the cause, that child is being relegated to a position outside the circle of intimacy, outside the realm of knowledge which serves as a bonding factor among other family members.

Children who are not told the truth are being required to live a lie. Further, they may be given a set of ideas about their loved one which do not fit what they know to be true. Consider, for example, these possible situations.

Lie: Daddy was happy, and on his way home from work when he had a heart attack and died.

Child's recall of the facts: Daddy never *seemed* happy. He yelled at us and didn't come home sometimes at night. When he did, he and mom would fight and I would hear her beg him to quit drinking.

Truth: Dad went to a bar after work where he drank excessively. Then he drove to an isolated spot on the river bank and shot himself with his hunting rifle which he had put in the trunk the day before.

Lie: Your brother was killed in an automobile accident on his way to a high school football game.

Child's recall of the facts: Once my brother took a lot of pills and had to have his stomach pumped out. Everybody was really upset. This morning my brother had been crying in his room. Then he went to school but never came home.

Truth: Brother, who had previously attempted suicide, went to school carrying a brown paper bag, walked to the middle of the football field, pulled a pistol out of the bag and shot himself.

A child can't be expected to uphold the lie and the accompanying inaccuracies. Specifically, a child can't feel an emotion that does not evolve from the *real situation* — his firsthand experience with his loved one. Moreover, if the child can't feel the emotions he is supposed to have to fit the lie, he will have the multiple burden of being conflicted, confused, guilty, and outside the mainstream of the family.

A child often has the additional burden of thinking he or she caused the death. Because this belief can have extremely damaging effects, it is important for an adult survivor to explain the suicide in terms of the victim's unhappiness with *many* things. The child should be told that the victim was not able to understand that others were willing to help. It is wise also for the child to be made aware of the part played by contributing factors — drugs or alcohol — since he or she will doubtless find it out from someone else.

After a general, truthful explanation is given, the amount of information that should be furnished to the child can be gauged by what he or she asks about, or comments upon. If the child is old enough to conceive of a question which shows considerable thought, that question deserves a serious, thoughtful reply.

If, on the other hand, the suicide victim's name is not mentioned and the family pretends the person never lived, the child will probably follow the cue, suppress emotions and avoid asking questions for fear of upsetting the remaining family members.

The child may also fear the remaining parent or sibling will commit suicide. While it would be unwise for the surviving parent to state this specific fear (that is, to suggest the possibility of another suicide) the remaining parent *should* assure the child of the parent's continued presence on into the future. This can be accomplished, in part, by mentioning things that will occur in upcoming months or seasons: Your grandmother would like *us* to come visit her at Christmas. This summer *I* will teach you to swim. When you go back to school you can help *me* make the lunches. A sense of continuity is implied. The child hears the message — that the parent is indeed planning on being there. Also, the child is reminded of any existing family unit, which constitutes an important security factor.

Additionally, the child of a suicidal parent is left with any number of beliefs. Among them are:

- I was so bad my father or mother wanted to get away from me.

- I caused my parent to die by wishing it.

- I was supposed to "watch Mommy" and I didn't.

- I found Daddy but I could not save him. I didn't know who to call. (I called the wrong number, was not strong enough to help, did not understand the garage door was supposed to be opened, etc.)

Because of such beliefs and others like them a child needs the opportunity to talk, to ask questions, to receive assurance, emotional support and to be given permission to mourn. In addition, the child's value and importance should be confirmed.

When appropriate, the child's self-esteem can be enhanced by accepting him or her as a participant in "grown-up" activities, praising his performance at home or school, encouraging him to instruct a younger child in a task, or letting him read to you, draw you a picture, tell you a story, or dance for you.

The life forces of all survivors must be encouraged and appreciated more than ever after a suicidal death.

(See *Surviving Loss During Childhood* for additional information regarding the child's healing process.)

Nonfamily Survivors

Emphasis needs to be placed on one unusual dynamic associated with suicide; that is, often the nonfamily members may be more closely involved in the death than the spouse, children, siblings or parents of the victim. A friend is often the one who hears the threat, receives the note or call for help, or finds the victim. For this reason, it is extremely important for the friend to be recognized as a survivor with extremely legitimate needs of his or her own. The nonfamily survivor should be included within the network of the family as the members come together for support.

There are, of course, cases in which this would be inappropriate due to a stressed prior relationship between family and the friend, or due to geographical distance. Whenever possible, however, the friend's burden, especially of guilt, should be recognized and eased.

9

Surviving a Murder

Our world was shattered. In the first few weeks we were literally held up by friends and neighbors, who surrounded us with love and caring. Then there came a time when this dropped off, as it naturally does. People have their own lives to live, and they went back to them. But a very vital part of the family was gone. My world would never be the same. And it amazed me that the rest of the world went on as usual. How could I do things like shop for groceries or clean house when my Lisa was dead? I couldn't think of anything else.

CHARLOTTE HULLINGER, WHOSE DAUGHTER
WAS BLUDGEONED TO DEATH BY AN
EX-BOYFRIEND, *PEOPLE MAGAZINE,* MARCH 16, 1981

As reflected in this mother's statement after the murder of her daughter, a survivor experiences amazement that "the rest of the world" can go on as usual after such a tragedy.

This amazement is a normal reaction because from the instant you are notified of the homicidal death of a loved one, you are set off from the world as you have always known it. You occupy a "world apart" and you experience an immediate sense of isolation, a sense of belonging to a tragic minority. In the months following your loss you grapple with a jumble of feelings—anger, horror, confusion, impotence, impatience, guilt, and perhaps even your own murderous impulses toward the person who killed your loved one.

Reactions

Because of the nature of the death and the special circumstances it presents, you have many unique, painful reactions to deal with. These reactions are, in most cases, more severe than those experienced by the survivor of a natural death.

Feeling Stunned

At first, you may be encompassed by shock and a resistance to believe what has happened. This state of disbelief and shock has its purpose. It provides you with protection against a reality which is too painful to assimilate all at once. As a result, your ability to function is impeded and you behave with robot-like detachment. You do not overtly or aggressively indicate your needs. In fact, because you are numb you appear to others to be "bearing up" quite well.

> Not having gone through it before [homicidal death of a loved one] you don't know what to expect. In the beginning, for maybe one, two, or three weeks, you're completely numb and your friends and neighbors say, "Oh, she's doing so well." But it's only because it hasn't really sunk in yet. Your body has not accepted it. You go through the funeral and the burial and just about the time everyone is going home it begins to sink in. *(Mother of a murdered victim,* PEOPLE MAGAZINE, *March 16, 1981)*

As the numbness lessens, any number of feelings rush forth. Among the most prominent of these is anger.

Feeling Anger

While enduring the loss the death brings, you may:

1. feel the need to have a target for your anger.

2. experience difficulty restraining your own murderous impulses.

3. feel frustrated as you wait for the apprehension of a suspect, a trial, or both.

You may direct your anger toward one or more "targets," the suspect, police, your neighbors, your spouse, your child's friends or teachers, the family of the suspect, yourself, God, or the world in general. Your rage may be so unshakable and acute that you think you are losing your mind. As the mother of a murder victim stated, "Violent death brings anger so intense most people can't stand it."

Another woman survivor, whose sixteen-year-old son was murdered by a man who stabbed him sixteen times, recalls feeling "like my brain was going to explode."

As with other types of loss, anger commonly goes hand-in-hand with guilt during the initial stages of the grieving process. Most often, these feelings will be prominent for approximately two weeks to four months.

Feeling Guilt

Self-blame can assume proportions which are life-denying, in the sense that they deprive you of any normal life. Instead of living, you exist within a torturous framework surrounded by your own accusations.

- I should have met my little brother when he got off the school bus.
- I should have recognized that my daughter's boyfriend was dangerous and talked to her about it.
- I should have gone to my friend's house and investigated when she didn't answer the phone.
- I should not have allowed my son to work in that high crime district at night.
- I should have made sure my daughter had lessons in self-defense before she went away to college.
- I should have insisted that my husband keep a weapon behind the counter in the shop.
- I should have taken better care of my wife's car and she would not have been stranded on the highway.

You will have your own "I should have's." They will be based on the belief that if only you were clairvoyant this death would not have occurred, because you would have known you needed to prevent it. Except in the rarest of cases, the claim against yourself has no valid relationship to the crime. Your accusation is the product of your need to direct the blame somewhere, so, being the most convenient and perhaps the most vulnerable target, you aim the blame at yourself.

Judicial Involvement and Media Intrusion

As soon as you were notified of the tragedy, you became the focus of media attention and, simultaneously, you were involved with law enforcement agents. Interviews, telephone calls from strangers, visits to police stations, and courtroom appearances may still dominate your life.

Because this activity occurs when you have little or no mental energy and only a minimum of emotional strength, you may feel as if your very sanity is being threatened.

> At first, the pain is so excruciating you think you can't live. You think if you do survive you'll go crazy. (Mother of murder victim)

Unfortunately, the way you feel has nothing to do with the responsibilities you are expected to fulfill. During this period of impaired or reduced emotional and mental capacity, you must supply information, often taxing your memory for the smallest detail which could be crucial to the investigation. You must contribute logical, influential evidence and provide convincing testimony.

You may worry that you are forgetting something, supplying inaccurate information, or, because of your strained emotions, impeding the judicial process.

You may be extremely displeased with what appears to be an inoperative or ineffective judicial system. As one parent lamented, "Will the pain ever lessen? Will justice be done?"

During this period, your stress may be amplified by:

1. delays, preliminary hearings, continuances, or plea bargaining.

2. police or other law enforcement agents who lack compassion and who make disparaging references to your loved one's affiliations or activities.

3. your own lack of understanding regarding the procedures and requirements of the judicial system.

Betsy Parks, the daughter of Ross and Betty Parks, was murdered on the North Carolina State University campus in Raleigh. The Parks waited seven years for a murder trial. Betty Parks explained the emotions provoked by their situation.

> It was...six and one half years after Betsy died, when Gary Coleman was extradicted from a prison in Georgia to North Carolina and charged with her murder. For the next fourteen months he was able to delay going to trial with motion after motion—thirty-one of them at one point.

> These continued delays kept us off balance all of one year. I felt helpless, frustrated, and angry, wanting the trial behind us, but also wanting the preliminary steps done correctly. If Coleman had

indeed murdered Betsy, I didn't want him escaping conviction through a technicality. *(SURVIVORS Newsletter, August 1984)*

This experience reflects the additional problems of dichotomous feelings—you want it over with, but you want it done right.

Facing the trial. The trial, with its multiple stresses, is another endurance contest. Some of the pressures are ones of which you are aware; others may affect you without your realizing it. For example, any number of the following factors may be extremely debilitating.

1. You see the murderer or the suspect, perhaps for the first time.

2. You may have to listen to defense attorneys make negative references to your loved one, directly attacking his or her background or character.

3. You may have to listen to character witnesses speak in support of the offender.

4. You may feel that "purgery without penalty" is occurring in the courtroom.

5. You review and reexperience the details of the murder.

6. You are questioned by the media regarding your opinions and feelings in relation to the events taking place in the courtroom.

7. You must control crying and suppress your rage, shock, or revulsion—sometimes all at the same time.

8. You are required, frequently without much instruction, to understand your role throughout the trial.

9. If an appeal is filed, you may have to wait years for a resolution.

As long as the trial continues, you are unable to grieve overtly and, until the judicial procedures conclude, you cannot rid your mind of thoughts about the death because each day you must face them again. The trial may seem the most torturous phase of the grieving process.

When the trial finally draws to a close and the criminal has been sentenced, you may have the expectation that you will feel "normal" again and your life will begin to make sense. When this doesn't occur, you are dismayed. You think something is wrong with you because you are not experiencing recovery now that it is "all over with." But what is over is the public part of death. The private part continues.

Immovable Memories

A series of visual images are associated with the death of your loved one. If you were actually present at the death you have a set of memories that involve a specific place, real people, actions and conversation. If you were not a witness, you have other mental images. These are the ones you have constructed to go along with what you *imagine* to be true. The imagined, at times such as these, can be more agonizing than reality.

A mother whose murdered twenty year old daughter was found abandoned in the mountains, a victim of rape and bludgeoning, had sought additional information from the police for months. There was evidence that the suspect tortured his victims for weeks prior to their murder, yet there was no definite proof that her daughter had been murdered by this particular killer. "If only I knew," she lamented, "if I could just *know* she wasn't tortured. But I keep imagining that those things he did, the things that were in the paper about the other women, happened to her, too. I haven't slept for six months."

This kind of personal torment has no limitations and no schedule. Your memories and speculations do not confine themselves to the daytime. The images also surface in your dreams. You may have unbearable nightmares which cause you to prefer sleeplessness to the anxiety of your dreams.

Experiencing Isolation

Since the tragedy first occurred, you have been consigned to another world that is not understood by the majority of the population. When people avoid you because they are distressed about what to do or say, your situation is made worse. Even a spouse can become distant and physically unresponsive. You hug and you don't get hugged in return. You may want the tenderness and intimacy that accompanies sex, and you are rejected. The "real world" seems too cold, unpredictable, cruel and imposing.

Some survivors, once they have isolated themselves, will begin to use or increase their use of tranquilizers or alcohol. By doing this, they distance themselves even further from the mainstream, shutting out a spouse, family members, a boyfriend or girlfriend, even their children.

Paranoia. Paranoia sometimes precedes withdrawal; other times it may emerge after one has sought isolation. Numerous fears supply you with seemingly sound reasons not to rejoin or trust the community around you. You will get mugged. Your car will break down and someone will pick you up and assault you. Your other daughter's boyfriend is potentially violent. There is a rapist next to you on the bus. A man in your apartment building is following you to work.

This kind of suspicion is a logical outgrowth of the violent shock you have undergone. Because your loved one's life was wiped away with no warning, you believe the same thing could happen to you or to another member of your family. You could not feel more vulnerable.

A middle-aged man described the way he reacted to his wife's murder which occurred in a seemingly serene neighborhood of elegant homes. "I went from being a happy-go-lucky person to carrying a gun. I thought people were out to get me." He began drinking to "keep the demons at bay," and eventually needed counseling in order to restructure his life, and regain his position in the world of the living.

The Healing Process

There is, of course, no way to obliterate your tragedy, but there are several ways to help yourself heal. You have undergone an ordeal that must not be consigned to silence because it cannot be "cured" by silence.

Father Kenneth Czillinger of Cincinnatti, who has done extensive work with grieving parents, offers this advice:

> When people ask you how you are doing, don't always say, "Fine." Let some people know how terrible you feel. Talking with a true friend or with others who have been there and survived can be very helpful. Those who've been there speak your language. Only they can really say, "I know, I understand."

As You Talk, You Heal

You need to tell your story; not once, but repeatedly. The old phrase, "You need to get it off your chest," has a great deal of truth because you do feel heavier at heart, indeed some people experience a pressure in the chest, or chest pains, as a result of the tremendous stress endured while dealing with a murder.

As you recount your experience, you benefit by both a physical and emotional release. You begin to assimilate what has happened because you hear yourself saying it. It becomes a reality. Roberta Anderson ("Parents of Slain Children," *Newsweek,* 1982) had a son who was killed when the drugstore in which he was working was held up. She said, "You talk and you talk. You keep telling your feelings and maybe one day you'll believe that it really occurred."

When other people don't want to hear you talk, when they don't want to listen to what you have to say about your feelings, your situation is made more difficult.

Charlotte Hullinger recalled her experience after her daughter's murder.

> I went back to teaching two weeks after the funeral and nobody said a word. They had sent me flowers, but I would say something about Lisa's death and they would quickly change the subject. I guess they think they are doing you a favor. They're not. Anyone in the situation needs to talk about it.

Another mother of a murder victim stated: "People don't know what to say to you so they avoid you like you have a disease." Because of other people's reactions, you may try not to talk about it or to show your feelings. Suppressing what you are thinking and feeling may win you the admiration of your friends, relatives, and co-workers. They may say how "strong" you are and how well you're coping, but that brave behavior will not benefit you, nor will it help you heal. Examine whether or not you are taking pride in being "strong and silent." If you are, try to be more lenient with yourself. Something terrible and unjust has happened to you. It is all right to feel sorry for yourself. You can cry and appear to be sad because you *are.* You can appear weak because your spirit, life, and physical body are indeed weakened by what you are going through.

Getting Support

If you are the parent of a murder victim, there is a place where you can find people who know your agony and understand your needs because they are victims of the same type of loss. *Parents of Murdered Children* is a national organization based in Cincinnati, Ohio, with over 45 chapters in the United States and at least one contact person in each state. The organization, which charges no dues, provides ongoing emotional support for many parents. This is accomplished by telephone, correspondence, or in person—either on a one-to-one basis or in group meetings. The national network also provides support through their literature, which includes a monthly newsletter. Their goals are as follows.

1.   To support any person who survives the violent death of a loved one.

2.   To provide contact with similarly bereaved persons and establish self-help groups which meet regularly.

3.   To provide information about the grieving process and the criminal justice system as both pertain to survivors of a homicide victim.

4.   To communicate with professionals in the helping fields about the problems faced by those surviving a homicide.

5.   To increase society's awareness of the problems associated with surviving the murder of a child.

A member of POMC will write or telephone any parent of a murdered child and will, if it is possible, link that parent with others in the same vicinity who have survived their child's homicide.

If you are surviving the murder of a spouse, sibling, friend or other loved one, you may set up a support group of your own. (See *Guidelines for Support Groups* in chapter ten.)

In a group of people who know what you are going through and who may still be going through the same feelings themselves, you will not feel judged, afraid, or embarrassed. You won't have to listen to people telling you to "Get on with your life and just block the death out of your mind," or offering similarly offensive advice. *Forgetting* is impossible. *Continuing on* will be possible only when you are ready.

If, because of your geographic location, you do not have access to a group, or if you do not wish to participate in group sharing or discussion, you need to identify one or two people who are willing to hear you discuss your concerns, ask your questions, and voice your fears. A family member, friend, neighbor, community worker, counselor, minister, priest, or rabbi who is a nonjudgmental and responsive listener can be of tremendous help.

As previously noted, most Hospices have lay counselors who can offer extraordinary support and guidance during your time of crisis.

Writing of Your Experience and Feelings

Besides talking about your experience, you may also write about it in order to gain relief. Write about the things which make you feel angry, guilty, helpless, or hopeless. Record your story from beginning to end, or report only the aspects of your experience which you find most confusing, frightening, or frustrating. Do any kind of writing that is necessary to vent your feelings. If you don't censor yourself, your important feelings will surface naturally. You do not need to share what you have written in order for it to serve as an emotional release and you may gain additional benefits if your writing allows you to formulate some helpful insights into your situation.

There is another kind of writing which will also provide emotional benefits. This is correspondence which has a specific and important purpose. This type of writing must be directed, focused, controlled and succinct. A letter to the chief of police, your legislator, or the editor of the local newspaper can be of value to both you *and* the recipient.

Seeking Information and Retribution

Regardless of how complicated the investigation of the crime, or how remote and cool the law enforcement officials appear to be, you need to continue to press for the information you feel would solve the missing parts of the puzzle—physically, emotionally, or both. Once you know as much as possible about what happened, who was involved, to what degree your loved one suffered, and over what length of time, you can begin to experience the relief, however small, that comes from knowing the details. As disturbing and dismal as this may sound, you can begin recovering from a specific set of circumstances, rather than from a tragedy that has no bounds, is surrounded by mystery, and augmented by your greatest fears.

You may decide to seek retribution for your loved one's death. If so, you may find that the actions necessary to the pursuit of this goal will serve as a force which mobilizes and unites the family. Working toward a common cause allows you to strategize, implement, provoke reciprocal behavior, and hopefully experience some small sense of empowerment in the face of loss.

Twenty-seven-year-old Christopher Coombs, of Wheaton, Illinois, was bludgeoned at the side of the road by two teenage strangers. As his attackers fled the scene, Chris stumbled away from his car and fell into a ditch where his frozen body was found ten hours following his death. After Chris's parents had endured the devastating initial impact of their son's murder, they were able to put their grief into action. Ten months after his death, they formed a POMC chapter in Illinois. After another year, the Coombs contacted the Illinois Attorney General regarding the needs of those who survive the murder of a family member. As a result of this meeting, the Attorney General appointed them to a Task Force on Crime Victims, which drafted a Victim's Bill of Rights. It insures that the murder victim's family members are *also* recognized as victims. The bill includes provisions stating that the family is entitled to information regarding the progress of the murder investigation; they are to be notified of indictments, of the need to appear in court, and of any cancellation of court appearances. The Bill further states that it is the family's right to have the verdict explained, in non-technical language, by the state attorney's office. The family is to be notified of any plea bargaining or sentencing hearing. They are to be informed about the ultimate disposition of the case and informed by the parole board of the impending release of the inmate. They are to be informed by a victim's advocate of the social services or victim's compensation which may be available. The family also has the right to make an impact statement at the sentencing or at the parole hearing.

Another kind of action was taken by POMC members in Philadelphia. They were told by the district attorney to attend the trials along with the members whose children had been murdered. In numbers, it was explained, they would have an impact on what occurred in the courtroom. As a result of this suggestion, eight members of the local chapter went to the trial of the accused murderer of one of the member's sons, a young man who had been stabbed 207 times and run over with a truck. Day after day, the contingent of POMC members appeared in the courtroom to serve as a constant reminder of the victim's rights. The accused was found guilty of murder. Action of this type can help the survivor to feel as if some progress is being made and that some effect is possible in the war against violent crime.

Informing The Public

Your complex and tragic experience is unique. All the horror and the hearings and trials have given you insights, and fostered in you strong beliefs about surviving a homicidal death. In addition, you have learned a great deal about the grieving process itself. Each day of your life as a survivor, you add one more bit of knowledge to what it means to deal with the murder of a loved one. There may be a time when you would like to use what you know to benefit others. By speaking of the various aspects of your experience, your feelings associated with it, and your view of how your experience as a survivor could have been made less stressful, it is possible for you to educate others. You could, for example, offer yourself as a speaker to any one of the following:

1. a local law enforcement agency.
2. local mental health clinics.
3. community education programs at hospitals.
4. religious organizations.
5. criminal justice classes at local colleges.
6. the Chamber of Commerce, private organizations, and clubs.

Your personal experience can benefit any group interested in learning about the issues relating to homicide survival, citizens who are concerned with having a better awareness of crime and the operation of the criminal justice system, and professionals who work with the bereaved. If you make known your availability as a resource, you may be surprised by the type and number of responses you receive from individuals and organizations who welcome the chance to become more informed about issues relating to your tragedy.

If you decide not to join a group, exert any leverage privately, or express any opinions publicly, you might consider offering moral support to someone who does. Those who do "go public" about their ordeal can benefit by having other individuals who will accompany them, give them feedback, or just provide a haven for talking over experiences.

Reaching Out

Regardless of the crime which has affected your life and the ordeal you have subsequently endured, you can enjoy positive feelings by doing something that is remarkably simple: Reaching out to someone else.

When your spirit undergoes a "relapse," when you find yourself feeling despairing, bitter, and without anything to look forward to, take notice of another person who needs help emotionally or physically. Offer to provide help to that person, *regardless of how minor your assistance seems to be.* Do an errand for your elderly neighbor. Take flowers to someone ill. Encourage a distressed co-worker to join you for coffee, a movie, or a game of golf. In other words, turn away from yourself and respond to the need of another. You will feel better for having done it.

The Renewal of Energy

Approximately eighteen to twenty-four months after the death, you will experience an increase in physical energy. This is made possible by stabilization of your sleeping patterns and eating habits. It should be easier for you to attend to everyday demands such as grocery shopping, banking, commuting, or various job-related tasks. These will be the same responsibilities, in fact, that seemed overwhelming or even physically impossible in the first months or year of bereavement.

If your physical energy does not return in this length of time remember that you must not expect yourself to be on any kind of schedule. It may take much longer for you to feel noticeably better. *Don't expect more of yourself than your body feels capable of giving.* Surviving a violent death is one of the most debilitating experiences a person can endure.

Progressing in your own way. A couple who survived the murder of their daughter sum up progress this way.

> People ask us if things get better as time goes by and my answer is that things get different. Different, in that we are not continually waiting for a trial. Different in that we are confident that Betsy's murderer will be in prison for a long time. Different in that our work in POMC gives us a place to use our energies constructively with people." (*Betty Parks,* SURVIVOR NEWSLETTER, POMC, August 1984)

Having some personal goals will help clarify your direction in the days ahead. It will allow you to move forward, to experience change that leads to new discoveries. You did not have any choice regarding whether or not the tragedy occurred in your life. You do, however, have a choice about how you react to it, what you say about it, and choose to do about it.

III.

Getting and Giving Help

10

Getting Help

The ways in which you react to the loss of a loved one are usually similar to the ways you have reacted to previous traumas in your life, even though they may not have been as serious.

During the grieving period, your instinctive reactions are magnified. If your pattern has been to withdraw during a trauma, you may now withdraw to a greater degree or for a longer period of time. If you usually enlisted the aid of others, you will now be likely to seek and receive sympathy and assistance from relatives and friends. If, in the past, you resorted to drink when in extremely stressful situations, you may now drink more than ever. The point is, *in the face of loss by death, you do not suddenly develop a whole new mode of behavior.*

Your individual resources—your psychological, physical, and genetic make-up—serve as your primary or basic support. Your parents, spouse, or children constitute your "second string" support. Beyond that, sequentially, are your friends and support group, followed by professional caretakers and counselors. Closely linked to these are various social agencies. Finally, this hierarchy of support extends to your own system of cultural beliefs and values. The total grief support system, portrayed in its simplest form, looks like this:

survivor
spouse, parents, children
friends and support groups
professional caregivers and counselors
social agencies
cultural beliefs and values

Though this is the general progression of the support system, the sequence will not apply to every survivor. For example, you may find that your friends are closer to you, seem to understand you more readily, and provide more support than your family; or perhaps a church group offers the necessary and ongoing support.

Any survivor needs support from others and will have much less difficulty during the grieving process if he or she does not feel separated from the interaction, sympathy, and assurance that is provided by others.

> The more isolated a person is, the more difficulty he or she has. When people feel isolated, they don't heal. *(Professional counselor and support group facilitator)*

In each of the preceding chapters dealing with a specific type of loss, various coping strategies have been presented. It has been repeatedly emphasized that you need to talk about your loss and seek support from one or two individuals, or a group of survivors who have experienced a loss similar to your own. The names of various national support groups and agencies have been included in the hope that you will seek one out to aid you during your grieving process.

Sometimes family members or friends turn away from you because they themselves are grieving. They think that if they interact with you and express their feelings of sadness or despair, they will compound your grief. Others simply feel you should "move on," "be through with it," "snap out of it," or "not dwell on it."

> Other people often want you to eat and drink and get on with your life. A lot of people don't want to see you hurt any more. They just want you to live your life again. *(Couple who lost a son to cancer)*

You cannot get through grief unless you experience it. If you hide it, deny it, or dull it, it will only be prolonged. Your emotional pain must be lived through in order for it to be lessened, and gradually eliminated. Meeting and talking with other people who have gone through this process will help you immensely.

If your support system with friends or family does not meet your needs or expectations, you will be likely to feel disappointed, uncared for, or even angry. While these feelings are generally normal, you should not keep hurting yourself if the support you require is not where you expect it to be. Look for it where it really is.

> Survivors need a place where people can talk about what happens to them without the other person running away. What happens when people are grieving is that the other people run out of gas with them. They don't want to hear them. They don't want them to cry or talk about the experience. They don't want them to exhibit their grief. People in a support group can cry, talk about what

happened, can do anything they really want to do, and be guaranteed that no one is going to run away. *(Support group facilitator)*

When you are in a support group, you are someplace where you don't feel isolated. You see people who serve as models. They have had a similar experience and have come out of it okay. When I see people who have done so well with it, I think I can do that, too. *(Mother of a teenaged accident victim)*

You may live in a remote geographical area far from Hospice or an appropriate support group related to your specific type of loss, such as a SIDS survivor's group, Survivors of Suicide, or Parents of Murdered Children.

Survivors who can't avail themselves of an established local group and survivors who prefer to select the people with whom they meet often start their own groups.

Guidelines for Support Groups

There are some recommendations and procedures which facilitate the founding and operation of a successful support group. Each of these will be discussed in the material which follows.

Founding Your Own Group

Ideally, your support group will be composed of people whose loss is similar to your own; for example, due to accidental death, the death of a child, or the death of a spouse. The group can, however, operate just as efficiently when its individual members are experiencing the aftermath of differing types of death.

Finding a location. When you are seeking a location for your meetings, it is best to use "neutral territory," such as the public room of a savings and loan building or library, or the home of one of the group members. If possible, avoid using hospitals or churches. A hospital will likely invoke memories and emotional associations so strong the survivor doesn't wish to be placed in such a vulnerable position. The use of a church may indicate to the survivor that the group is religiously affiliated, or that the potential group member must hold certain religious beliefs in order to attend.

Locating prospective members. Newspaper accounts of deaths similar to that of your loved one (accidental, suicide, during childhood, etc.) can be a resource for identifying potential members. You can also contact hospitals and mortuaries. Be cautious about using the police department or sheriff's office as a resource. This procedure may prove successful in some cases, as when locating parent survivors of the Sudden

Infant Death Syndrome, for example, but it may not be wise to use it to identify the survivors of a murder because many murders are committed by family members or are drug related.

Prospective members can be contacted by sending out a notice or brochure giving this information:

- *State who may be interested in the meeting.*
  (Parents who have lost a teenager to an accidental death, suicide survivors, parents of cancer victims, widowers within a retirement community, parents of AIDS victims, etc.)

- *Identify the organizer.*
  (Dick and Linda Clifford are the parents of a teenaged suicide victim; Jack Gillespie is a widower who lost his wife to cancer; Janet Bell lost a newborn baby, etc.)

- *Specify where the meeting will be held.*
  (Include a map if the location is not well-known to most community members.)

- *Include both the starting and finishing time.*
  (The group will begin promptly at seven o'clock and will conclude at nine.)

- *Indicate if refreshments are to be served.*
  (Coffee and dessert will be served, wine and cheese, etc.)

- *Mention that the group is free.*

Along with the notice, attach a personal note which explains the group's purpose, invites the prospective member, and offers transportation. Here is a model which can be modified to meet your needs.

Dear Mr. and Mrs. Randolph:

The purpose of this survivors' group is to provide support to parents suffering the loss of a child to leukemia. The group offers a safe place to meet and share with other parents who have had similar experiences. I recognize, of course, that even though a group such as this has been found to be helpful to many survivors, it may not appeal to everyone.

I will call on Thursday to ask if you are interested in joining us. If you would like to visit the group, I would be happy to pick you up.

The size of the successful group is usually between eight and fifteen people. A group that is too large may prevent people from sharing, either because they are inhibited or there is not enough time for everyone to have a turn to speak. A group that is too small may suffer from low energy and minimal input if two or more participants fail to attend.

The facilitator. The person who serves as the group facilitator should have experienced the loss of his or her loved one at least a year prior to assuming a leadership role. Someone who is newly bereaved will find it very difficult to act as a coordinator or discussion leader.

It is usually unwise to publish the names or phone numbers of group leaders in the newspaper. The names can, however, be given to the social service worker or pastoral care worker at the hospital or to your physician to relay to survivors who could be potential members.

Support Group Procedures

A reasonable amount of time for a meeting is two to two and a half hours. You should state clearly that the meeting will begin promptly, and then every effort should be made to keep to a schedule. People are more likely to attend a group when they know exactly what to expect in terms of a time commitment.

At the first meeting, introduce yourself and explain that you formed the group because you needed it and thought it would be helpful to others in the community who had experienced similar losses. Point out that you are not a counselor (unless, of course, you are).

Orientation. Explain that survivors' groups usually begin by sharing experiences. Inform them that sometimes the group may decide to invite a professional to discuss a special concern, or the members may wish to designate a specific topic of interest to be discussed among themselves at a future meeting. To relieve any possible anxiety the members may have, explain that you will start the sharing by telling something about your own loss. Then you will invite others to do the same. Emphasize that they can say as little or as much as they like. If they don't wish to say anything, that is perfectly acceptable. If anyone feels the need to step outside for a while, everyone will understand.

Mention that even though a member may feel compelled to add to what someone else is saying, the group will work better and be more effective if no one interrupts while another person is speaking.

Sharing. After the orientation, start the sharing by telling who you lost, and a little something about when and how the loss occurred. After you have talked for a few minutes, ask for someone else to introduce himself or herself.

> We go around the room and everyone tells their story. The purpose is to allow the time and space to share without someone judging or saying, "It's time to get on with your life. You shouldn't feel that way now." *(Mother survivor of a neonatal death)*

As experiences are related and discussions initiated, some important procedural guidelines should be observed.

Procedural Guidelines

- The facilitator needs to give each person a chance to speak and, at the same time, to move the discussion along so that the meeting does not run overtime.

- Each person needs to have an opportunity to talk, but if any survivor wishes to listen without sharing, his or her preference should be respected.

- Explain to the survivors that there is a difference between actively listening to what another person is saying, and expiating their own grief. Sometimes survivors will automatically use other's experiences as a springboard to relay their own experiences. They may say, "Oh yes, well, when that happened to *me...*" Warn members against using another person's grief experience to launch into a discussion of their own grief.

- When members are absent from the group, don't discuss them beyond sharing any necessary information. ("John is not well and it would be nice if one or two of us called and offered to help." "The Johnsons will not be here for a month because they're visiting their parents in the east, etc.") No judgments should be made about how those who are absent from the group should act or feel. If someone begins such a discussion, the facilitator should change the topic.

Organizational Guidelines

- Make sure you schedule a meeting before holidays or as close to the holiday as possible. Thanksgiving, Christmas, Hanukkah, or Easter may be very difficult times for survivors.

- Invite members to suggest topics or speakers for upcoming meetings.

- Record the death date and birthday of each survivor's loved one. Call that member on each of those dates. Both are critical times for the survivor and he or she will need support.

- Suggest an exchange of telephone numbers among the members.

- Invite members to bring in and tell about books they have found exceptionally helpful during their time of mourning.

- After the group has been together for a few months, suggest a potluck or swim, a barbecue in the park, or some similar event which invites sharing, participation, and feeling of community.

Special Considerations

There are several factors, related to support group dynamics, which deserve special attention. These are (1) the emotional and physical drain that is inevitable during group participation, (2) male participation, and (3) overdependency.

Emotional and physical drain. You can help beginning members by explaining that participating in the group will be a draining experience, especially when they first begin to participate. Some members feel the first two or three meetings are the most difficult.

> It is an exhausting experience. The first three meetings are probably the hardest because you are so tired. After the first meeting, some people go home and say, "Why did I go? It was terrible. I'll never go again." *(Parents of an accident victim)*

When members are forewarned, they are able to recognize that their experience is normal, and to anticipate that it will be less difficult each time. Once they get beyond the initial meetings, the survivors will feel less taxed.

Being a facilitator is also an extraordinarily exhausting experience. This person, who is also a survivor, must be alert, organized, innovative, a dedicated listener, and, when the need arises, a program coordinator. If the facilitator begins to experience burnout, there should be a second survivor who can fulfill the same role. When there is no survivor whose loss occurred a year or more before, the group may like to set up a series of guest speakers or facilitators to present special topics for four or five meetings. You may, for example, invite a counselor, psychologist, or pastoral care worker to discuss particular issues such as guilt, anger, depression, social isolation, or siblings' reactions to the death of a brother or sister.

To find speakers you can call a local Hospice, the Public Health Department, public relations department of the hospital, Family Service Agency, or you may call local authors who have written in the field of grief. When calling agencies or institutions ask to speak to the director, then explain your group's needs and interests. You will most likely obtain several referrals.

Male participation. Because men have a more difficult time than women expressing their grief, most of them will be reluctant to attend a support group. Some men will be completely resistant.

A group facilitator makes this observation, "It's a big step for the men to come, but once they come, they talk." A man who does attend the group will initially "go for his wife" so his wife will not have to participate by herself. After the husband has visited the group, he is usually more positive and will often admit that he is glad he was willing to give it a try.

In comparison to their wives, men are more inclined to check out the group to see if it is safe before they talk about anything personal. They have to be absolutely certain they can trust the other participants not to misjudge or evaluate them.

> I feel safe talking to this group but I don't feel comfortable any more talking to other people. There isn't the same trust. *(Father of a teenaged accident victim)*

Though men are not generally inclined toward group sharing they may have a pronounced need for an outlet. Men often do not take (or are not entitled to) more than a few days respite from their jobs after a death occurs in the family. It is usually imperative for them to return to work and to uphold their responsibilities *as if nothing had happened.* Because of pressures at work, and other demands, the man's grief is not resolved. An evening support group offers a forum for the working man's grief. (This is also true, of course, for women who must return to work immediately, and for young mothers who must take care of preschoolers during the day and have no time to attend to their own emotional needs.)

Ask for a male participant in the group to volunteer to contact any potential male members. The seasoned participant can explain the group's purpose and offer to pick up the grieving father, husband, son or brother for the next meeting.

Overdependency. Though it is not a frequent problem, there exists the possibility of a survivor becoming overly dependent on the group.

When a survivor becomes a participant on a regular basis, he or she naturally becomes part of the group's social network, one that can be invaluable during a time of deep sorrow. A special bond is created, telephone numbers are exchanged, and people select those to whom they will confide in private.

> A lot of people have said to me, "I have two sets of friends. I have the people I have known all my life. They are my friends who know what has happened to me before my child died. And I have my friends who know what has happened to me after. These are two sets of people and they are very different. One I can talk to about my experience and the other set I can't."*(Professional counselor and support group facilitator)*

Interaction with members of an accepting group is enormously beneficial as long as it is not to the exclusion of all other social interactions over a prolonged period of time. A member who becomes extremely dependent on the group and builds a whole life around the group meetings and activities for longer than two years may be in danger of becoming a "professional mourner." The survivor in this role will dimiss other valuable friendships and forsake other meaningful roles in his or her life.

A member who begins to develop this kind of attachment should be gently and discreetly encouraged to reach out to others and to invest personal energy in other activities. A professional could even be invited to speak to the whole support group about the importance of not gaining one's identity from grief.

Assessing Your Own Progress

As pointed out previously, you will react to the death of a loved one in much the same way as you have reacted to other severe traumas. There are those survivors who say, "I deserve to survive this." They recognize their own self-worth and importance and seek ways to have their own needs met. Other survivors with different personal histories and levels of self-worth will not have the needed impetus to undergo the change and growth necessary for healing. Instead, their emotional distress is unrelenting and unchanging.

Still others vascillate between depression and pleasant, successful behavior. Any survivor whose negative behavior dominates or restricts his or her life will benefit by obtaining professional help.

If you do not have a completely clear perspective of the ways in which you have been affected by your loss, you may wish to compare your own behavior with the actions or patterns noted below.

A survivor who is likely to have a poor outcome may:

- engage in excessive drinking or eating

- be accident prone

- develop a chronic health problem such as asthma, ulcers, or allergies

- have excessive weight loss and suffer from insomnia

- enter into poor business transactions

- spend disproportionately to his or her income

- enter into an abusive relationship with another person

- engage in compulsive caregiving

- reject other close and healthy relationships

- be irrationally overprotective with family members

- have violent or agonizing nightmares which involve the dead loved one

- perceive himself or herself only as a burden to others

- fantasize about suicide

- resent other people's happiness or well-being to such a degree that he or she behaves spitefully

- be plagued by guilt or anger

- lack all powers of concentration

- talk about the dead person in the present tense

These negative conditions are compounded by two other factors: *grief itself,* and the survivor's *constant awareness* that he or she is experiencing misery.

> I once read the sentence, "I lay awake all night with a toothache, thinking about the toothache and about lying awake." That's true to life. Part of every misery is, so to speak, the misery's shadow or reflection: the fact that you don't merely suffer but have to keep on thinking about the fact that you suffer. I not only live each endless day in grief, but live each day thinking about living each day in grief. (*A GRIEF OBSERVED, C.S. Lewis*)

Just as your awareness of *how much* you are suffering can cause you to suffer more, the awareness of the transient nature of emotional pain can cause you to suffer *less.*

Recognize that pain, no matter how intense it is, does not last forever and that it does, in fact, come in *waves.* By being aware of this fact, you will be better able to endure each wave, knowing that it will eventually be followed by a period of numbness.

The natural order of things prevents you from experiencing more pain than is possible for you to endure. You will never have more pain than you can stand because it will shut off. You can help yourself by trusting this process.

The nerves of a burn victim have intermittent moments of numbness when the pain will not register. So it is also with the person who experiences emotional pain. You will not have more than is endurable. Your mind will function like a safety mechanism that shuts off or numbs out and it is during that time of relief that you can have a breathing spell. Each time you begin to feel overwhelmed by pain, *remember* that the breathing spell is coming. In the middle of the wave of pain *remind yourself* that it will not last forever.

> Perhaps the best illustration of the oscillating nature of pain is grief. The sense of loss whelms up, a feeling so intense that one cannot imagine an end to it. But then, after a time, the numbness comes, a period of calm and relief. Soon numbness is replaced by another wave of loss. And so it continues: waves of loss, calmness, loss, calmness. This is the natural cycle of pain. As soon as you reach an overload, your emotions shut off, you literally stop

feeling for a little while. These waves continue, with smaller amplitudes and longer rest periods, until the hurt finally ceases. *(SELF-ESTEEM, Matthew McKay and Patrick Fanning)*

Sometimes when you are feeling better, you may be thrust instantly, and without warning, into misery as the emotional wave swells and descends. Remind yourself that you have had the feeling before and that eventually it passes. Think of these waves of emotion as having a purpose. Each wave will wash away some inner dependence, denial or hurt. These peaks are not relapses; they have a function. They bring you closer to the day when the pain will subside permanently.

You can also take action to reduce your emotional suffering by seeking counseling. Professional counseling serves as a private, individualized support system and is found to be helpful to the survivor who wants to have an open forum for the expression of feelings, or to the survivor who feels as if he or she is not able to function normally.

I go to counseling whenever I feel the need to talk to someone who is not directly involved in the situation. *(Mother of a teenaged cancer victim)*

Any survivor can benefit from additional support resources. Short-term help can make daily life considerably less stressful following the death of a loved one.

I knew that the time I had to myself, the quiet time, was important. But I also knew I needed quality time with other people, on whatever level that was, whether it was work or time with my family. There was part of me that felt I was going to need some counseling but I didn't feel ready for it right away. I waited about a year. *(Widowed nurse)*

While you may feel ready for counseling, you may not know how to select a professional counselor, psychologist, or psychiatrist. One or more of the following referral sources should prove helpful:

- your family physician
- a trusted friend or relative who had gone to the professional for counseling, therapy or treatment
- the pastoral care office or social services department of a hospital
- the psychiatric department of a hospital
- your minister, priest, or rabbi
- the local Hospice (or closest Hospice)

The Benefits of Professional Help

In a group of twenty survivors who were interviewed about the death of a loved one, all of them found professional help to be extraordinarily beneficial during their grieving process.

> There should be a requirement that every person who goes through grief should have some counseling. The burden is too heavy to carry alone. I had to know that I was not going to go crazy, or drink too much, or lock myself up in my house and not ever come out again. *(Mother of a teenaged accident victim)*

There are some survivors who simply must function alone. They spend more time resenting and resisting help than benefiting from it. These people, however, are in the minority. Most people will gain from counseling.

> Relatives just want to fix you. A counselor doesn't take the same approach. *(Mother of a teenaged cancer victim)*

> I went to counseling after my husband died. I lost my friends and I was taking it personally. I didn't realize that death is threatening to other people. *(Sixty-two-year-old widow)*

> I spent many hours "on the couch" after my father's death. I had a lot of issues to deal with. I could not have functioned even somewhat successfully without professional help. It kept me going. *(Forty-two-year-old dentist whose father died)*

> You can admit things to a stranger. There were times when I just wanted to get away from the whole scene. And I did. I worked a full-time job. I dated and had a terrible romance. My counselor helped me through all of those things. Of course, they were all interrelated but I didn't know it at the time. *(Mother of a teenaged daughter who died from leukemia)*

> I didn't want to go to any kind of counseling because I had the feeling that I was going to be talked out of it (how I felt), that he was going to try to talk me out of it, and I would be told how to feel. I *needed* to feel the way I felt. *(Widow)*

The goal of professional help is not to transform you beyond your natural capacities nor to defy your instincts. *Counseling takes you where you are.* It is also not a forum for vilifying or idealizing your loved one, but for viewing the *total person* and the *total relationship* the two of you shared. Counseling allows you to acknowledge each feeling and express it without fear of retribution. It permits you to delineate those aspects of the relationship that were valuable and positive and explore those which were destructive or painful. Memories may be recalled, fears explored, motivations brought up from their hidden depths into the light.

These are some of the definite guidelines for gauging the progress of your own grieving process. To determine the degree to which you are experiencing healing, ask yourself these questions:

- Is less of my time taken up with actions or thoughts that are negative and self-destructive?

- Am I able to integrate moderately into social situations?

- Am I able to talk about my loved one without experiencing great emotional pain or despair?

- Do I use the past tense when I talk about my deceased loved one?

- Can I perform my job and concentrate on the task at hand?

- Are my dreams of my loved one often pleasant and reassuring?

- Do I enjoy any close relationships with other people?

- Am I genuinely interested in other things and other people?

- Am I able to smile and laugh without feeling guilty?

When you are healing successfully, your life embodies a purpose, a future, and an appreciation for those components of your being which make you the most human. The *same* components which produce deep grief after your loved one's death also serve to make life worthwhile and something to be treasured. To have a life free of grief, you would have to live without love. No one would willingly choose such an alternative.

11

Helping Those Who Grieve

There was a friend who said to me, "I know this is the anniversary of Janet's son's death but I don't know what to do. I don't want to call Janet and see how she is because then I'll remind her of it." I told the friend, "Go ahead and call her. She hasn't forgotten that her son died."

SISTER OF JANET, MOTHER OF AN ACCIDENT VICTIM

Survivors commonly report that friends and relatives assume they are being helpful if they don't mention the death of the survivor's loved one. Therefore, they act as if nothing has happened or they rapidly change the subject if death is mentioned. A woman survivor, the mother of a murder victim, gave this advice:

> Friends and relatives need to talk about it. It is as if people believe if you're not talking about your loss, you're not thinking about it. That's as ridiculous as assuming if you're not thinking about breathing, you're not doing it.

A father whose son was a cancer victim remarked that when he and his wife were with close friends the friends would talk about anything other than what was most immediate and important to the grieving couple.

> We would go out with people and they wouldn't even bring up the topic. It was all we wanted to talk about and nothing else.

Reacting to the Grief of a Friend or Relative

You can't help a grieving friend or relative if you ignore the fact that a death has occurred in the life of that person. As obvious and simple as that fact is, there are those who fail to recognize it. Once you have accepted that the death cannot be ignored, there are four fundamental guidelines for reacting to the grief of a friend or relative. They are: (1) Do not withdraw from the survivor. (2) Do not compare, evaluate, or judge. (3) Do not expect sympathy for yourself. (4) Do not patronize the survivor.

Withdrawing. After the funeral is over, the survivor needs support on a continuing basis. Unfortunately, it is at this same time that friends and relatives often withdraw. A health professional observed, "There are people who are very close to the survivor during the period when the spouse, child, or friend is dying. Then, after the death, they drop out. They isolate the survivor even further by doing so."

Shock and initial grief after the funeral are pronounced; yet some friends and relatives assume that because the burial service has taken place, it is also time to bury feelings and go on with life. Instead, the mourners need others who can offer consistent comfort and consolation, who are there to talk over what has occurred, or to reminisce about some important moments from the loved one's final days.

When you contact a person during the period of initial grief, first ask how the person is doing and feeling.

> The people who would come over and say, "How are you doing now? It's been a week (or a month). How are you feeling?" Those are the people I really appreciated. *(Mother of a young cancer victim)*

Comparing, evaluating, or judging. "Why are you crying all the time? Pull yourself up by your bootstraps. Look at John—he has it worse." As crass as this sounds, similar remarks are heard, all too frequently, by survivors. Some people even suggest the survivor will experience some positive outcome from the death such as, "It has made your family more closely knit, more caring." "This has been a lesson to your other children not to experiment with drugs." Or, "Now your husband will appreciate his home more."

Equally devastating are suggestions that the death could have been prevented, the wrong hospital was chosen, the doctor was unskilled, the person was not cared for, or did not feel needed. No judgments will bring back the loved one or help the survivor. They will only exacerbate anger, guilt, confusion, recrimination, doubt, or shame.

Sometimes well-meaning friends will rationalize the legitimacy or need for the death. As an example, the parent survivors of a neonatal death may hear, "The baby would never have been able to lead a normal life, so he is better off." The dead baby's parents may heartily disagree. They may, in fact, have wished to raise their baby to adulthood, regardless of whether or not he had all the physical or mental capacities which qualified him as "normal" in the eyes of others. In addition, this type of remark infers that the parents were responsible for producing an abnormal human being. People in circumstances such as these are already dealing with despair and self-blame. They do not benefit from others' awkward attempts to legitimize the parent's loss.

Eliciting sympathy.

It disturbed me when people came seeking support because they didn't know how to handle their own feelings. It became an added responsibility. So many people wanted us to buoy them up. *(Parents of a cancer victim)*

In an effort to show their sorrow and empathy, some people display their own grief and talk about how they are affected by the loss. They seem to expect the survivor, who had the primary relationship with the deceased, to listen and help them through their own grief.

To the contrary, the mourner must use all of his or her resources to continue life, maintain a home and, in addition, may need to give support and affection to children who are feeling bereft as a result of the death.

Patronizing. The condescending behavior of others does not help the survivor. This type of interchange often implies that the survivor is child-like, adrift in society, or doomed to grieve for the rest of his or her days. A middle-aged widow described it as the oh-you-poor-dear-what-in-the-world-will-you-do-now syndrome. This type of reaction is superficial, uncaring and unconstructive.

Helping the Survivor

You can actively help a survivor by:

- Accepting the survivor's feelings, concerns and actions.
- Listening to the survivor.
- Displaying patience.

- Maintaining a positive personal perspective.

- Providing practical help.

- Providing social support and promoting interaction.

Some of these procedures, more than others, will be compatible with your personality, lifestyle, and preferences; you will naturally find it easier to help in some ways, more than others.

Accepting

Accepting the survivor where he or she is — *how* the person is — is the first major step. It is not important for the survivor to be where you think he or she *should be* in terms of feelings, concerns and behavior.

The survivor may say to you, "All I can do is cry." Or, "I can't start talking to you because I'll cry." Crying is natural and normal. It is part of feeling the emotional pain which must be experienced before it can be reduced. Accept the survivors' need to cry and offer assurance. Statements similar to these will help:

> Please don't worry if you cry in front of me. It's hard to feel so sad and not to cry.

> It is natural to cry — and I hope you feel comfortable enough with me not to have to feel embarrassed or sorry about doing it.

> If you didn't cry, then there might be some cause for concern. When you're able to cry, I know you're going to get through this.

Casual remarks like these help the survivor understand that he or she does not have to worry about shocking or embarrassing you, or causing you to withdraw. More than anything, *the survivor needs to know that his or her crying will not cause you to run away.*

Let the survivor know that it is completely acceptable to feel anything he or she is inclined to feel. Make the person aware of your receptivity to any thoughts, or feelings the survivor wishes to express. Let your relative or friend know you're not going to try to talk him or her out of it. You are not going to remove your support.

If your relative or friend is depressed and expresses *nothing*, don't feel as if you must start a conversation or *do* something. You can provide support by sitting in the same room, holding the person's hand, or giving him or her a silent hug.

If the survivor seems to reject physical gestures of affection, respect the person's reserve. Some survivors see intimacy as another responsibility (they have to hug you back), or as an assault (they might break down). Some survivors do not wish to be personally invaded in any way.

When you are unsure of what to do, you may extend a hand or a touch on the shoulder, and if the survivor stiffens up, you will know it is best to offer your presence silently and without additional physical gestures of sympathy. You might even say, "I'll sit here with you for a while, if you don't mind. When you want me to leave, I will understand. Please just tell me and I will go."

It is important for you to understand that in the initial stages of grief *all the grieving person wants is for the dead one to be alive.* Because of this, you may sometimes feel as if you are being resented, cut off, rejected, and ignored. Don't take such actions personally. Even though you may want more than anything to help the mourner, he or she is not able to fully appreciate or respond to anyone.

The survivor may even behave as if he or she thinks the dead loved one will be brought back to life by wishing and pining for the person. This yearning and longing are normal and should not be discouraged or denied by others. This helps the mourner assimilate the reality of the loved one's permanent absence. The finality of the loved one's death will be recognized as a result.

Listening

Every survivor needs an attentive, accepting and caring listener. By being such a listener, you provide the most valuable support possible. The survivor has a need to:
- retell the details of the loved one's final months or weeks
- review various aspects of the relationship shared by the two of them
- express feelings such as anger, guilt, remorse and yearning

Retelling the Details

Every time you talk about it, every time you go through your story and talk about some part of the grief process, as painful as it might be at the moment, it becomes easier. Some people need to continue to talk about it a few times. Some people need to continue to talk about it over and over again. I felt the need for a long time to tell the story. At least a year. *(Survivor of a neonatal death and a support group facilitator)*

Most survivors have a compelling need to retell the details of the final hours, days, even months of their loved one's life. In general, they will talk about the who, what, when, and how of the loss. They will go over details which vary, depending of course on the type of death and the specific situation. The survivor may talk about the diagnosis of the loved one's illness, what medical personnel said, what the parent said during his or her last weeks of life. If the loved one was the victim of an accidental death, the survivor may talk about having strong, intuitive feelings prior to the accident, thinking that something was wrong, that the husband, son or mother was "in danger," "in trouble," or even dead. The survivor may repeat the victim's last conversation before the fatal accident, tell how the victim looked going out the door, talk about which person was first notified of the accident and what he or she said or did.

These details are extremely important. The survivor must review and recall them, for by remembering, the survivor holds onto the person. Couples who recount the loss of a child, for example, may interrupt and correct each other about the smallest of details, such as what a particular nurse said, whether or not the door to a bedroom was open or closed, which doctor spoke to them. The sequence of events is equally important. The survivor will be persistent in clarifying the order in which actions occurred. The car skidded into the tree and *then* went to the right side of the road. They notified their oldest son *before* their daughter. The hospital clerk gave them papers to sign *after* they talked to the priest, etc.

Usually the survivor will retell details for three or four months. Each detail adds to the loved one as a person and verifies the reality of the loved one's existence. *When the survivor is assured that he or she will not lose the memory of the loved one, clinging to the details becomes less important.* The "picture" takes its place in the memory process. The survivor begins to let go of some information and associated feelings, but keeps what he or she needs in order to validate the death.

Reviewing the relationship. In addition to retelling the details, the survivor needs to review the relationship he or she shared with the loved one. This may include talking about certain aspects of the relationship such as the companionship, dependency, affection, and shared goals, and remembering conversations, anecdotes, or shared traumas. The survivor is testing the relationship, the reality of it, and often, silently soliciting *verification* and *validation* of the relationship from the listener.

When a loved one has gone through a long and painful terminal illness, the survivor appreciates, more than ever, affirmation of that lost loved one's active, vital self before he or she became debilitated. This need is expressed in the following excerpt from a letter written by the wife of a cancer victim to relatives and friends. At her request, it was read at her husband's memorial service.

> For almost five years now I have seen Hugh grow thinner and older and physically powerless, moving indomitably but with great pain and difficulty. The man so strong he once cracked a friend's rib in a casually exuberant hug could no longer do the spading and lifting and repairing that he felt to be his part of the chores. The man who had eaten and loved and laughed and worked with such gusto, now ate only by an act of will, his tongue so cracked from the chemotherapy that he had to rinse his mouth with an opium solution before mealtime.
>
> I watched this happen twenty-four hours a day for months on end, and gradually that was the only person I could see. Sometimes it was hard to recall the vibrant, joyous larger-than-life man I immediately fell in love with such a short time ago. I thought then I would surely die if I couldn't marry him.

When Hugh died and your messages and phone calls and letters began to pour in, the incredibly rich fabric of our twenty-six years together came to life. With your memories and your love, you have recalled the Hugh who could — and did — move mountains, and you have given him back to me. I am grateful. *(From "A LETTER FROM DOROTHY," Dorothy De Lacy)*

You can help the survivor not only by affirming the loved one's character and personality but by augmenting personal anecdotes the survivor may tell you. Join the survivor in the telling of a recollection. "Yes, I remember how Dad always wanted you to walk with him after dinner." Or, "She was proud you were her sister." Or, "I remember how he loved to challenge his brother to a tennis match." Or, "Yes, Jeff was always borrowing your best clothes to wear to school. He wanted to be like you."

As the survivor tells you about the relationship and recalls specific pieces of it, he or she is also separating from it, putting it outside the self, and eventually integrating it as an entity into an ongoing life.

Expressing feelings. It is inevitable that the discussion of feelings will accompany the recall of details as well as the review of the relationship. The survivor will experience strong associative emotions or conditions, such as guilt, anger or despair. In addition to facilitating emotional expression by being accepting, as previously discussed, you may also help the survivor recognize emotions relevant to certain issues. Sadness may accompany a memory of celebrating a wedding anniversary. Anger may be linked with the family's reaction following the death of a child, or guilt may dominate nearly every memory.

As you accept without judgment, shock, or embarrassment the feelings the survivor expresses, you may also be able to ease any feelings of remorse and self-blame the survivor has. When you hear those feelings expressed, you may offer questions which give the survivor a realistic perspective of his or her responsibility for certain acts. If, for example, a survivor of a suicide or accidental death is taking responsibility for the death occurring, you may ask: "What would you have had to do to prevent that from happening? Would that have been possible? How do you know it would have been effective? Is there anyone else who could have taken the same step? Did they? Are you really being fair to yourself?"

A survivor who sees the death as a punishment for his or her perceived misdeed (wishing the person would go away, resenting the attention the person received, etc.) may benefit from suggestions such as, "No one is fully loved, fully wanted, or fully appreciated every minute of his or her life because no one feels the same way about another person *all of the time*. Every relationship between any two individuals has some degree of ambivalence." "People don't die because of others' wishes, resentments, or limitations." (See "Understanding and Dispelling Your Guilt" in chapter two.)

Following the loss of a loved one, an older survivor may tend (now, more than ever) to voice feelings and concerns regarding his or her own death. Again, it is important not to gloss over, ignore, or deny what you are hearing. Acknowledge what the survivor is expressing. If, for example, your seventy year old father wants to talk about how he feels about dying, or if he wants to specify certain desires regarding his own death and funeral, hear him out. Appreciate that he is trusting you, thinking coherently about an inevitable event and expressing legitimate concerns and preferences which may ease decisions for you later. If your son says he is afraid he will die in the same way as his brother, let him express his fear.

Offer reassurance and don't tell the survivor "not to talk about it," or to "forget it." *He can't.* Voicing the feeling is better than pretending it doesn't exist. Talk it out with the survivor coolly and logically, acknowledging that the feelings of your relative or friend are real and deserve attention.

Displaying Patience

As you exercise acceptance and listen to the survivor, you may have to possess an inordinate amount of patience. This is especially true when the survivor's key response to loss is irrational anger. You may even become the target for the anger. In such a circumstance, it is necessary to remember that anger, within reasonable bounds, is a natural, healthy response. Don't blame the survivor for striking out. Depersonalize what is happening and wait; the anger will subside.

If your relative or friend grows silent and remote, don't prod the person with questions. Moodiness is part of grief and often total silence is an absolute necessity.

> My friend insisted that I take a short trip with her a few months after my husband died. All I could do was go, I couldn't participate. My friend got upset with me for being quiet. She wanted me to be outgoing. *(Widow)*

Remember, no schedule exists for healing. A survivor is raw with grief and must endure much pain before healing takes place. The only course you can take is to avoid appearing restless or annoyed with the survivor. If you think that your friend or relative is beyond the bounds of normal grief, you will be interested in reviewing "Recognizing Potentially Unfavorable Outcomes" later in this chapter.

Maintaining a Positive Perspective

It may be difficult for you to achieve a balance between *acknowledging the loss* that caused the survivor pain, and *maintaining a positive perspective* in the face of that loss. You cannot help the survivor by blocking reality or steering a survivor away from painful reminders of the loss, but at the same time, you need to maintain a positive perspective while facilitating grief.

You can do this by validating the person who died, talking about how the person touched or enriched the lives of other people. When the opportunity arises, mention facets of life in which the survivor has formerly shown interest. Make a mental list of those activities or people who gave the survivor enjoyment. Keep the sparks of those natural interests alive or at least present, by mentioning them — the garden, the pets, the survivor's favorite shopping area, golf partner, or community interest. By doing this, you are indicating to the survivor that *there has been a past* and *there will be a future* with these same things, people and places in it.

Providing Practical Help

Well-intentioned friends or relatives will sometimes call the grieving person and say, "If there's anything I can do, let me know." It is the rare survivor who will respond, "Could you drive me to the doctor on Tuesday?" Or, "My house hasn't been cleaned for two months." Or, "The children are too much for me to handle today." In other words, if you genuinely wish to provide help, you need to:

1. Survey the grieving person's situations and needs.
2. Decide on two specific tasks or ongoing responsibilities you are willing to assume.
3. Call and offer to do the most difficult of the two; if that offer is rejected, propose to do the second.

After one offer for help has been accepted by the survivor you can more easily identify additional ways in which you can make life less stressful and burdensome for the survivor.

In the list of suggestions which follow, some, more than others, will be applicable to your situation and will meet the needs of your friend or relative:

- Prepare and deliver dinner on a specific day of the week that has been agreed upon beforehand.
- Babysit for a day.
- Mow the lawn or take care of the garden.
- Feed the pets.
- Bring fresh flowers to the house.
- Write notes expressing your love, encouragement, and availability for specific tasks.
- Accompany the survivor to the cemetery.
- Offer to house sit if the survivor must leave town.
- Make phone calls that are difficult for the survivor, such as notifying distant relatives, calling the child's school or the person's place of employment, calling the social security office,

talking with the insurance representative, etc.
- Do the grocery shopping.
- Drive the survivor to the doctor.
- Give the survivor a book on grief.
- Help answer correspondence.
- Take the laundry home and do it.
- Take the pets to the vet.
- Wash the survivor's car.

Don't force yourself on the survivor. Make sure it is okay to perform the task before you undertake it. Also, make certain what you do for the survivor will benefit him or her. Some survivors have remarked that people sometimes offer to do things that will make *them* feel better, rather than the survivor.

> I appreciated it when a friend gave me a book on grief. Books can make the person feel less isolated, can reaffirm what they know, and can allay fear. *(Young widow)*

> I liked to have my friend go to the cemetery with me. I realized that she cared about my brother, too, and that she wasn't afraid of me exhibiting emotion. She was quiet, but she was there. *(Sister of an accident victim)*

There are some pleasantly innovative ways friends and relatives have helped survivors. A couple who lost a teenaged son in an automobile accident reported that a crew of high school students came to their house every month. The teenagers dusted, vacuumed, cleaned, and mowed the lawn for the grieving parents. A young widow who lived in a dark, rural area told of her closest neighbors keeping their lights on at night, and having music playing when she came home in the dark. They were making sure there were some signs of life at their house so she would feel less isolated.

As you look for ways to help, think of the *whole family unit.* You may be able to provide support to a family member who has been ignored or forgotten by others. Remember, to children death is exceptionally confusing, painful and frightening. You may be able to meet a child's intense need for reassurance, companionship, and compassion. (See chapter six, *Surviving Loss During Childhood.*)

There are a variety of ways to help a child of your friend or relative.

- Let the child talk about death to you.
- Read the child a story.
- Take the child for a walk.
- Make or buy the child a puppet or gather together some art materials.
- Help the child with homework.
- Take the child with you when you shop for the family's groceries.
- Encourage the child's positive activities and interests.

Helping a survivor of *any age* through the grieving process is one of the most valuable things you could do in your life. Establishing yourself as a person committed to an ongoing and caring relationship with the survivor will ultimately benefit you both.

Providing Social Support

It is safe to say no survivor will find it easy to reenter into normal social interaction after the death of a loved one. You can assist the survivor in this process by:

- being aware of, and sensitive to, the courage it may take for the survivor to go out in public

- offering to accompany the survivor in public when it is appropriate

- making a mental inventory of those activities which were once enjoyed by the survivor—then providing invitations which coincide with the survivor's interests

A young widow tells of beginning to cry in the bank because she had to explain to the teller a name change on her account. A widower tells of feeling shunned by former friends because he no longer fit in—and because a "grieving person does not make a great dinner guest." A couple who lost a teenager tells of being avoided by former friends in the supermarket. They confide that they felt hurt when people turned away, pretending not to see them. A young mother tells of having to listen to other mothers at a school meeting complain about their children's behavior or performance. She said, "I wanted to scream, 'But you still *have* your children! Stop complaining about them. They're alive!' "

These anecdotes represent only a sampling of the hundreds of similar disturbing situations which occur in the lives of grieving people. They illustrate the need for a great awareness on the part of the family, friends, and neighbors. To many survivors, *every type* of social interaction is a potentially painful situation. They may not want to talk. They may be afraid they will cry. They may even feel tainted or rejected because of the nature of their loved one's death.

Once you recognize the courage required of the survivor you can show your understanding by offering to drive the survivor or accompany him or her in public when it is appropriate. For example, you may accompany a widow to a meeting with her tax consultant. Offer to drive a teenaged survivor on her first day back to school, or take a grieving friend to lunch or dinner on the person's first day back at the office. You might offer a widower a ride to church or offer to accompany him as he shops for groceries. In such cases, you are volunteering support for the survivor as he or she continues the practical, functional aspects of living.

In addition to helping with the unavoidable, everyday activities, you can promote a recreational activity by drawing the survivor out for the sake of fellowship and pleasure. The best way to approach this is to first take a mental inventory of the activities which were once enjoyed by the survivor, issue verbal invitations which coincide with the survivor's former interests, and provide the means by which to pursue those interests.

To accomplish this, you will need to give some serious consideration and attention to the pleasurable or interesting aspects of your friend's or relative's life before the death occurred. For example, prior to her loss, your sister may have loved browsing in secondhand shops. Your friend may have enjoyed jogging. Your brother may have enjoyed computer games. Your dad may have expressed an interest in writing, building a wine cellar, or going boating. Whatever the survivor's natural interests were, you may now help the survivor by extending invitations. Ask your sister to go with you to a newly discovered secondhand shop. Invite your friend to jog with you several times a week. Offer to help your brother save for a new computer game. Encourage your dad to take a creative writing course at the local adult school or community college. Give him a book on wine tasting. Invite him to go to a boat show with you.

There is a special need to recognize the social isolation felt by widows and widowers. Invite the widow or widower to dinner. Too often, senior citizens who lose a spouse suddenly are dropped or ignored even though there is probably no other time in their lives when they need as much consistent emotional and social support. Single women, in particular, get fewer invitations from couples than their male counterparts. Because they are often seen as a threat to married women, they are consigned to interacting only with other widows, women who have never married, or single parents. Unfortunately, this situation does not allow for the enriching interaction which can result when people of various lifestyles, concerns, experiences, and interests get together. A middle-aged mother and businesswoman who has defied narrow social arrangements says, "When you invite single people, people of various age groups and backgrounds into the lives of the married couple, it is like playing a piano selection using the whole keyboard instead of one octave. Which would you rather listen to?"

The social interaction of the survivor cannot be adequately dealt with without recognizing two major outcomes of grief, both of which have been previously discussed. They are (1) the tendency to the grieving survivor to change his or her priorities, and (2) the highly charged emotional needs which often cause the survivor to alternate between interaction and withdrawal.

When a survivor undergoes severe priority changes following the death of a spouse, friend, child or sibling, he or she may have no interest in an activity which had formerly provided enjoyment. For example, a young businessman who once spent his free time reviewing marketing publications no longer finds that a compelling or valid way to spend his time. A saleswoman who once spent a lot of free time taking aerobic classes and going to the spa now wants to pursue a more "other-oriented" activity, so she is taking a psychology class.

There are hundreds of ways in which a survivor's priorities can change and you may find that such is the case with the survivor whose interests you are trying to spark. Your role is simply to offer, but not to insist, that a person pursue a former interest. Accept and respect a negative response without feeling personally rebuffed. Dealing with death changes people in ways which are not always possible for those close to the survivors to completely understand.

One young woman complained, "My mother was a terrific landscape artist. But since my father died she won't pick up a paintbrush. She hasn't painted for two years. She says painting is too self-indulgent, a waste. The only thing that interests her is volunteer work at the hospital."

This woman chose to turn from a solitary activity to one which seemed more socially beneficial and meaningful. The choice in this case, as in all others, is the survivor's. It should not invite judgment.

Recognizing Potentially Unfavorable Outcomes

Most survivors have periods of deep despair or withdrawal and long periods of crying or insomnia. The reactions to the loss of a loved one, which are thoroughly discussed in Sections I and II, are varied and numerous. No definite guidelines can be given regarding the *number* of reactions any survivor can be expected to experience, nor what amount of time he or she will spend in deep consuming grief. Generally, as previously noted, there will be some positive signs of recovery, *however minor*, at a period between six months to a year following the death of the loved one. For bereaved parents, this gradual recovery process will usually be of longer duration.

You may feel uncertain about being able to distinguish your friends' or relatives' normal, natural grief responses from signs of severe disturbances. Some specific guidelines can be offered in this regard. The following list contains conditions which, when prolonged, indicate that the mourner's grieving is not likely to reach a favorable and unchanging outcome:

- an all-encompassing helplessness which finds the survivor stripped of normal defenses and completely dependent on others
- a sense of worthlessness accompanied by self-blame and inertia
- overt hostility without provocation; frequent, severe tantrums
- remote characteristics; withdrawal, lack of attempt to communicate
- abuse of alcohol or drugs
- obsessive conversations about wanting to be with the loved one who died
- physical deterioration such as lack of hygiene, grooming and mobility; extreme loss of weight
- fantasies about death

It has been noted previously that with very few exceptions survivors will benefit from individual counseling. Sometimes, in order for the survivor to make it through the grieving process and regain a sense of normalcy in his or her life, outside professional help is recommended. (See "How To Find a Counselor," in chapter 10.)

A survivor who exhibits any of the behavioral patterns discussed here should be assisted in obtaining professional help.

Suicide and grief. Any caregiving person who deals with the grieving should be aware of the signs which may indicate the survivor is prone to suicide. An accountant, worried about his son, echoed many survivors when he asked, "Once you become alarmed, how do you decide how severe the situation is?"

In general, a person who is capable of committing suicide is one who is experiencing a great degree of stress or fear, pronounced physical or psychological changes, or unbearable sadness or grief. In some cases, of course, an individual could be experiencing all of these conditions simultaneously and intensely.

There is no definitive, complete profile of a typical suicide victim. The person can be any race, rich or poor, young or old, and educated or uneducated. There are, however, some factors which remain constant: The largest percentage of suicide victims are white males. Older men who lose their wives are in a high risk group. Further, suicide is more likely to be viewed as a viable solution if a friend or relative of the survivor has committed suicide.

An individual who decides to take his or her own life does not recognize any other alternative. Death seems to be the only feasible way to be released from an unbearable condition. The person's coping strategies are gone.

Following are behaviors which are prevalent among those in *all age groups* who are suicidal:

- hopelessness
- withdrawn, remote behavior
- perfectionism and a high degree of self-criticism
- low self-esteem
- depression and feelings of worthlessness

The suicidal person may also:

- have frequent conversations about suicide
- exhibit a lack of energy
- experience drastic changes in eating and sleeping habits
- have sudden and drastic changes in behavior
- participate in alcohol or drug abuse
- be a victim of domestic violence
- dispose of possessions
- write notes, journal entries or letters which indicate the acceptance of suicide as an alternative to misery

In addition, the *adolescent* suicidal person may exhibit the following behavior:

- not be conversant with classmates or teachers
- listen to music, read stories, and play games that have death themes
- fail in school or be classified as truant

In addition to the common behaviors, *adults* may do the following:

- purchase a gun
- put business affairs in order
- change a will
- make funeral plans within a short period of time after a loved one's death
- make arrangements to become an organ donor
- stop medical treatment for a chronic disorder

If you are concerned that a survivor is having thoughts of suicide, but you cannot be certain, the best course is to ask directly. Say something like, "I know you've had a very hard time. Has the pain made you think sometimes of suicide, have those thoughts crossed your mind?"

If you feel your loved one may be suicidal, you can help by following the suggestions in the preceding material, but you should also *recognize your own limitations* in such a situation. Regardless of how much help you give, it may not change the outcome for the survivor. Encourage the survivor to seek help. A person whose feelings of hopelessness, helplessness and despair are so extreme as to make him or her consider suicide will not be enthusiastic nor resourceful about seeking help. You may call a local agency which deals with suicide and ask for the names of professionals who the agency recommends to deal with high risk survivors.

Do not tell your friend or relative that "Everything will be all right," to "Look at the bright side," or "Your troubles aren't all that bad." This says that you do not accept what the grieving person is telling you, that you are ignoring the individual's pain, and that the survivor should do the same. A person who is severely depressed and despairing wants to be understood. If he or she ventures to explain deep feelings, the survivor wants those feelings to be acknowledged. The emotions or beliefs are not a figment of the survivor's imagination. They are very real.

Keep in contact with your loved one and discreetly suggest to other friends and relatives that the person is going through an exceptionally difficult period and needs love and support.

Keeping the Survivor's Grief in Perspective

As has been stated, any grieving person is affected by six major factors:

- The quality and type of relationship the survivor had with his or her loved one.

- The type of death (sudden, unexpected, lingering, suicidal, etc.)

- The support, availability and response of friends and community.

- The previous unresolved loss of a loved one, or more than one loss within a relatively short period of time.

- Other severe stresses or traumas which are concurrent with the death (loss of job or home, a major move, a physical illness, etc.).

- Socio-demographic factors (age, sex, religion, occupation, economic position and culture).

- The survivor's personality characteristics.

All of these will influence the resolution of the loss, the survivor's adjustment to life without a loved one, and the degree to which the survivor can become involved in ongoing relationships.

Some survivors are very difficult to help.

> If you extend your help and your support, or even the hand of friendship, you need to be able to understand that sometimes it will not be accepted. It will be rejected. *(Parents of a teenaged accident victim)*

This statement warns that no matter what you do, and regardless of how well-intentioned, skillful, or compassionate you are, the survivor may not let you help. If you experience a similar rejection, realize it is not personally directed at you. In such a situation, the only remedy would be for you to *be* the person's dead loved one. Remembering this will help you to keep the survivor's reactions in perspective. Offer, but don't insist. Be available, but not domineering.

Most relatives, friends, lay counselors and professionals who work with survivors have the opportunity to experience the great pleasure that comes from seeing the survivor evolve from an existence of sadness, pain and despair to a life that once again offers pleasure and reward. It is a life where people talk and smile, see the colors, and hear the music. But most of all they have a deep regard for one another as caring, loving beings who have been given this time on earth to develop expectations, exercise potential, and experience the essence of unique, life-enriching forces.

The father of a four-year-old leukemia victim talked about this transformation:

When I was grieving the loss of our child I realized there is something incredible inside all of us. When you reach down inside yourself and pull it out, you become much more than you think you are. More than you could ever imagine possible.

References

Alvarez, A. *The Savage God.* New York: Random House, 1970.

Axelrod, Julius, and Terry D. Reisine. Stress hormones: their interaction and regulation. *Science,* Vol. 224, May 4, 1984.

Baechler, Jean. *Suicides.* New York: Basic Books. 1979.

Beck, Aaron T., Robert A. Steer, Maria Kovacs, and Betsy Garrison. Hopelessness and eventual suicide: a 10 year prospective study of patients hospitalized with suicidal ideation. *American Journal of Psychiatry,* Vol. 142, May 1985.

Berlinsky, Ellen B., and Henry B. Biller. *Parental Death and Psychological Development.* Massachusetts: D.C. Heath and Company, 1982.

Bowlby, John. *Attachment and Loss,* 2 vols. New York: Basic Books, 1969-1973.

_____. *Attachment and Loss.* Vol. III. London: Hogarth Press, 1980.

Cain, Albert C. *Survivors of Suicide.* Illinois: Charles C. Thomas, 1972.

Checkups. *Family Health,* May 1981.

Cutter, Fred. *Art and the Wish To Die.* Chicago: Nelson-Hall, 1983.

Donnelly, Katherine Fair. *Recovering From the Loss of a Child.* New York: Macmillan, 1982.

Durkheim, E. *Suicide: A Study in Sociology.* Trans. John A. Spaulding and George Simpson. Glencoe: The Free Press, 1951.

Edelstein, Linda. *Maternal Bereavement.* New York: Praeger Publishers, 1984.

Ellison, Craig W. *Loneliness.* New York: Christian Herald Books, 1980.

Emery, Gary. *A New Beginning.* New York: Simon and Schuster, 1981.

Fleming, Joan, and Sol Altschul. Activation of mourning and growth by psychoanalysis. *International Journal of Psychoanalysis,* Vol. 44, 1963.

Fletcher, J.C., and M.I. Evans. Maternal bonding in early fetal ultrasound examinations. *New England Journal of Medicine,* Vol. 308, 1983.

Freud, Sigmund. Mourning and melancholia. *Collected Papers,* Vol. IV. New York: Basic Books, 1917.

Furman, Erna. *A Child's Parent Dies.* New Haven and London: Yale University, 1974.

Furman, R.A. A child's capacity for mourning. *The Child in His Family: The Impact of Disease and Death.* ed. E.J. Anthony and C. Koupernick. New York: Wiley, 1973.

Greenberg, Samuel I. Managing the potentially suicidal patient. *Physician and Patient,* Vol. 3, Feb. 1984.

Hendin, Herbert. *Suicide in America.* New York: W.W. Norton and Company, 1982.

Izard, Carroll E. *Patterns of Emotions.* New York: Academic Press, 1972.

Jacobs, Jerry. *Adolescent Suicide.* New York: John Wiley and Sons, 1971.

Jahr, Cliff. A Voice for Today. *Parade Magazine,* June 9, 1985.

Kapleau, Philip, ed. *The Wheel of Death.* New York: Harper and Row, 1971.

Kennell, J., H. Slyter, and M. Klaus. The mourning response of parents to the death of a newborn infant. *New England Journal of Medicine,* Vol. 283, 1970.

Kirkley-Best, E., and K. Kellner. The forgotten grief: a review of the psychology of stillbirth. *American Journal of Orthopsychiatry,* Vol. 52, 1982.

Kirsch, Charlotte. *Facing the Future.* New York: Penguin Books, 1983.

Koestenbaum, Peter. *Managing Anxiety.* New Jersey: Prentice-Hall, Inc. 1974.

Koestenbaum, Peter. *Is There an Answer to Death?* New Jersey: Prentice-Hall, 1976.

Krementz, Jill. *How It Feels When a Parent Dies.* New York: Alfred A. Knopf, 1981.

Kubler-Ross, Elizabeth. *On Death and Dying.* New York: Alfred A. Knopf, 1981.

_____. *Questions and Answers on Death and Dying.* New York: Macmillan, 1974.

_____. *On Children and Death.* New York: Macmillan, 1983.

Legg, C., and I. Sherick. The replacement child—a developmental tragedy: some preliminary comments. *Child Psychiatry and Human Development,* Vol. 7., 1976.

Levine, Stephen. *Who Dies?* New York: Anchor Books, 1982.

Lewis, C.S. *A Grief Observed.* New York: Bantam Seabury Press, 1963.

Lewis, E., and A. Page. Failure to mourn a stillbirth: an overlooked catastrophe. *British Journal of Medical Psychology,* Vol. 51, 1978.

Lindemann, E. Symptamatology and management of acute grief. *American Journal of Psychiatry,* Vol. 101, 1944.

Lohmann, Jeanne. *Granite Under Water.* c. 1965 (unpublished manuscript).

Lonetto, Richard. *Children's Concepts of Death.* New York: Springer Publishing Company, 1980.

Macon, L. Help for bereaved parents. *Social Casework: The Journal of Contemporary Social Work.* November, 1979.

Maddison, D.C., and B. Raphael. Normal bereavement as an illness requiring care: psychopharmacological approaches. *Journal of Thanatology,* Vol. 2, 1972.

Maddison, D.C., and A. Viola. The health of widows in the year following bereavement. *Journal of Psychosomatic Research,* Vol. 12, 1968.

McKay, Matthew, and Patrick Fanning. *Self-Esteem.* California: New Harbinger Publications, 1986.

Miller, Marv. *Suicide After Sixty.* New York: Springer Publishing Company, 1979.

Osterweis, Marian, Frederic Solomon, and Morris Green, eds. *Bereavement: Reaction, Consequences, and Care.* Washington, D.C.: National Academy Press, 1984.

Parks, Betty. We waited seven years for a murder trial, *Survivors* newsletter, Vol. IV, No. 1, August, 1984.

Parkes, Colin Murray. *Bereavement.* London: Tavistock, 1972.

Parkes, Colin Murray, B. Benjamin, and R.G. Fitzgerald. Broken heart: a statistical study of increased mortality among widows and widowers. *British Medical Journal,* Vol. 1, 1969.

Poduska, Bernard. *You Can Cope.* New Jersey: Prentice Hall, 1976.

Pollock, G.H. Anniversary reactions, trauma and mourning. *Psychoanalytic Quarterly,* Vol. 39, 1970.

Pouschine, Tania. By their own young hands. *Forbes,* October 21, 1985.

Raphael, Beverley. *The Anatomy of Bereavement.* New York: Basic Books, 1983.

Ring, Kenneth. *Life at Death.* New York: Coward, McCann and Geoghegan, 1980.

Robins, Eli. *The Final Months.* New York: Oxford University Press, 1981.

Sabom, Michael B. *Recollections of Death.* New York: Harper and Row Publishers, 1982.

Sachs, Hans. Beauty life and death. *The Creative Unconscious.* ed. A. Roback. Massachusetts: Science Art Publishers, 1942.

Sarton, May. *Shadow of a Man*. New York: W.W. Norton, 1950.

Schiff, Harriet Sarnoff. *The Bereaved Parent*. New York: Crown Publishers, Inc., 1977.

Schoenberg, Bernard, Arthur C. Carr, Austin H. Kutscher, David Peretz, and Ivan Goldberg, eds. *Anticipatory Grief*. New York: Columbia University Press, 1974.

Seligman, Martin E.P. *Helplessness*. San Francisco: W.H. Freeman and Company, 1975.

Shaffer, Martin. *Life After Stress*. New York: Plenum Press, 1982.

Sharkey, Frances. *A Parting Gift*. New York: St. Martin's Press, 1982.

Smith, Gudmund J.W., and Anna Danielsson. *Anxiety and Defensive Strategies in Childhood and Adolescence*. New York: International Universities Press, Inc., 1982.

Stearns, Ann Kaiser. *Living Through Personal Crisis*. Chicago: Thomas More Press, 1984.

Stringham, J., J.H. Riley, and A. Ross. Silent birth: mourning a still-born baby. *Social Work,* Vol. 27, 1982.

Tavris, Carol. *Anger*. New York: Simon and Schuster, 1982.

They won't forget. *Survivors* newsletter, Vol IV, No. 1, August 1984.

Trouble. *People Magazine,* March 16, 1981.

Waas, Hannelore, and Charles A. Corr. *Helping Children Cope With Death*. New York: Hemisphere Publishing Corporation, 1982.

Wilson, A., J. Lawrence, D. Stevens, and D. Soule. The death of the newborn twin: an analysis of parental bereavement. *Pediatrics,* Vol. 70, 1982.

Worden, William J. *Grief Counseling and Grief Therapy: A Handbook for the Mental Health Practitioner*. New York: Springer Publishing Company, 1982.

Other New Harbinger Self-Help Titles

Father-Son Healing: An Adult Son's Guide, $12.95
The Chemotherapy Survival Guide, $11.95
Your Family/Your Self: How to Analyze Your Family System, $11.95
Being a Man: A Guide to the New Masculinity, $12.95
The Deadly Diet, Second Edition: Recovering from Anorexia & Bulimia, $11.95
Last Touch: Preparing for a Parent's Death, $11.95
Consuming Passions: Help for Compulsive Shoppers, $11.95
Self-Esteem, Second Edition, $12.95
Depression & Anxiety Mangement: An audio tape for managing emotional problems, $11.95
I Can't Get Over It, A Handbook for Trauma Survivors, $12.95
Concerned Intervention, When Your Loved One Won't Quit Alcohol or Drugs, $11.95
Redefining Mr. Right, $11.95
Dying of Embarrassment: Help for Social Anxiety and Social Phobia, $11.95
The Depression Workbook: Living With Depression and Manic Depression, $13.95
Risk-Taking for Personal Growth: A Step-by-Step Workbook, $11.95
The Marriage Bed: Renewing Love, Friendship, Trust, and Romance, $11.95
Focal Group Psychotherapy: For Mental Health Professionals, $44.95
Hot Water Therapy: Save Your Back, Neck & Shoulders in 10 Minutes a Day $11.95
Older & Wiser: A Workbook for Coping With Aging, $12.95
Prisoners of Belief: Exposing & Changing Beliefs that Control Your Life, $10.95
Be Sick Well: A Healthy Approach to Chronic Illness, $11.95
Men & Grief: A Guide for Men Surviving the Death of a Loved One., $11.95
When the Bough Breaks: A Helping Guide for Parents of Sexually Abused Childern, $11.95
Love Addiction: A Guide to Emotional Independence, $11.95
When Once Is Not Enough: Help for Obsessive Compulsives, $11.95
The New Three Minute Meditator, $9.95
Getting to Sleep, $10.95
The Relaxation & Stress Reduction Workbook, 3rd Edition, $13.95
Leader's Guide to the Relaxation & Stress Reduction Workbook, $19.95
Beyond Grief: A Guide for Recovering from the Death of a Loved One, $10.95
Thoughts & Feelings: The Art of Cognitive Stress Intervention, $13.95
Messages: The Communication Skills Book, $12.95
The Divorce Book, $11.95
Hypnosis for Change: A Manual of Proven Techniques, 2nd Edition, $12.95
The Chronic Pain Control Workbook, $13.95
Rekindling Desire: Bringing Your Sexual Relationship Back to Life, $12.95
Visualization for Change, $12.95
Videotape: Clinical Hypnosis for Stress & Anxiety Reduction, $24.95
Starting Out Right: Essential Parenting Skills for Your Child's First Seven Years, $12.95
Big Kids: A Parents' Guide to Weight Control for Children, $11.95
My Parent's Keeper: Adult Children of the Emotionally Disturbed, $11.95
When Anger Hurts, $12.95
Free of the Shadows: Recovering from Sexual Violence, $12.95
Lifetime Weight Control, $11.95
The Anxiety & Phobia Workbook, $13.95
Love and Renewal: A Couple's Guide to Commitment, $12.95
The Habit Control Workbook, $12.95

Call **toll free, 1-800-748-6273**, to order. Have your Visa or Mastercard number ready. Or send a check for the titles you want to New Harbinger Publications, Inc., 5674 Shattuck Avenue, Oakland, CA 94609. Include $3.80 for the first book and 50¢ for each additional book, to cover shipping and handling. (California residents please include appropriate sales tax.) Allow four to six weeks for delivery.

Prices subject to change without notice.